DEMOCRACY RULES

House Republicans stand together
alongside social distancing boxes prior to a press
conference on Capitol Hill. (Saul Loeb / AFP)

DEMOCRACY
RULES

JAN-WERNER
MÜLLER

FARRAR, STRAUS AND GIROUX

NEW YORK

Farrar, Straus and Giroux
120 Broadway, New York 10271

Copyright © 2021 by Jan-Werner Müller
All rights reserved
Printed in the United States of America
First edition, 2021

Library of Congress Cataloging-in-Publication Data
Names: Müller, Jan-Werner, 1970– author.
Title: Democracy rules / Jan-Werner Müller.
Description: First Edition. | New York : Farrar, Straus and Giroux, [2021] |
    Includes bibliographical references and index.
Identifiers: LCCN 2021002667 | ISBN 9780374136475 (Hardcover)
Subjects: LCSH: Democracy.
Classification: LCC JC423 .M78558 2021 | DDC 321.8—dc23
LC record available at https://lccn.loc.gov/2021002667

Our books may be purchased in bulk for promotional, educational,
or business use. Please contact your local bookseller or the Macmillan
Corporate and Premium Sales Department at 1-800-221-7945, extension
5442, or by email at MacmillanSpecialMarkets@macmillan.com.

www.fsgbooks.com
www.twitter.com/fsgbooks • www.facebook.com/fsgbooks

10 9 8 7 6 5 4 3 2 1

CONTENTS

Preface

Democracy? It is a dream to suppose that we already know
what it is, whether out of satisfaction with our present
state or to attack its misery. It is simply a play of open
possibilities, inaugurated in a past still close to us, and we
have barely begun to explore it.

—CLAUDE LEFORT

Everybody thinks they know that democracy is in crisis, but
how many of us are certain what democracy actually is? The
reasons for a pervasive sense of crisis seem plain: a steadily
rising number of authoritarian regimes; increasing levels of
dissatisfaction with politics within democracies; and, beyond
abstract numbers, the double trauma of 2016, with Brexit and
the election of a reality TV star as president of the world's oldest and (still) most powerful democracy.

Does the elevation of an evidently unfit candidate to the
highest office in the land automatically prove that democracy
is in crisis? Or was conclusive proof only supplied by the fact
that this man-child, in the very last days of his presidential
term, incited followers to storm the legislature? Or did American democracy on that occasion demonstrate its resilience, ultimately absorbing the shock to the political system? Not every
shock signals crisis. In the original ancient Greek meaning,
krisis denotes a moment of stark choice: a patient would either
die or recover, a defendant would be judged guilty or innocent

(in fact, "judgment" was the other meaning of the term).[1] If so, was Trump's election perhaps a moment when it was voters who were judged—as unfit for democracy? As we now know, a president tweeting falsehoods or spouting them in live press conferences can certainly turn into a matter of life and death—if members of his audience take him seriously and literally during a pandemic. But did lying about Lysol undermine democracy? Does the decision to leave a supranational organization, following a referendum initiated by one of the world's oldest political parties, namely the Tories in the United Kingdom, constitute a fatal blow to democracy as such? There are plenty of outcomes in democratic polities one might find abhorrent, but to presume more or less casually that they'll kill the system is to engage in what Saul Bellow once derided as "crisis chatter." Just what are plausible criteria for declaring a "life-and-death moment"? And is there a way for such criteria not to look immediately partisan?

That question cannot be answered without a proper understanding of democracy to begin with. True, we think we know it when we see it. But many leaders determined to subvert democracy have become very adept at making us believe that there's something there long after it is in fact gone. What is truly essential for democracy? Is it one thing only, or perhaps more than one thing? Is it elections, or a set of basic rights such as free speech, or a more elusive matter of collective attitudes, for instance, citizens being disposed to treat one another in a civil, respectful manner?

We won't get very far in answering these questions without first returning to basics. It's the move Machiavelli recommended when he wrote that addressing a crisis requires nothing less than a *riduzione verso il principio*, a "return to first principles." This book seeks to offer such a route. Inevitably, we walk with our backs to the future, but having some sense of where we're coming from and what the path so far has looked like can help in figuring out whether we have really lost our way (which is not to say there's necessarily only one way).

It's a mistake to assume that all thinking about democracy today needs to be fashioned as a response to the new authoritarians. Yet we also can't pretend that nothing happened. Thus, the first chapter of this book will revisit the question Hillary Clinton posed in her instant memoir: What happened? And why is it still happening, after so many self-declared defenders of democracy have sounded the alarm bells?

There have been two convenient but ultimately very misleading responses. One is to blame the people themselves. This has been true of liberals in particular, who prioritize individual rights, are more or less content with capitalism, and tend to value diversity as such, but who also labor under an inherited notion that democracy is perennially in peril of deteriorating into a tyranny of the majority. They have taken what is often dubbed "the global rise of right-wing populism" as license to revive clichés from nineteenth-century mass psychology—the kinds of ideas one should not really utter in polite company, even if one is convinced that civics-education pieties hardly ever match political realities: the masses bring all kinds of disasters on themselves; ordinary folks—ill-informed and, even if well-informed, plainly irrational—are always ready to be misled by demagogues. The obvious lesson is to re-empower what are gingerly called gatekeepers—which is often really just to say traditional elites.[2] More concretely put, we must reengineer political primaries so as to minimize the decision-making power of those who in the United States are often (strangely) called everyday citizens:[3] let's be done with referenda and other irresponsible exercises in direct democracy; let's just recognize that politics is a profession.[4] After all, we must not forget that two-thirds of Americans can name at least one member of the jury of the TV show *American Idol*, but only 15 percent are able to identify the chief justice of the Supreme Court.[5] Amateurs may applaud a particularly virtuous performance of "politics" in a TV debate, but during and especially after the show they must be kept safely on the sidelines. Those holding such views—lest they be thought of as just indulging good old demophobia, that is, fear of ordinary people—usually rush to back up their suspicions about the masses with timeless insights from social psychology: the people are prone to tribalism; polarization, as in enmity between groups, is the default of all politics; and we should devise psychological exercises such as "mindfulness" to make ordinary people tone it all down a bit.[6] Those despairing of the masses also point to surveys supposedly proving that citizens across the globe are more and more inclined to back "strong leaders," or even military rule.

What's wrong with this picture? To begin with, most surveys are ambiguous at best, and in any case surveys have hardly ever predicted either the life or the death of democracy; they certainly do not demonstrate conclusively that the people are thoroughly disenchanted with ideals of self-rule.[7] There's a reason why the instigators of military coups—be it in Thailand or Egypt—do not officially disavow democracy. Rather, they fake democracy, as in General Sisi's Egypt, or they promise a swift return to self-government as soon as the conditions are right, as in Thailand (even if there are always reasons to put that return off again).[8] It's wrong to assume that there is now an unstoppable wave of authoritarian populism—or, as the English Brexiteer Nigel Farage, who evidently felt the image of a wave didn't do justice to his world-historical role, put it, a "tsunami." True, parties that can plausibly be labeled populist—and I'll say more about that highly contested designation shortly—have increased their vote shares in many countries. But the notion that majorities are inevitably clamoring for authoritarians fails to take note of one simple fact: until today, in no Western country has a right-wing populist authoritarian party or politician come to power without the collaboration of established conservative elites.[9] Moreover, the supporters of those elites don't think of themselves as getting rid of democracy when they vote for conservative and center-right parties.

A quick glance at history (and, of course, one shouldn't glance just quickly) would suggest that there are few—possibly no—instances of democratic majorities clearly deciding to be done with democracy. Fascist thugs marched on Rome, but Mussolini didn't: he arrived by sleeper car from Milan, because liberal elites and, not least, the king had decided that the future *Duce* should have a try at cleaning up the mess of parliamentary politics. Obviously, his Fascist Party had highly committed supporters, as did the National Socialists in Germany. But there as well, the crucial decision to empower Hitler was made by parts of what might as well be called the conservative establishment of the day. Those searching for one-line lessons from history should take note: apparently, it is not the people who decide to be done with democracy; it is elites.[10]

Of course, this notion would seem to play right into the hands of those who assign blame to the powerful for the political upheavals of our time. Indeed, there is much to criticize in what can be understood as a kind of *secession* of the most privileged from particular polities, but it does not do justice to the complexity of our moment simply to claim that its problems are all caused just by the rich and powerful being bad, corrupt, or, to coin a phrase, "crooked" characters, whether that claim is made by the left or the right. The powerful do what they do because they have the power to do it, and the power was given to them ultimately through the institutions of our democracies. We must reexamine the latter, as opposed to getting stuck with shaming particular figures (even if doing so is often justified, and also fun: think of the billionaire on American TV prompted to tears by the specter of somewhat—in fact just *slightly*—higher taxes). In other words, the focus on individuals is misguided, whether it stresses the many—as in the casual contempt for the allegedly irrational and proto-authoritarian masses—or the few, as in the satisfying but ultimately cheap attacks on selfish elites.

To think about institutions is not to reduce politics to process and procedure; what matters is to probe the principles that animate and justify the rules of the democratic game and its informal norms.[11] One of the important insights from students of politics is that such uncodified norms can be at least as important as laws; they actually keep the democratic game going (and crucially constrain the players in ways not found in the rule book).[12] Yet neither rules nor norms are in and of themselves a good thing, and especially not when they enable a game that rests on spoken or unspoken injustices. Southern gentlemen in the twentieth-century U.S. Congress no doubt graciously observed norms of civility (and even an imperative to compromise on a range of issues, oiling bipartisan politics with bonhomie). But the system of racial exclusion that they defended was fundamentally incompatible with democratic principles. As the American law professor Jedediah Purdy has observed, "Norms are like the statues of dead leaders: you can't know whether you are for or against them without knowing which values they support."[13] We need to go beyond rules and norms and ask about the animating principles—or, as some political thinkers would have put it in a bygone era, the *spirit*—behind them. It's not enough to appeal to rule following in the hope that we can get going again a process (or game) that has been blocked by more or less authoritarian figures; after all, the point of democracy surely is not just for different elites to cycle in and out of power.[14]

Then what is the point? A conventional answer is that democracy can be justified only with an appeal to the principles of freedom and equality. A rule like "majority decides" isn't good because it produces the best results or is most efficient; it's right because it reflects respect for citizens' equality, and it takes the form of counting every individual vote. This rule is opposed to acclamation by crowds, as we affirm that everyone matters (and assume that everyone is capable of political judgment).[15]

Democracy is not exhausted by the equal freedom to vote. There are also freedoms of speech, assembly, and, not least, association. Organizations multiply the value of individual rights of political expression, but, less obviously, they also undermine equality; those with more resources or, for that matter, better and more eloquent arguments will have more influence when it comes to making collective decisions. Democracy is not just irenic equality; it's friction on the basis of people using their freedoms. Yet without associations—political parties, above all—there is also no way to rectify inequalities; sometimes the tools that built the master's house can be useful for remodeling it into a home for equals.

Whether one likes it or not, democratic conflicts are still predominantly structured by intermediary institutions, political parties and professional media in particular. These have been considered crucial for making representative democracy function properly ever since the nineteenth century. It is conventional wisdom that both are in deep crisis today, and by crisis I *mean* crisis, for plenty of media and parties *are* dying. Before we can even get to addressing this twin crisis, however, we should take a step back and ask—*riduzione verso il principio*—in what ways exactly these institutions provide (or at least used to provide) a critical infrastructure for democracy: a way for citizens to reach others, and be reached by them in turn, comparable in a sense to the postal service that Trump sought to destroy, thinking that in a free and fair election with a proper infrastructure for mail-in voting he was bound to lose (a correct assessment, as it turned out). Once we see the principles behind this infrastructure, and democratic institutions more broadly, we'll also be less frightened of replacing some of them. Rebuilding democracy after authoritarian populism does not have to mean more of the same, but can include innovative machinery that is in fact more likely to work in tune with democracy's underlying principles.[16]

Yet it's naive political solutionism to expect that *one* product of what has become a kind of global democracy innovation industry—be it internet voting, assemblies of randomly chosen citizens, or what have you—will get us out of our difficulties. Nonetheless, the renovation of democracy's critical infrastructure is a crucial first step. *Pace* the demophobes, this can be done without simply reinstating traditional gatekeepers; rather, as I explain in the last chapter, the people themselves are able to determine the ways in which intermediary institutions—parties and media, above all—should be refashioned.

To be sure, intermediary powers—or, for that matter, any new democratic machinery—need to be constrained by one nonnegotiable principle: they cannot deny the standing of particular citizens as free and equal members of the polity. If one undermines such standing, the game—in which anything else, from material interests to sexual identities, can become subject to conflict without suspending the civic bond as such—will be over; one can say all kinds of unfriendly things to other citizens in political battle without disrespecting them, but one can't say, "You're a second-class citizen" or "You don't really belong here" (as Trump did, for instance, when he told progressive congresswomen of color to "go back" to their countries). Some states have provisions to penalize, or even simply prohibit, parties that, in effect, seek to shrink the demos or in other ways violate fundamental rights. The banning of political actors goes back as far as the ancient Athenian democracy, but is it ever really justifiable, given the obvious danger that such apparent measures for democratic self-defense might bring about the very demise of democracy that they are supposed to prevent? After all, a country in which the basic right to free association is infringed on or someone is told they don't belong (and, as a result, ostracized and sent away, as happened in Athens)—albeit all in the name of saving democracy—can hardly claim to be a proper democracy anymore.

If rules enable and at the same time constrain the democratic game, rule breaking must be bad. But is it? Democratic politics is never exhausted by rule following and sometimes might positively require upsetting the game; it is not an accident that the ancient Athenians praised their polity for its capacity for innovation, while their enemies charged them with being capricious.[17] Not all norm breaking is the same.

Rules can be broken while one remains faithful to their underlying principles; sometimes, to preserve the very meaning of the game, people want to engage in forms of disobedience designed to serve or even deepen democracy. In the eyes of skeptics, such disobedience paves the road to anarchy or to authoritarianism, because no citizenry has ever put up with anarchy for long (and critics of democracy, from Plato onward, have warned that "too much freedom" results in tyranny). But, then again, many of those aghast at the antics of today's enemies of democracy have at one point or another wondered, just why aren't we on the streets challenging authoritarians right now? Why aren't we stopping *this*? How come we're obsessed with lessons from history, and yet we seem to be standing by as passively as many of our ancestors did? Is there a threshold beyond which democratic disobedience becomes legitimate, as opposed to looking as if one were just a bad loser in electoral contests (or, in the worst-case scenario, risking civil war in fighting for one's partisan convictions)?

THIS BOOK IS not a political manual. One of its wagers is that we still have time—and ought to make time—for thinking about first principles. The latter do not dictate highly specific institutions or detailed political rules; democracy isn't just one thing, and there's more than one way of doing democracy (just as there is more than one way of faking it). In line with the insights of the great French political philosopher Claude Lefort, some probably have not even occurred to us (though by the same token some strategies for undermining democracy have not occurred to *them* yet). Another wager is that democracy does still rule—in the sense that plenty of people around the globe view it as deeply desirable. They still dream it as a political system that has enormous problems but that remains best able to avoid domination, and to give people a chance to experience a decent life in common.

DEMOCRACY RULES

1. FAKE DEMOCRACY: Everybody Has Their Reasons

The awful thing about life is this: Everybody has
their reasons.
—Octave in JEAN RENOIR, *The Rules of the Game*

I have lived for the last month . . . with the sense of having
suffered a vast and indefinite loss. I did not know at first
what ailed me. At last it occurred to me that what I had
lost was a country.
—HENRY DAVID THOREAU

They do not all look the same; plenty of differences are obvious. But group them together and they clearly make up one political family: Orbán, Erdoğan, Kaczyński, Modi, undoubtedly ex-president Trump, perhaps Netanyahu, but Brazil's president Jair Bolsonaro for sure. It is imperative to understand what is often described as a global trend in authoritarianism.

The obvious danger is that the effort to do so will homogenize what, after all, remain fundamentally different national trajectories. The causes for the rise of right-wing populism in particular are not identical. But radical right-wing populists have developed a common strategy and even what might be called a shared authoritarian-populist art of governance—hence the family resemblances.

The spread of this populist art has put paid to a particular post–Cold War illusion: not that History had ended (did anybody *really* believe that?), but that only democracies could learn from their own mistakes and from one another's experiences. Authoritarian regimes, so the assumption went, could not adapt to changing environments and innovate; they were all fated to end like the Soviet Union in 1991. The new Authoritarian International—whose members can try out and refine techniques of radical right-wing rule—puts that complacent liberal-democratic self-conception to rest; best authoritarian practices (or should we say worst?) can be copied across borders.

Broadly speaking, the authoritarian-populist art of governance is based on nationalism (often with racist overtones), on hijacking the state for partisan loyalists, and, less obviously, on weaponizing the economy to secure political power: a combination of culture war, patronage, and mass clientelism. To be sure, the nationalism often amounts to a simulation of sovereignty, a studied performance of collective self-assertion, when in fact not all that much is changing; plenty of anti-globalization rhetoric turns out to be perfectly compatible with the continued deregulation of capital flows across borders and other measures that enrich elites in other countries.

These specifics are missed by political diagnoses that equate contemporary right-wing populism with fascism, or see populism as a new, internationally successful ideology, or assume that "ordinary people" just brought all this on themselves with their supposed craving for authoritarianism. Historians have sought precedents for what we are witnessing, often with a view to drawing "lessons from the past." Of course, exercises in comparison are valuable, and there cannot be blanket prohibitions on finding parallels between the present and the atrocities of the twentieth century, for, without first comparing, we could not appreciate the differences. Still, analogies all too often lead to shortcuts in political judgment; we are more likely to see the similarities, or even engage in motivated reasoning, that is, pick evidence in order to justify our preferred political strategy for today. As James Bryce—today virtually forgotten, but a highly influential diagnostician of democracies at the turn of the twentieth century—put it, "The chief practical use of history is to deliver us from plausible historical analogies." That's a note of caution which always applies; more specific to our age is Tony Judt's observation that we have become extremely skillful at teaching the lessons of history but probably quite bad at teaching actual history.

The truth is that today's threats to democracy barely even rhyme with many twentieth-century experiences. Many of those who after November 8, 2016, rushed to buy *1984* or *The Origins of Totalitarianism* might well have given up after a few dozen pages. Fascism specifically—as distinct from authoritarianism or racism in general—is not being revived in our era: we do not see the mass mobilization and militarization of entire societies;[1] and while hatred against vulnerable minorities is being fanned, no systemic cult of violence that glorifies mortal combat as the apotheosis of human existence is being instituted. Nor are states being thoroughly remade on the basis of racism, which is not to deny that racial (and religious) animus has been legitimated from the very top in Hungary, Brazil, and the United States.

We are all in favor of learning from history, but we implicitly assume that only good people learn from it. One of the reasons we are not witnessing the second coming of a particular antidemocratic past is that today's anti-democrats have also learned from history. They know full well that highly visible human rights violations on a mass scale should not form part of today's authoritarian repertoire: that would be too uncomfortable a reminder of twentieth-century dictatorships.

Large-scale repression, as perpetrated by Erdoğan since 2016, must be understood as a sign of weakness, not strength. Trump sending his "army" of far-right hobby warriors, conspiracy theorists, and the occasional country-club Republican in the direction of the Capitol was a matter of desperation, not proof of a master plan for a fascist takeover. Precisely because we might recognize it as a historical precedent, it by and large isn't happening. So, what then is happening?

But What Is Right-Wing (or, for That Matter, Left-Wing) Populism Anyway?

I've so far used the term "populism" as if its meaning were self-evident. It's not. It is positively misleading to equate populism with "criticism of elites" or "anti-establishment attitudes." While such an equation has become conventional wisdom, it's actually based on a rather peculiar thought. After all, any old civics textbook would instruct us that keeping an eye on the powerful is a sign of good democratic citizenship, yet, nowadays, we are told incessantly that such conduct is precisely "populist" (and, by implication, according to many observers, dangerous for democracy and the rule of law). Now, it's true that populists, when in opposition, criticize sitting governments (and, usually, also other parties). But, above all, they do something else, and that is crucial: in one way or another, they claim that they, *and only they*, represent what they often refer to as the "real people" or also the "silent majority."

At first sight, this might not look particularly nefarious; it does not immediately amount to, let's say, racism or a fanatical hatred of the European Union or, for that matter, the declaring of judges and particular media "enemies of the people." And yet this claim to a distinctly moral monopoly of representation has two detrimental consequences for democracy. Rather obviously, once populists assert that only they represent the people, they also charge that all other contenders for office are fundamentally illegitimate. This is never just a matter of disputes about policy, or even about values; such disagreements, after all, are completely normal and, ideally, even productive in a democratic polity. Rather, populists assert that their rivals are corrupt and simply fail to serve the interests of the people on account of their bad, or indeed "crooked," character. What Donald J. Trump said about his rival in the 2016 election (and then also about his opponent in 2020) was extreme but not exceptional: all populists engage in talk of this kind.

More insidiously, populists also claim that those who do not agree with their ultimately symbolic construction of the people (and hence usually do not support the populists politically) might not properly belong to the people in the first place. After all, the suggestion that there is a "real people" implies that there are some who are not quite real—folks who just pretend to belong, who might actually undermine the polity in some form, or who at best are second-rate citizens.[2] Just remember Trump's habitual condemnation of his critics as "un-American," or think of Jarosław Kaczyński's railings against Poles who he said have treason in their genes, or listen to what's really being said with the pronouncement of BJP politicians that "the division . . . is just in the mind of certain politicians, but, as a society, India is one and India is harmonious."

Populists always claim to unify the people or simply uncover the unity that is always already there, but their de facto political business model is to divide citizens as much as possible. And the message that only some truly belong to the people systematically undermines the standing of certain citizens.

Obvious examples are minorities (whose status in the polity might already be vulnerable for one reason or another) and recent immigrants, who are suspected of not being truly loyal to the country. Think of Modi's policy of creating a register of genuine citizens. Ostensibly, this is supposed to help identify illegal immigrants (referred to as "termites in the soil of Bengal" by Amit Shah, when he was head of the BJP). Hindu nationalists understand perfectly well that the entire exercise is meant to affirm the "real"—that is, Hindu—people and put fear into one particular minority, namely Muslims.

Where populists come to power, one consequence of this exclusionary stance can be that some citizens no longer enjoy full equality before the law (or even protection of the law at all): they are treated differently in conspicuous ways, perhaps not necessarily by judges in court, but in many ordinary encounters with bureaucrats who have understood perfectly well what is expected from the very top.[3] That is not even to mention the unleashing of hate on streets and squares. There is significant evidence, for instance, that Trump rallies were associated with a local increase in politically motivated assaults; Asian Americans were attacked more frequently during the pandemic; Trumpist vigilantes clearly felt empowered by the Republican Party's showcasing a suburban couple training weapons on Black Lives Matter protesters; and, lest we forget, anti-Semitic "incidents" also hit an all-time high in the United States in 2019 (numbers for 2020 were not available at the time of writing).[4] The philosopher Kate Manne's term "trickledown aggression" perfectly captures this phenomenon.[5]

Note how this radicalization of the right in the name of the people is not the same as nationalism per se. The latter implies that every cultural nation is entitled to its own state, that compatriots are owed more by way of moral and political obligations than foreigners, and that the imperative of preserving the nation has moral weight as such.[6] To be sure, all populists need to provide some content for their notion of "the people," and it is hardly an accident that right-wing populists have so often reached for an ethnically defined nation to do so (or opted for outright nativism). But, in principle, one can be a populist for whom the definition of the people is primarily political or ideological—just think of Hugo Chávez's notion of Bolivarian socialism for the twenty-first century; what matters in this case is that those who disagree with the supposedly uniquely authentic representative of the people are declared illegitimate and quite possibly put *hors la loi*.

An Art of Governance

Authoritarian-populist regimes, then, constantly seek to divide their societies and, more particularly, hold up ideals of the "real Turk," the "real Indian," the "real American," and so on. But these attempts at solidifying cultural domination have gone hand in hand with something much more mundane: a propensity for crony capitalism. Many of today's authoritarian regimes are in effect also kleptocracies (a term coined by the Polish-British sociologist Stanislav Andreski in the late 1960s). There is one straightforward explanation for this: the absence of legal and political constraints makes self-dealing so much easier, which in turn reinforces the need to maintain a tight grip on the judiciary and the political system in order to avoid punishment in the future. But there is also a political logic: involving others in criminality compels their loyalty to the regime; mass clientelism—rewarding supporters with patronage—solidifies mass allegiance; and threatening those who might not support the authoritarian populists with loss of jobs or benefits solves the problem of how to exert control over societies without too much direct political repression.

Such dynamics, which go beyond traditional kleptocracy, are what the Hungarian sociologist Bálint Magyar has in mind when he refers to the rise of a "mafia state" in his native country.[7] A mafia state is not about large envelopes with cash changing hands under the table; rather, it is the use of state structures and what on the surface are legal means—in particular public procurement processes where, strangely, only one bidder ever shows up, or where the crony is paired with a phony bidder. A mafia state is controlled by and benefits what Magyar calls extended "political families." (This might well include the ruler's actual family, as in the prominent examples of Trump's, Orbán's, Bolsonaro's, and Erdoğan's children, with especially nefarious roles reserved for sons-in-law.) Absolute loyalty is given in exchange for material reward and, equally important, protection for an indefinite future. "The main benefit of controlling a modern bureaucratic state," a Hungarian observer has noted, "is not the power to persecute the innocent. It is the power to protect the guilty."[8]

Here ideology can also function as a reliable indicator of political and familial submission; going along with provocations and outrageous norm breaking by the leader becomes a litmus test for those who might otherwise be suspected of having retained a belief in proper democratic standards. What's more, since violating norms compromises members of the political family, they must stick together for mutual protection, which helps establish reliability and trust—a defining feature of the original form of the mafia, of course.

Not only are the new authoritarian-populist states not fascist in the familiar historical sense; in one important aspect, they turn the pattern of Nazi rule upside down. As the political scientist (and German exile) Ernst Fraenkel demonstrated, the Nazi polity was not characterized by complete lawlessness and chaos, in the way traditional accounts of tyranny or of totalitarianism tended to suggest; there were plenty of areas of life that proceeded in normal, predictable ways: marriages were concluded and annulled, business contracts written and enforced. Alongside these areas of relative legal normality, however, there was always the threat of the "prerogative state," which could act in completely unpredictable and unaccountable ways. Fraenkel coined the term "dual state" to describe this split between ordinary, rule-governed life and unpredictable repression.[9]

What if today we are once more facing dual states, but with a difference? Now the realm of politics remains, in many respects, relatively normal but for some legal-looking manipulations, while in the economy one is subject to the arbitrary exercise of power. Or perhaps not so arbitrary, for if it is correct that loyalty to the political family is crucial for economic success, punishments are in fact foreseeable. Instead of sending muscle to collect the cash, the government simply asks the tax authorities for some extra audits. And, lo and behold, they always find something. As a consequence, powerful businesspeople not obviously loyal to the regime are made offers that they cannot refuse to sell their holdings; this has regularly happened to oligarchs in Hungary who were perceived to be aligned with the opposition socialist party. As the sociologist Kim Lane Scheppele has pointed out, these patterns are not always easily discernible to outsiders, for actions that are essentially political can always be represented as having been dictated by economic and financial necessity (in the same way that Trump's brazen attack on the postal service was couched in the language of efficiency, even if it had the plainly political purpose of making mail-in voting in 2020 more difficult).[10]

Not all right-wing populist governments operate fully fledged mafia states, and in general mafia states are harder to establish in the internationally exposed parts of the economy. It is received wisdom that right-wing populists are enemies of neoliberalism, but a figure like Orbán evidently made his peace with international investors. He offers the German car industry what one Hungarian observer has called "Chinese conditions" in the middle of Europe: mostly pliant unions, where there are unions at all, and swift clampdowns on anything that looks like environmentalist protest, for instance, against the major Audi factory in Győr; as one critic has put it, the system is as much an "Audi-cracy" as an autocracy.[11] "We are pragmatic," Mateusz Morawiecki, the head of Poland's right-wing populist government, emphasizes: "We have a problem with a part of the European political elite and with journalists, but not with the normal people. For example, 97 percent of all foreign investors would come to us again."

If they have sufficient power, populists try to colonize the state itself. One of the first changes Orbán and his party, Fidesz, sought after coming to power in 2010 was a transformation of civil service law that would enable them to place loyalists in what were supposed to be nonpartisan bureaucratic positions. The justification they gave was that the liberal left controlled the state and had to be purged; in line with their self-conception as the only true representatives of the people, populists could also claim that the state was there for the people, so that if they took possession of the administration, it was simply the people themselves appropriating what was rightfully theirs. Trump took longer to understand this logic, but eventually he also purged inspectors general who were supposed to check for fraud and favoritism in the federal government.

Both Fidesz and the Law and Justice party (PiS) in Poland moved no less smartly to control the courts and exert power over the state media. It was made clear that journalists should not report in ways that violated the interests of the nation, equated with the interests of the ruling party. Like Napoleon III, they would typically counter any criticism from jurists or journalists by demanding, "Who elected you?" India's finance minister declared that "democracy can't be the tyranny of the unelected"; the Polish justice minister, engaged in relentless attacks on the independent judiciary, felt it necessary to explain that Poland was a democracy and not a "courtocracy."

Trump has not been the only one given to declaring the independent media "enemies of the people." Yet the capture of the media by authoritarian populists does not have to be complete; again, too obvious a *Gleichschaltung*—a homogenization of political content—would remind both citizens and outsiders of paradigmatic twentieth-century dictatorships. Independent websites and a major German-owned commercial TV station continue to operate in Hungary, for instance, but virtually all the country's regional newspapers have passed into the hands of government-friendly oligarchs. Many of the latter were kind enough at the end of 2018 to "donate" their holdings to a new foundation tasked with "promoting activities that serve value creation and strengthen Hungarian national identity in the print, radio, television, and online media platforms that make up Hungarian mass communication." According to the social scientist Gábor Polyák, the foundation—comprising in the end around five hundred media outlets and registered at the holiday home of a major Orbán ally—controls about 16 percent of all revenue in the Hungarian media market. On the basis of a special clause in competition law, the government declared the merger to be of "strategic national importance," thereby preempting any action by the authorities officially charged with mitigating concentrations of media power.

In some countries, critical or even just potentially critical media outlets have been shut down completely. The coronavirus pandemic has equipped governments with new powers to halt the spread of misinformation or outright disinformation, but in the hands of the new authoritarians any criticism of the government's response has often been equated with "spreading fake news" and "scaremongering." In Hungary, police have detained several citizens who had posted comments finding fault with the government's policies for the pandemic; they confiscated phones and computers and made sure that videos of their repressive conduct were displayed on Facebook.

Where such outright threats are too risky, it is often the government itself that tries to create as much misinformation as possible. Trump's playbook has included not just the individual intimidation of journalists (especially female ones) but the strategy of "flood[ing] the zone with shit," in the words of Stephen K. Bannon, one-time chief strategist of Trumpism, then accused of defrauding Trumpists donating to build the wall, then pardoned by his political padrone (alongside many others who conspicuously looked like mafia-types). Professional journalists find it virtually impossible to deal with such "manufacturing of confusion" (in the words of the media critic Jay Rosen) from the very top; they know the statements to be false, but since a president is making them, they have to be covered (or so it seems). They also find it no less difficult to deal with a figure like Bannon who frames professional media as "the opposition" and hence puts pressure on the latter to prove their impartiality through ever more contorted presentations of "balance" and "objectivity" (for instance, by finding experts who did not outright deny the idea that injecting disinfectants might help against the coronavirus). Other journalists have marketed themselves relentlessly as truth tellers and defenders of democracy, though making oneself into the press department of the resistance would appear to confirm precisely what the likes of Trump and Bannon have been saying about the media all along (we'll get back to this point in the final chapter; there is a way to reinforce the basic rules of democracy against right-wing populists while maintaining a credible commitment to objectivity—though not neutrality—at the same time).

Protest from within civil society poses a particular problem for populists: it potentially undermines their claim to be the exclusive representatives of the people. Their solution is to follow a strategy already perfected by Vladimir Putin (in many ways a role model for today's right-wing populists, and a real innovator when it comes to the kleptocrat's tool kit): try to "prove" that civil society isn't civil society at all and that what seems like popular opposition on the streets has nothing to do with the real people. On one level, this is perfectly consistent with the logic of populism: if one asserts "we and only we represent the people," then by definition it cannot be the case that people are out there protesting on the street against their unique authentic representatives; clearly, they must be fake people, so to speak.

And what makes them fake? The answer is always ready at hand. Right-wing populist regimes have gone out of their way to portray NGOs and ordinary protesters as the tools of external powers, and even pass laws that declare them "foreign agents." Trump, for instance, described the millions who came out against his proposed "Muslim travel ban" as "paid-up activists" and used the term again about critics of his Supreme Court nominee Brett Kavanaugh (for good measure, he also declared them "evil").

Governments can always trot out the usual suspects—the CIA is behind it all, or Soros—but for the truly creative conspiracy theorist there are no limits: the Gezi Park protests, an Erdoğan adviser eventually explained, were the doing of Lufthansa, which allegedly feared increased competition from Turkish Airlines after the opening of Istanbul's new airport (by some measures now the largest in the world, or, at any rate, large enough to push the Germans into procuring and organizing fake Turks).

At the same time, populists might positively come to like protest: it is fuel to the fire of the culture wars on which they thrive. This is why, in the first year of the Trump administration, Bannon described the "resistance" as "our friend" (by the same logic, the opposition-friendly "fake media" were also the Trumpists' friends). The lesson here is not, of course, that citizens should refrain from taking to the streets to protest, only that one must be aware of how swift and sophisticated populists can be in turning dissent to their own advantage, to justify what always ends up as a form of exclusionary identity politics.

Identity politics of this kind is not about beliefs; it is about proving that you belong to the real people. One less noted legacy of the Cold War is that we assume the terms of political conflict must be traceable to the ideas of important thinkers. Want to understand Putin? The intellectual power behind the throne of the new czar is said to be the "Eurasianist" philosopher Alexander Dugin, talked up by Western pundits as "the most dangerous philosopher in the world." Care truly to comprehend the bizarreness of Bolsonaro? Study the YouTube channel of Olavo de Carvalho, self-taught Brazilian philosopher, former astrologer, and chain-smoking conspiracy theorist (who resides among real Americans in Virginia). We were told over and over that the man to watch if we wanted to make sense of Trumpism was the political sage Bannon, whose secret reading list is said to include such figures as the Italian traditionalist Julius Evola, a major inspiration for the European New Right.

Instant intellectual history of this sort takes it for granted that we are dealing with political actors inspired by comprehensive worldviews; it also assumes without much evidence that far-right parties succeed because voters find particular philosophies attractive.[12] In fact, leaders do not want to be constrained by intellectuals who might criticize them for failing to implement ideas properly, and in any case most citizens know little about the esoteric musings of the alleged powers behind the throne.

It isn't hard to see why liberal (again, in the broadest sense of that term) thinkers have inadvertently been building up their opponents into philosophical giants of illiberalism: it gives them something to work with as political theorists. And even if Bannon, asked about Evola's philosophy of traditionalism, replies, "I'm just some fuckin' guy, making it up as I go along," the disavowal of deep political ideas can be read as a perfidious way to conceal them.[13]

The Will of the People

Not all liberals necessarily want to explore esoteric realms of astrology and theories of how Aryans originated in the Arctic—the kind of stuff the Dugins and Carvalhos specialize in. As an alternative, one can always indulge the view of the people as ill-informed, irrational, and itching for authoritarianism—what in fact has been a kind of default position for many liberals ever since the early nineteenth century. As Hillary Clinton put it in a remarkably evidence-free interview, right-wing populism meets what she calls "a psychological as much as a political yearning to be told what to do."

But do citizens really crave that strong hand? Have large majorities truly been converted to the views of the far right? Contrary to the domino theory propounded by pundits and populists themselves—first Brexit, then Trump, then Le Pen, and so on—the fact remains that until today no right-wing populist has come to power anywhere in western Europe or North America without the collaboration of established conservative elites. Farage did not bring Brexit about all by himself; he needed his Michael Gove, a longtime Tory cabinet member, and his Boris Johnson, who assured voters that Brexit was a jolly good idea. Trump was not elected as the leader of a spontaneous grassroots movement of, as the cliché would have it, angry white working-class males; he was the candidate of a very established party. The Republican heavyweights Chris Christie, Rudy Giuliani, and Newt Gingrich in effect vouched for Trump's character. What happened on November 8, 2016, was in one sense explicable with the most banal political science account of all: partisanship. Citizens who identify with the Republican Party came out and did what most voters do on Election Day: they cast a ballot for their party—something utterly normal, except that the candidate was obviously not quite so normal.[14] It happened in 2016, and it happened again in 2020.

The abnormality did not go unnoticed, of course, but it could be overridden by other concerns. Some Republicans went on record saying that they considered Trump unqualified to be president. And then they revealed that they had just voted for him. The explanation of that seemingly schizophrenic position is that an increasing number of elections are less about enthusiastically endorsing a mandate and more about resoundingly rejecting someone or something else. Political groupings are brought together not by what John Stuart Mill called "common sympathies" but by what one might name "common antipathies," or what political scientists refer to as "negative identity." Clearly, for many on the American right (and some on the left), Hillary Clinton was unelectable no matter what;[15] for many Brazilians, it was of supreme importance to vote against Lula's Workers' Party.[16] In Hungary and Poland, Orbán and Kaczyński did not campaign on the promise of dismantling the rule of law in the decisive elections of 2010 and 2015, respectively. Instead, they presented their parties as mainstream center-right (in the case of Hungary, that self-presentation was certified by Europe's most powerful Christian Democrats—the Bavarians with their car industry). And citizens, rather than revealing deep-seated yearnings for authoritarianism, did exactly what democratic theory would have told them to do in a two-party system where one of the major contenders had become discredited—in Hungary because of the Socialists' corruption and disastrous economic record, in Poland because Donald Tusk's Christian Democratic Civic Platform had become complacent after too many years in power.[17] Only after resounding victories did Orbán and Kaczyński declare that it was time to remake political institutions.

Populists in power assert that a triumph at the ballot box translates into everyone's now having to accept that they, *and only they*, represent the will of the people (and if that claim is accepted, other details aren't all that important; as an acquaintance from India put it to me, as long as you support Modi, you can eat a burger). Never mind that these figures often did not reach an actual majority (let alone a supermajority): the BJP, for instance, won a mere 37 percent of the vote in the elections in India in 2019 but, as a result of the first-past-the-post system, received a majority in parliament (a similar outcome could be observed in Poland in 2015, where the Law and Justice party, on the basis of 37 percent of the vote share—19 percent of eligible voters—gained a majority in the Sejm and took this as a mandate to dismantle the rule of law). In Hungary, Orbán declared the 2010 election, in which his party received a majority of the votes and a supermajority in parliament, a "revolution at the ballot box"—construing a comprehensive mandate for constitutional as well as far-reaching social and political changes, even though a new constitution had not been part of the election manifesto.

It's a mistake to read authoritarian outcomes back into some mystical will of the people, as though whatever has happened under right-wing authoritarian populists is what all citizens really wanted all along. It is also a mistake to think that such populists have gotten the people more involved in day-to-day governance. True, an Orbán has trumpeted his "national consultations"—regular countrywide polls on specific policy questions. He describes these exercises as a sign that ordinary folks have been empowered to resist the impositions of liberal elites, in particular what the Hungarian leader calls the "liberal nihilists" in Brussels, the EU headquarters. But these exercises are highly manipulated: the questions are leading or outright nonsense; for instance, Magyars were asked to express an opinion on a "Soros plan" for refugees that does not exist. Even so, to make sure the people give the right answer, the government spends millions on propaganda to incite hatred of immigrants and the European Union. Tellingly, when one such consultation proved invalid because of insufficient turnout, Orbán claimed the mantle of unique representative of the people's will anyway: right-wing populists don't even respect the rules they themselves have created, because it's always possible to invoke a quasi-mystical notion of the real people's will in contrast to mere numbers at the ballot box.

This tells us something more general about the relationship between populism and direct democracy. We should disregard the conventional wisdom that associates populism with a principled defense of letting the people speak without representatives and intermediaries. For referenda have a very specific meaning for populists: they are *not* understood as an open-ended process in which citizens exchange views, argue with one another, and so on. Rather, the correct collective answer to a question is always already known, because it can be deduced from the—in the end, symbolic—understanding of the real people propounded by populists. The role of the people is not permanently to participate in politics; rather, they should just tick the right box and confirm what populist leaders have always been claiming about the popular will. There is not meant to be any uncertainty about the outcome.

It is not an accident, then, that in the countries discussed so far populist regimes have not transformed the political system so as to make it more open to ordinary folks; on the contrary, where possible, such regimes have taken as much uncertainty out of elections as possible, be it through voter suppression, gerrymandering, or the populist arts of governance already discussed.

But doesn't this then prove Clinton's point? People crave the strong hand or are at least willing to put up with it. True, some of the leaders mentioned so far have genuine popular support, but this should not be read as a clear collective wish for authoritarianism. The problem is not that ordinary people wish to be done with democracy; the problem is the choices on offer in highly polarized and increasingly fragmented societies.[18]

The Double Secession

Populism is not uniquely responsible for polarization, but it's important to understand that populists' key strategy simply *is* polarization. They seek to divide polities into homogeneous groups and then insinuate that some groups are fundamentally illegitimate or even pose an existential threat. Instead of being characterized by identities and interests that cut across different political groups, the political world is simplified and rendered in terms of one central cleavage that's of existential importance (along the lines of "if the wrong side wins, we shall perish"). The victory of the other side spells not so much a temporary defeat; rather, it poses a grave threat to a common life or even the end of the polity as such (according to a Pew survey in 2016, 45 percent of Republicans and 41 percent of Democrats saw the other party as a "threat to the nation's well-being"[19]).

Polarization, contrary to many laments in the United States in particular, is not somehow hardwired into us; human brains are not programmed for tribalism. It is easier, however, for political polarization entrepreneurs to do their work in deeply fragmented societies. But why are societies fragmented? Why do they have trouble agreeing on who the people are, and just why they are in this (polity) together? A conventional answer points to the increasing number of refugees and immigrants in a range of countries (countries, one should say, to which people with the luxury of writing and speaking about theories of peoplehood would pay attention). There are also anxieties about supposed demographic decline and, more particularly, the shifting ethnic composition of the demos due to differences in birthrates among various ethnic groups (both of which have fired the imagination of right-wing populists eager to stoke fears of a "great replacement" of current populations).[20] But these answers are simplistic; they assume that one particular policy challenge more or less determines the political divisions in society.

Brexit and Trump are commonly mentioned together to

illustrate the rise, or sheer political power, of populism. One curious fact has rarely been noted. The campaigns supporting Hillary Clinton and Remain had similar-sounding slogans— ones that seemed to have spectacularly failed to resonate with large parts of the electorate: "Stronger together" and "Stronger in Europe." Evidently, a significant number of citizens felt that they might be stronger precisely by *not* being together.

I don't want to make too much of this coincidence, and campaign slogans don't decide outcomes. But it may indicate something crucial: what "together" means today has been put profoundly into question. In France, 35 percent of people claim that they have *nothing* in common with their fellow citizens.[21] Just *why* are we in this together, many people are asking, and what exactly do I have to do with the fate of these *other* people?

So, what has changed, such that the question of who precisely is part of the people is more in play than previously in the postwar era? It's not just immigration (which, in any case, is not a new development of the last few years); it's also what I shall call the "double secession," a problem further aggravated by the increasing stress middle classes are experiencing in the contemporary era. Let me explain.

The first secession, to put it bluntly, is that of the most privileged. They are nowadays often lumped together under the category of "liberal cosmopolitan elites," an invective thrown around by right-wing populist leaders but also a term employed by a growing number of pundits and social scientists. That designation is misleading in two respects: first, while it is true that many elites are very mobile (at least potentially if not always in fact), they are not necessarily cosmopolitan in any strong moral sense—if by "cosmopolitan" we mean not folks with the highest frequent-flier status but those committed to the idea that all humans stand in the same moral relation to one another, or, put more simply, that borders have no real moral significance. Rather obviously, being mobile is not the same as being universalist; this should have been clear ever since illusions about railway travel eliminating nationalism were debunked in the nineteenth century. On the other hand, one of the greatest universalist moral philosophers—Immanuel Kant—virtually never left his hometown of Königsberg in East Prussia.[22]

True, prominent members of various elites—including globally recognizable stars—make a big show of international charity work, but one searches in vain for advocates of what in political philosophy would be called genuine global justice: a real worldwide redistribution of resources and life chances. It is telling that in the 1990s and the early years of the twenty-first century the cheerleaders of globalization justified it not with its *globally* beneficial effects but with the advantages it would bestow on national constituencies.

"Cosmopolitan" is misleading in yet another way: the "mobility" of the privileged is often a matter of having options and day-to-day frequent-flier experience but not of actual migration. In many Western countries, economic and administrative elites still follow education and career paths that are distinctly national.[23] At the same time, they appear to be able to retreat from any real dependence on the rest of society (I say "appear" because they of course still rely on police, halfway usable roads, and so on). Not every one of them might literally live in a gated community, but the underlying trends of "self-sorting" and homogenization in wealthy enclaves are clear enough: the well educated and the well-off marry each other, live near one another, and reproduce many of their privileges over the generations. None of this is in and of itself immoral (would we want to go back to the glory days when bosses married secretaries? Would undoing all gentrification make inner cities great again?). But it has consequences for how society is understood and, specifically, for how citizens view one another: for those able truly to "socially distance," it is indeed not obvious why they should think of themselves as being in this together with the rest of the people. In fact, never mind anything like moral interdependence; it's not even obvious for what exactly one *needs* one's fellow citizens, practically speaking. With the globalization of supply chains, workers do not have to be in the same polity; with "free trade" regimes, consumers do not have to be in the same country; and with the shift away from mass armies after the end of the Cold War, one also no longer depends on one's fellow citizens to serve as soldiers.[24] Even "essential" workers are, as the 2020 pandemic demonstrated, more essential for some than for others; the privileged get to use "concierge" medical services to have access to doctors, nurses, and, of course, testing with results available in thirty minutes, all reserved exclusively for them.

An openly avowed, though also quite cartoonish, version of this secession of the economically powerful is provided by the Silicon Valley billionaire Peter Thiel. Thiel self-identifies as libertarian (and ended up as not only an adviser to Donald Trump but one of the figures trying to adorn Trumpism with actual ideas, after he declared that candidate Trump had to be taken seriously but not literally).[25] In a programmatic statement, he writes that "in our time, the great task for libertarians is to find an escape from politics in all its forms—from the totalitarian and fundamentalist catastrophes to the unthinking demos that guides so-called 'social democracy.'"[26] He is putting his hope into "some sort of new and hitherto untried process that leads us to some undiscovered country." Since, alas, there appear to be very few "undiscovered countries," Thiel is betting on "cyberspace," "outer space," and "seasteading" (as in "settling the oceans"); others count on the conquest of time more than space as they invest in cryonics (as in "freeze me now, resurrect later")—a kind of secession from the life of ordinary mortals altogether.

Thiel's dismissive remarks about the demos did not go unnoticed, in particular his sentence stating that "since 1920, the vast increase in welfare beneficiaries and the extension of the franchise to women—two constituencies that are notoriously tough for libertarians—have rendered the notion of 'capitalist democracy' into an oxymoron." He later clarified that he did not advocate stripping people of the vote. Indeed, the whole point was that one couldn't do much with a hopeless demos, even a suitably shrunken one; the best one could hope for was to seek distance from it. This attitude may as well be described as a desire for secession. It is not often expressed so directly (let alone justified with more or less philosophical-sounding techno-clichés as in Thiel's case). But the secession of the wealthy surely is happening.[27] The sordid realities that correspond to Thiel's pining for undiscovered countries are the acquisition of second passports, residency in more or less glamorous tax havens, third or fourth homes in supposedly apocalypse-proof places such as New Zealand, and, not least, transnational accounting tricks with entirely stateless entities. As two distinguished economists observe, "US firms have in 2016 . . . booked more than 20% of their non-US profits in 'stateless entities'—shell companies that are incorporated nowhere, and nowhere taxed. In effect, they have found a way to make $100 billion in profits on what is essentially another planet."[28] Such acts of secession are not undertaken by actual "citizens of nowhere" (nor does the money really end up nowhere); nor does any of this have anything to do with moral or even cultural cosmopolitanism, even if right-wing populist leaders, ever ready to wage culture wars, portray things that way. But the criticism of elites contains a kernel of truth: some citizens in effect take themselves out of anything recognizable as a halfway decent social contract.

To be sure, none of this is entirely new: the leading French revolutionary Abbé Sieyès, writing about French aristocrats, already observed that "the privileged actually come to see themselves as another species of man." They eventually found out that they were not, just as some today will eventually discover that there are no undiscovered countries and that during pandemics, even with concierge services at hand, one is in the end probably only as safe as the least safe place (as long as a virus could be *anywhere*).

Still, social distancing today is also not quite the same as it was in previous gilded ages; again, we are not dealing with any real "return of the past." Inequalities are often hidden, rather than openly justified, as was obviously the case in aristocracies; the opacity of democratic politics in complex societies with a highly developed division of labor can make it seem as if we are all in this together, when the reality is different rules for different people.

Cutting through the complexity (and breaking a political taboo), social scientists have asked whether some democracies—the United States above all—are not today de facto oligarchies. This does not mean equating America with, for instance, the kleptocratic Russia of the 1990s, or post-civil-war Lebanon, where, irrespective of election outcomes, the crucial political positions are controlled by the same self-enriching religious-cum-political leaders. Oligarchy might exhibit two different characteristics, and they don't necessarily have to go together. An oligarch, according to Aristotle's first criterion, was not just someone of immense wealth but also a figure ruled by his own appetites and the sheer need to grasp more and more (what the Greeks called *pleonexia*). As candidate Trump put it in a speech in Las Vegas in February 2016, after winning the Republican primary in Nevada,

> It's hard for me to turn down money because that's what I've done in my whole life, I grab and grab and grab. You know I get greedy I want money, money. I'll tell you what we're going to do, right? We get greedy right? Now we're going to get greedy for the United States we're going to grab and grab and grab. We're going to bring in so much money and so much everything.[29]

Obviously, not every rich person, and not everyone ruled by greed, is an oligarch (and it's very debatable whether Trump himself ever was one, other than by the grab-whatever-you-can criterion). For the second aspect of oligarchs—also highlighted by Aristotle—is that they can deploy their wealth to create dependencies and distort the political process. The effect, to put it bluntly, is that individuals with concentrated (and at the same time easily accessible) wealth operate in a different political universe. The political scientist Jeffrey Winters highlights the crucial dividing line between the run-of-the-mill wealthy and those who have so much excess cash that they can afford the pricey services of what Winters calls the "income defense industry."[30] Only those able to retain accountants and lawyers who can construct tax shelters in the Cayman Islands will have lower taxes than their own secretaries (in Warren Buffett's infamous example).[31]

Contrary to the cliché of the ultra-wealthy as liberal do-gooder globalists, the actual economic policy preferences of the 0.1 percent are extremely conservative. And they make sure that such preferences count for much more than those of the rest of the population, though not necessarily on all policy questions; oligarchs don't single-handedly decide about gun and abortion rules, for instance. But on taxes and trade, their preferences tend to win out, and because the policy details are so complex—often on purpose—many in the public, and even plenty of professionals for that matter, might not understand how the exceptionally wealthy benefit from particular decisions (without having ever appeared in public saying they want to "grab and grab and grab").[32] Even if they do, they might find it difficult to mobilize against, for instance, Republicans who stuffed emergency legislation during the 2020 pandemic with gifts for corporations, and the real estate industry in particular.

In the United States, figures one might plausibly describe as oligarchs have aligned themselves with an increasingly radical right, prominent counterexamples notwithstanding; they have been perfectly willing to accept the populist strategy of a Trump that, in the end, yielded no real wall for the real people but a tax cut for Wall Street: more than 80 percent of the 2017 Tax Cuts and Jobs Act giveaway went directly to the 1 percent (Republican donors had made it clear that if taxes were not slashed, funding would stop). Trump had promised to keep the Mexicans out; instead, his signature legislative achievement was to enable the most powerful Americans to take themselves out of common fiscal obligations and to live in what we may as well call a concierge society. Hemingway famously responded to F. Scott Fitzgerald's lines in his story "The Rich Boy"—"Let me tell you about the very rich. They are different from you and me"—with the observation that the rich are indeed different, because they have more money; it turns out that they have not only more money but, crucially, also more power to protect that money.

Note how this de facto secession relies not on any kind of conspiracy but on controlling one of the two major political parties (and having influence on the other one as well, of course). As Jacob S. Hacker and Paul Pierson have pointed out, Republicans and their financial backers are well aware that their policy preferences do not enjoy broad support among the electorate; they need to tie their economic agenda to a strategy of permanently waging culture war to have any chance of winning, and even wins are made possible only by the structural advantages rural voters enjoy in the American political system, in particular their gross overrepresentation in the Senate.[33] And, as a fallback, there is always voter suppression and other means to ensure that what is nominally a democracy becomes a de facto tyranny of the minority—a scenario about which the very founders Republicans claim to worship were in fact deeply worried.

We should be less concerned, then, about the psychology of the rich and famous—*pace* Aristotle. It makes more sense to worry about the underlying infrastructure of democracy—in particular, the nature of the party system and the rules concerning campaign finance that crucially shape it. It is this infrastructure that facilitates something like a secession of the wealthiest.

The other secession I am concerned with is much less visible. It's not like the *secessio plebis* in the Roman Republic, when the plebs literally trekked out of the city under protest, organizing a kind of general strike to bring about major political changes and leaving the wealthy in the lurch. It's also not like the poorer citizens in ancient democratic Athens discovering that the rich really were good for nothing. As Plato (admittedly, not an unbiased observer) describes that moment of recognition,

> A poor man, lean and suntanned, is stationed in battle next to a rich one, reared in the shade and carry-

ing a lot of excess flesh, and sees him panting and
completely at a loss . . . [H]e believes that it is because
of the cowardice of the poor that such people are rich
and . . . one poor man says to another when they
meet in private: "These men are ours for the taking;
they are good for nothing."[34]

But such a change of mind—terrifying for all who worry
that democracy always holds the possibility of the poor
soaking the rich—is not at all what we are witnessing today.

Rather, the second secession is this: an increasing number
of citizens at the lower end of the income spectrum (to put it
very neutrally) no longer vote or participate in any other form
in politics. Of course, I do not suggest that this de facto self-
separation is based on a conscious program in the way Thiel's
space (or spaced-out) fantasies are; there is no "undiscovered
country" for them; there's only the land of deprivation and
quiet despair, which can be as much inside people's minds as
it is on maps of what are sometimes euphemistically called
"disadvantaged communities."[35]

Such a largely invisible secession can easily become self-
reinforcing: political parties have no reason to care for those
who don't care to vote; this in turn strengthens the impression of the poor (to the extent they can afford any attention
at all) that there's nothing in it for them when it comes to politics. The result is declining and, specifically, also ever more
distorted participation. The German political scientist Claus
Offe sums up the logic at work: "As people are conditioned to
'waste' their rights and political resources, and as competing
political elites and political parties *come to understand* that
parts of the electorate are less likely than others to make use
of their political resources, those elites will concentrate their
platforms, campaigns and mobilization strategies upon those

segments of the citizenry who actually 'count' and neglect others."[36] In short, a vicious cycle, as a result of which political elites and poorer citizens will be driven ever further apart.

The pandemic of 2020 has been like a Rorschach test: everyone could see in it the political lessons they had always favored anyway ("we need to strengthen the state!"). But it was also an X-ray: it made structural problems visible (it did not create them). The privileged could retreat into their homes, the very privileged could retreat into their second homes (of which there are 3.4 million in France, for instance), and the oligarchs could go to their hotel-like compounds in the Hamptons or, creating more distance still, sail off on their yachts (though this caused the conundrum of whether and how to quarantine with the servants). By contrast, those already disadvantaged kept dying, confirming that in the United States a nominal democracy remains in many ways a racial caste society: the poor were much more likely to have underlying conditions and to live in cramped spaces. Even the thought that the better-off depended on the health of delivery workers seems not to have led to any real sense that, as the clichéd phrase went, "we are in this together" because we actually depend on one another (and that, to paraphrase the poet W. H. Auden, this was a moment when we must help one another or die). To acknowledge dependence would not have meant the end of conflict or political disagreement, but it would have exposed some of the absurdities of the culture wars, where even wearing a mask out of consideration for oneself and others became coded as the wrong political identity. Instead, Benjamin Disraeli's description of Britain in the nineteenth century seemed a perfect fit for some Western countries in the twenty-first:

> two nations; between whom there is no intercourse
> and no sympathy; who are as ignorant of each other's

> habits, thoughts, and feelings, as if they were dwellers
> in different zones . . . who are formed by a different
> breeding, are fed by a different food, are ordered by
> different manners, and are not governed by the same
> laws.

At the top, the nation features citizens highly engaged in politics but who have everywhere else to go; the separate nation at the bottom consists of men and women highly disengaged who have pretty much nowhere to go. Of course, this is a radical simplification; there is also the challenge of an increasingly stressed middle, which in some countries can include what on the surface looks like an upper-middle class of affluent professionals. In the United States, the latter are increasingly anxious about rising tuition and narrowing paths to college (that is, means of reproducing privileges). When they think about "the great replacement," it's not Muslims who come to mind but machines that will substitute for jobs in accounting and management.

There is plenty of evidence for citizens' deepening pessimism about the economic future of themselves and their descendants: 60 percent of Americans and 64 percent of Europeans think their children will be worse off. As the political scientist Adam Przeworski observes, "This collapse of the deeply ingrained belief in intergenerational progress is a phenomenon at a civilizational scale." It's these conditions of perceived threat and prospective decline that best explain why middle-class citizens appear willing at least sometimes to condone breaches of democratic principles and the rule of law. Many citizens are at least somewhat aware that the Orbáns and Trumps of this world are chipping away at democracy. Yet, in highly polarized and increasingly unequal societies, they are willing to put up with the damage out of economic self-interest (whether illusory or real).[37] The problem is at its most severe when populists stoke a sense of "it's either us or them" or create a panic about "the country being taken away from us." As the political scientist Larry Bartels has shown, what he calls "ethnic antagonism"—enmity toward nonwhites supposedly grabbing power or at least making too many claims on the state—explains the weakening commitment to democratic principles among a significant number of self-identified Republicans in the United States. This isn't just about dispensing with niceties in defense of what they evidently re-gard as a kind of "ethno-state"; they are explicitly endorsing lawlessness, even violence.[38]

Today, then, some citizens are willing to engage in a trade-off between what they think is personally good for them—or helps them to provide a better future for their kids—and damage to democracy. And this impulse to trade democracy against something else isn't just a temptation for economi-cally (or, for that matter, racially) insecure majorities or fright-ened middle classes: the most privileged often in effect say that they're enthusiastic about democracy and that we all need to defend it, but only if their taxes don't go up. The orig-inal meaning of democracy was something like the whole people "going on together"; for democracy's enemies in an-cient Greece, it meant the poor threatening the rich, because the poor might want to advance their material interests (just as oligarchs do).[39] The wealthy's commitment to democracy has always been conditional.

During the 2020 primary campaign, Lloyd Blankfein, for-mer head of Goldman Sachs and a registered Democrat, ad-mitted, "I think I might find it harder to vote for Bernie than for Trump." Asked about Sanders's attack on the "billionaire class," he stated, "I don't like assassination by categorization. I think it's un-American. I find that destructive and intemperate. I find that just as subversive of the American character as someone like Trump who denigrates groups of people who he has never met. At least Trump cares about the economy."

So oligarchs can find something positive in right-wing populist parties because, as a matter of fact, they promote their economic interests ("at least Trump cares about the economy"): here is plutocratic populism. Meanwhile, middle classes can view those parties as saviors of the "real people" from various undeserving others, be it the poor or ethnic minorities (or both at the same time); as a leader of the far-right party in Germany put it, "We need the fearful to move majorities."[40] And the worst-off don't vote at all, or when they do, it's pure protest, with the right-wing populist candidate sometimes seeming to stand for "the biggest fuck-you" (to quote Michael Moore on Trump).

As the character Octave says in Jean Renoir's film *The Rules of the Game*, in many ways a film about the crisis of democracy in the 1930s, "Everybody has their reasons." It is unlikely that we can completely change what people think of as good reasons. But we might change their circumstances and the choices they are facing, which is another way of saying change democracy's critical infrastructure. To do that, we shall need a clearer sense of democracy's underlying principles—*riduzione verso il principio*. But before embarking on this journey back to basics, there is one more lesson we can take from the triumphs of right-wing populism.

A Hard Border

Right-wing and left-wing populists may have a point when they speak in their own way about the secession of the powerful. But they are wrong to reduce all conflicts to questions of belonging or to deem disagreement with them as automatically illegitimate ("those who disagree must be traitors"). This impulse is why genuine left-wing populists—that is to say, actors who claim a monopoly on representing the people, in the name of some left-wing ideology or other—are also prone to destroying democratic institutions: after all, there is no reason to protect the basic political rights of their opponents once the latter have been deemed not to deserve a place in the democratic game at all. Venezuela under Chávez and Maduro is the most obvious example.

Right-wing populists often engage in a curious political projection. Effectively, they conjure up something like an expulsion of the supposedly "real people," who very unfairly have been made to feel like strangers in their own country. Then again, the real people can hardly secede from their own homeland, though some of the far right are trying, when they seek to create a white supremacy wonderland in North Dakota (more on which later) or when Austria's right-wing populist party, the Freedom Party, acquired a picturesque small inn—Pension Enzian—where they hid gold with the argument that they might need a refuge in case a European civil war broke out. So, those who stoke fears of "losing the country" then themselves seek the expulsion from the polity of all those who allegedly do not truly belong to the people. Those excluded will hardly be the most powerful; rather, it is usually already-vulnerable minorities who will be harassed and have their rights denied. Never mind that the pandemic could have taught the lesson that "the real people" actually depend on those often framed as alien minorities: the migrant workers picking the fields in the United States; the Romanians and Bulgarians who ended up as the only highly mobile Europeans, since they were sent on chartered flights to process meat in German factories (while the supposedly liberal cosmopolitan elites were staying put and working from home).

Any such interdependence is denied by right-wing populists, for to acknowledge interdependence would be to acknowledge that others have claims on you and that these claims need to be properly engaged in a political process;[41] instead, these leaders make majorities feel like victims under attack, or at the very least form communities of shared outrage.[42] That outrage has a real cause, because minorities really are making demands. But it's not inevitable that such demands become understood by the voters of right-wing populist parties as "people who don't really belong here are taking stuff from us."

Does all this amount in the end to saying that "people talk" is inherently dangerous, perhaps automatically illiberal, or even outright exclusionary? The answer is no. In fact, it would be peculiar if one sought entirely to dispense with people talk in a democracy. For instance, what would one think of a professional politician who, when asked about her vision of the people, could only reply that she had no idea but could discuss some great technical fixes for the recent local sewage problems?

Politics as a profession includes the duty to have given some thought to what constitutes the people; there's nothing strange about that. What marks the difference between the populist and the non-populist politician is that the latter treats a conception of "the people" as effectively a fallible proposition, a hypothesis, so to speak, that can be rejected (at least temporarily) at the ballot box.[43] By contrast, the populist politician not only always already knows the uniquely correct answer to the query "who are the people?"; he also treats that answer as if it were a given, indisputable fact (which he just uniquely happens to know). It is a claim that can never be disproven with an actual election or referendum result; if it seems to be rejected, that only goes to show that there must have been fraud. Populists do not claim to both follow and *form* the will of the people, as, broadly speaking, democratic politicians would do; rather, they pretend that they are just *finding* it, because the collective will can be deduced directly from the one authentic understanding of the people.[44]

Of course, this difference, significant as it is, does not exhaust the question of what makes for a non-populist conception of the people. Debates among political philosophers around this question have been caught between two extremes: on the one hand, the position that a morally correct theory would clarify the shape of political boundaries once and for all; defenders of nationalism as a moral theory would decree, for instance, that all major cultural groupings must be politically self-determining. On the other hand, there's the view that such theorizing amounts to an undemocratic imposition by moral philosophers. Instead of the latter, one should leave the question of the people entirely to messy, unruly political struggle; from this angle, any criteria of togetherness decreed from on high look like an illegitimate way to cut off a genuine democratic fight (never mind that moral philosophers can only dream of having such power).[45]

Yet simply throwing up one's arms in the face of political conflict—let the chips fall where they may—would appear to leave one speechless in the event of politicians systematically disempowering or even disenfranchising minorities. At the same time, advocates of fighting it out in politics do have a point when they cast doubt on the notion of a uniquely correct moral answer, an answer, that is, which would leave the demos with no other role than gratefully accepting the right plan handed down by philosophers.[46] They cannot just take for granted that "contestation" necessarily results in inclusion; it could well lead to calls for shrinking the demos (through expulsions, for instance).[47]

Both answers, then, are unsatisfactory. Perhaps that's because the question is badly posed. We're not looking at a globe populated by humans and then asking what would be the correct way of dividing them into discrete peoples; we'd be searching in vain for an Archimedean point from which to do this.[48] I suggest we embark on a different route. What we are really interested in is not just "the people" in the abstract but the people as a *democratic* people. Of course, that's presuming a lot. In particular, it presumes that a distinct group is committed to realizing a way of life according to principles of equality and freedom.[49] I'll address the question of how exactly these principles relate to democracy in the next chapter; for now, I'll make yet another presumption—namely that a shared intention to live according to such principles has to translate into an imperative to maintain an institutional machinery (a state, for shorthand) that enforces such a shared commitment.[50]

One may well object that what needed to be proven has now just been presumed. But this very rough sketch of a democratic people does not prescribe a specific answer in the endless conflict over boundaries; it just limits possible conflict in two not so trivial ways.

First, a distinctly democratic people cannot expel or disenfranchise citizens (that is, exclude them against their will); it also cannot in more insidious ways deny the standing of particular citizens, for that conflicts with a commitment to democratic equality. Such conduct—or even just such rhetoric—is outside what we may as well call a *hard border* of democratic conflict. Denying the wishes of those who seek to expel or disenfranchise is not a violation of democratic principles, as such citizens fail to subscribe to the collective democratic project in the first place; less obviously, no particular effort to justify policies is owed to them, since they do not accept the shared framework of the polity at all.[51] I'll say more in the last chapter about scenarios where citizens determined to expel and disenfranchise others organize in political parties, thus posing a more serious threat than individual voices.

Second, in struggles over boundaries, one cannot simply assert a supposedly self-evident conception of the people. That is what defenders of a particular ethnic conception of the nation tend to do (such advocates do not necessarily have to be populists who assume that the popular will just somehow needs to be *revealed* by the leader).[52] The problem is not that a position which seeks to restrict immigration is necessarily outside democratic debate; at issue is not the substance of this view but the way it's being asserted: it actually tries to put peoplehood beyond political conflict altogether by pretending that it's naturally given. It's one thing to make the argument that immigration drives down wages of low-skilled workers (though the evidence for this claim is hardly conclusive); it's another simply to posit that only Christians can be Americans—end of debate! As the legal theorist Christoph Möllers has pointed out, "Where there is final certainty about the concept of the people, democracy has ended."[53]

That leaves plenty of room for democratic conflict. What it doesn't leave room for is the simple assertion of the people as given ("Americans must be white Christians, and the state belongs only to them"—the kind of thought that makes Republicans condone damage to democracy). Of course, one can wonder whether the hard border suggested above isn't also just an "assertion" that takes a question central for any polity and places it de facto outside politics. The point is that the border is justified with respect to an indispensable element of democracy—namely equality. And it's true that nondemocratic states don't have such worries (and such normative borders).[54]

These points do not translate into saying that actual borders should never be changed, or that any process at the end of which a demos has apparently shrunk is automatically illegitimate. Think of a permanently alienated cultural minority—such as the Kurds—that cannot express itself because a dominant group instrumentalizes the state to promote its own culture (including its own language) at the expense of all others; such a situation may be grounds for actual legal secession, which would leave a diminished demos behind (though even with separations and secessions among democratic peoples, there is no such thing as a right to expel).

Not surprisingly, then, questions of peoplehood drive us back to democracy (as long as we assume a democratic people), and democracy in turn forces us to take a closer look at equality. But note how the need to keep open the possibility of struggling over questions of belonging within what I've called the hard border also points to examining the quality of democracy's critical infrastructure. It's not one "people" who debate. As Judith Shklar once observed, in a piece tellingly titled "Let Us Not Be Hypocritical," "A people is not just a political entity, as was once hoped. Parties, organized campaigns, and leaders make up the reality."[55] That reality can be better or worse. Going back to democracy's basics helps us to see more clearly what exactly makes it better or worse.

2. REAL DEMOCRACY: Liberty, Equality, Uncertainty

How do you ever arrive at consensus before you have
conflict? In fact, of course, conflict is the vital core of an
open society; if you were going to express democracy in a
musical score, your major theme would be the harmony
of dissonance. All change means movement, movement
means friction and friction means heat.

—SAUL ALINSKY

Whence all this passion toward conformity anyway?—
diversity is the word . . . It's "winner take nothing" that is
the great truth of our country or of any country. Life is to
be lived, not controlled; and humanity is won by continuing
to play in face of certain defeat. Our fate is to
become one, and yet many.

—RALPH ELLISON, *Invisible Man*

Competition is for losers.

—PETER THIEL

Right-wing authoritarian populists insinuate that not all citizens are the real people; rather, some people do not belong at all or are at best second-class citizens. Even if this incitement of contempt or outright hatred does not result in "trickle-down aggression" (though why wouldn't it?), one is correct to think that a basic democratic principle is being violated: in a

democracy, citizens are supposed to enjoy a sense of fundamental political equality.

This is a widely shared intuition, one that also immunizes
democracy against a particular danger: if democracy is considered a good thing because it delivers prosperity and peace,
then it might as well be abandoned if another political system
can provide riches and stability more effectively (an idealized
authoritarian China, for instance). If people feel strongly that
they do not want to live in a society in which some are assumed to be fundamentally superior to others—a kind of caste
society—then they have reasons to prefer democracy to even an
authoritarianism with a supposedly human face; higher performance will not automatically beat messy, slow, often seemingly irrational democratic procedures.[1]

Note that there are two different understandings of
equality at work here: one is about equal rights; the other
is about "social equality"—the kind of ease among people
who consider one another equal (but not the same). It was
the lack of deference and power plays in everyday American life that so astonished the French aristocrat Alexis de
Tocqueville; Tocqueville, after all, hailed from a world in
which differences in status—even after the official end of
the ancien régime—were absolutely everything. This kind
of equality responds to a very basic human desire to look
one another in the eye; people don't want to spend their
lives scraping and bowing (and constantly calculating what
others think of them).[2] Such equal relations, by definition,
are impossible in a nondemocratic—that is to say, politically
hierarchical—society.[3] But of course equal social relations are
also not automatically assured in countries with free and fair
elections. Plenty of areas of contemporary life, from patriar-
chal families to corporations where employees may have to
soil themselves (because only a limited number of, or even

no, bathroom breaks are allowed), are characterized by domination: people who are nominally equal citizens of a democratic state are actually at the arbitrary will of the powerful.

If one takes social equality seriously, a neat division between official "politics"—the stuff that's usually first on the news at night—and lived experience in work and family breaks down.[4] This does not mean that all areas of life must feature elections in order to be acceptable; there exist hierarchies that can be justified and that do not translate into domination (I may tell my students what to do without assuming that they are somehow inferior, or violating their dignity, in the way a ban on bathroom breaks does). Still, democracy in this social sense "bleeds" into other areas of life, and that's a good thing, too; it puts pressure on power holders to justify their positions. Simply saying "the world must be run by men," "star professors ought to be allowed to interrupt female students," and so on won't do as justifications.

Equality, whether in the social sense or in the sense of equal fundamental political rights, does not mean sameness or homogeneity: the opposite of equality is not difference, which can be perfectly compatible with political equality, but inequality.[5] What's more, neither legal equality nor social equality requires that people agree. One of the most widespread misconceptions about democratic politics today is that somehow division and conflicts are inherently problematic or outright dangerous. General Mattis, Trump's ill-fated secretary of defense, stressed a society's need for "fundamental friendliness"—at first sight something like the easygoingness that so impressed Tocqueville—but then went on to lament the lack of "political unity" in his country.[6] The promise of democracy is not that we shall all agree, and it does not require that citizens exhibit "uniformity of principles and habits," as Alexander Hamilton demanded (another political thinker got closer to the truth when he said—or, rather, sang—"We're one, but we're not the same"[7]). Citizens have very different ideas about the good life for themselves and the common good more broadly. The differences are not all explained by irrationality, lack of information, or absence of the proper political education (or reeducation). What often enough explains the differences are diverging dispositions, diverse life experiences, and varying ways of weighing evidence.[8] In a society of free and equal citizens, all these differences—and hence conflicts—are not going to magically disappear.

But disagreement is not the same as disrespect. The latter is not simply "rudeness" or "incivility"; rather, it is an attitude that denies the status of citizens as free and equal members of the political community. If one accepts this more precise understanding of disrespect, the good news is that there is less "disrespect" than is often alleged (for instance by a figure such as Trump, who would effectively call any criticism—but especially criticism from females—"disrespectful"). The bad news is that real disrespect is a more serious challenge for democratic politics than usually thought. I'll return to the question of how to be confrontational—even *very* confrontational— without violating democratic standards at the end of the very last chapter of this book.

Now, in theory, equal relations among citizens could also be ensured if they all delegated decision-making power to a neutral arbitrator who is somehow guaranteed to have no interest in domination: think of the mythical founding figures who, in the works of Rousseau and others, set up a perfect polity and then magically disappear. Or imagine a giant computer that would take everyone's preferences into account with equal concern and produce a happy policy outcome such that no citizens could feel that they had been treated as inferior.

It's fairly obvious how a different intuition about democracy makes such a picture unattractive.[9] For one thing, there's a difference between being treated equally by an impersonal apparatus and people *actively* treating one another as equals, affirming their status as full members of the polity.[10] More important still, rather than being treated equally by a machine, people also want to have choices; they want to act and claim powers, as opposed to being mere recipients of decisions, albeit of a benevolently programmed machine (or, for that matter, a China that worked as if its own propaganda were true). Elections do not just serve the purpose of getting rid of bad rulers peacefully, as conventional wisdom has it; they also allow citizens to exercise a larger capacity for choice, to say and do something by making use of fundamental political rights such as free speech and assembly. Put differently, elections do not just promise something like a collective thumbs-up or thumbs-down about a government; they include the freedom to take the initiative and offer something new—be it novel forms of political speech or an unprecedented political association (this obviously doesn't happen every day, but it's vital that the opportunities for it remain open). Such moves will likely cause friction—to use Saul Alinsky's term—but, again, this is not in and of itself the same as the kind of pernicious polarization discussed in the previous chapter.

Freedom means one can become engaged in politics; freedom also means one can choose not to become engaged in politics. Some will canvass and argue on doorsteps with gusto; others, for good or not so good reasons, will conclude that politics isn't for them. That doesn't mean citizens can no longer treat one another with respect. To be sure, some of the civic-minded may look at the disengaged with disdain, but that is not the same as denying their standing in the democracy.[11]

Democracy needs both equality and freedom, but it is precisely the combination of equality with freedom that makes equal influence on matters of state, or even equal chance of influence, unlikely (though not conceptually impossible): citizens throwing themselves into campaign work will have a different impact from the indifferent; those taking the time to work out persuasive arguments will leave a different mark from those who don't. To appreciate the tensions between equality and freedom—and to be clear-eyed about the possible costs of emphasizing one or the other—it's helpful to revisit the original Greek version of democracy, especially in its most radical form. The Greeks' experience demonstrates that equal chance of influence is actually not a completely unobtainable ideal; it also relativizes the prejudice of the moderns that elections—and the notion of choice—must be the only core element of democracy.

President for a Day?

Could equality ever mean *equal likelihood* of citizens influencing political outcomes?[12] In democracies in which representatives are chosen by election, the answer would seem to be no: some candidates are persuasive and charismatic; others aren't. Some candidates are known to virtually the entire country because they play a businessman or a president on reality TV: one can hardly complain that a political system lacks equality because one happens not to be Donald J. Trump or Volodymyr Zelensky (who had the benefit of having the TV show *Servant of the People*, in which he appeared as Ukraine's president, replayed nonstop the day before the 2019 presidential election, when officially all political advertising was banned).[13]

Even for those without TV shows, a much more mundane

argument holds: actual equal influence cannot be inherently desirable, because it would lead to the demand that bad arguments or inaccurate information have the same weight as coherent claims based on facts. An imperative of establishing equal influence would also restrict the activities of some citizens (you are allowed to knock on only so many doors per election!) and force others who don't want to participate in politics to do so.[14]

This doesn't mean that equal chances or opportunity—as opposed to de facto equal influence—is an unattainable ideal. After all, in the ancient polis many offices were filled by an elaborate (and highly manipulation-resistant) system of lot, such that the idea of ruling and being ruled in turn, at least for men of ethnic Athenian descent, *was* a reality. For instance, every citizen had a decent chance of being the head of the Council, whose task it was to prepare the agenda for the citizens' assembly (where anyone who turned up could vote on decrees by raising a hand). Chair of the Council was also a ceremonial office whose occupant held the seal of Athens, kept the keys to the treasury, and represented the polis vis-à-vis other polities—but only for twenty-four hours (yes, they were *that* serious about frequent rotation of magistrates—for us, used to associating offices with specialized skills, virtually unimaginable . . .). The historian Mogens Hansen observes, "Every second citizen above thirty . . . served at least once as a member of the Council; and three quarters of all councillors in any one year had to serve for a night and a day as *epistates ton prytaneon* (and never again). Simple calculation leads to this astonishing result: every fourth adult male . . . citizen could say 'I have been for twenty-four hours President of Athens'—but no Athenian citizen could ever boast having been so for *more* than twenty-four hours."[15] Thus, opportunities to occupy that "presidency" (which, however, conferred no particular privilege when it came to charting the overall course of the polis) really were equal.

True, other offices in the democracy were elective. The *strategos*—the general, for shorthand—was chosen for his specific capabilities, and a Pericles was chosen again and again. Finances were also placed in the hands of those deemed particularly good with numbers. Precisely for this reason some political thinkers writing today have identified the election of representatives as a form of aristocracy, but in the best sense of the term and in contrast to a truly democratic mechanism such as a lottery.[16] After all, it is a common view that citizens are tasked with trying to select the *aristoi*—literally, the best—through their vote (and not the merely wealthy, that is to say, oligarchs).[17] We don't want just anyone to represent us; we need clear evidence of competence, charisma, or at least the ability to convincingly copy presidential demeanor on TV (Zelensky as president could at least play himself playing president; Trump only ever acted as Trump).

If we truly believed in equality, this line of reasoning goes, we would be completely at ease with the idea of a lottery.[18] As consistent democrats, we should assume that *all* our fellow citizens (now including women and ethnic minorities!) are equally qualified—or at least qualified enough—to conduct affairs of state. After all, we have no real preconditions for politicians to run in elections, other than, in some countries, a minimum age and being born on native soil, and today the office of citizen (yes, that is an office as well!) also does not come with the expectation that one first prove one's capabilities. So, if we *really* meant it, when we talk about political equality, lottery—the mechanism that guarantees equal likelihood of success—would be the obvious way to go.

Does the fact that at least some of us recoil from this

idea prove that we just don't mean it when we rhapsodize about political equality? No. Elections—and the principle of representation—while not in and of themselves democratic, are also not inevitably tied to an aristocratic conception of politics. Let me say for now (and I'll expand on these points later in the chapter), elections and representation allow us to deal with deep-seated and yet legitimate conflicts within the hard border I argued for in the previous chapter. Representatives—in particular leaders of political parties—can articulate different interests and ideas but also identities; they can suggest terms of political engagement and then take the fight (at the ballot box, on TV and Twitter, and so on) from there. The nature of the fight is not just given; the conflict is partly about how to define conflicts. As the political scientist E. E. Schattschneider, in his self-consciously realist take on American politics, put it, "Political conflict is not like an intercollegiate debate in which the opponents agree in advance on a definition of the issues. As a matter of fact, *the definition of the alternatives is the supreme instrument of power*; the antagonists can rarely agree on what the issues are because power is involved in the definition."[19] Citizens who then become party to the conflict have skin in the game; they feel they're in the game and represented. In ancient Athens, as we'll see momentarily, there of course were conflicts, but no stable representations of conflicts or groups—that is to say, parties—to deal with them (there weren't even political groupings sitting together in the assembly). In fact, there was no word for "party," or even "politician" for that matter.[20]

Elections for a representative assembly, with well-known candidates standing clearly for different sides in well-understood conflicts, are in one sense clearly superior compared with lotteries: elections produce results that, at least on one level, are not a matter of subjective disagreement; what anti-democrats sometimes derided as "King Number" has the advantage that numbers are not open to individual interpretation.[21] In this simple sense, elections serve conclusively to process conflict: they generate winners and losers in an unambiguous manner.[22] If we assume, again in a hard-nosed-realist sort of way, that politics takes place in the permanent shadow of civil war, then elections are about potential parties to a violent conflict flexing their muscles; they'll settle the question of who's stronger without any shots being fired.[23] Thus, elections—what Walt Whitman called "a swordless conflict, / Yet more than all Rome's wars of old, or modern Napoleon's"—ultimately make for peace.[24]

Lotteries, by contrast, show nothing about the balance of political strength among different groups; they also do not allow losers to regroup and try again at the next contest. They might affirm a collective belief in equal basic competence among citizens, but they don't help to deal with persistent conflicts.

That's all very well, one might say, but it doesn't weaken the charge that election to representative bodies has an aristocratic character. The decisive counterargument comes down to the fact that ultimately it's up to citizens to decide what conflicts are most pressing and how and who best to represent their views and, at least sometimes, achieve a resolution. We do not impose *criteria* on the basis of which one has to select candidates in an election. In other words, in a democracy there is no agreed-on, let alone naturally given, notion of "the best"; citizens remain free to choose those who propose (not impose) themselves on whatever grounds they, left to their own lights, deem best (and, at least in theory, they may think of putting themselves forward, if they don't find what they are looking for on the list of candidates).[25]

This conjures up exactly the specter of reality TV presidents of which liberals are so scared.[26] But it is nevertheless central to a notion of equal political freedom. Individuals remain at liberty to decide what matters to them most. It's beneficial to talk about what that might be, because it might inspire others or, for that matter, because others can set me straight if my choices are based on incorrect information (the reality TV tycoon can't even run his own company properly, it turns out). But I ultimately don't owe them an account of my criteria or my concrete final choice, if more than one candidate fulfills those criteria. While democracy is an inherently collective exercise, it is telling that the act of voting is an isolated and anonymous one.[27] Citizens go to what the French tellingly call *isoloir*. That self-conscious "isolation" was initially introduced to protect voters from pressure by the powerful, and also from corruption (after all, it made no sense to bribe people if you couldn't check whether they had made the choice for which you had paid them).

But what if the corrupting influence of money or, as was typical of nineteenth-century elections in the United States, copious amounts of whiskey could be done away with? Why do we still need to have the "little man, walking into the little booth" (as one of Winston Churchill's less well-known definitions of democracy went)? In the eyes of some political thinkers, when there's no undue pressure, public accountability for one's vote seemed the right principle; the need to reveal one's decision would make for better choices. A nineteenth-century liberal like John Stuart Mill declared that "when the voter's own preferences are apt to lead him wrong, but the feeling of responsibility to others may keep him right, not secrecy, but publicity, should be the rule."[28]

Never mind that pressures from the powerful—be they employers or patriarchs—have hardly disappeared from the face of the earth; it is telling that where "open"—that is to say, non-secret—elections exist at all, incumbents overwhelmingly tend to win.[29] More important, the starting assumption that one could so easily distinguish right and wrong in voting is problematic and goes against the basic freedom to think about criteria for oneself. Evidence suggests that most citizens actually sincerely want to vote for the common good;[30] the problem is that the demand to do so is both too weak and too strong. It's too weak because, as anyone who has ever attended a certain kind of committee or business meeting (or, for that matter, political gathering) can attest, it might be all too easy to find ways of presenting particular concerns as being in the general interest (to others and even to oneself). But it's also too strong a demand, because democracy doesn't ask everyone to be altruistic all the time; people can feel at home in a democracy precisely because they can confidently assert their interests and try to build coalitions on that basis (provided that the underlying principles of freedom and equality are not violated: I cannot say that I find my interests respected only if I can proceed with putting together my mass movement for the expulsion of half my fellow citizens).

Mill, incidentally, gives the game away as to what he was really worried about. He noted that, apparently, the age of "coercion by landlords, employers, and customers" had passed but that

> at present . . . a much greater source of evil is the selfishness, or the selfish partialities of the voter himself. A "base and mischievous vote" is now, I am convinced, much oftener given from the voter's personal interest, or class interest, or some mean feeling in his own mind, than from any fear of consequences at the hands of others: and to these evil influences

the ballot [secret voting, that is] would enable him
to yield himself up, free from all sense of shame or
responsibility.[31]

Mill concluded with horror that "the electors themselves
are becoming the oligarchy."[32] In other words, he worried—in
1859—that one class, the workers, would simply vote its material "interest" and not for the common good.[33] But there was
and is nothing wrong with citizens' articulating their interests,
provided it happens within a fair, free, and open democratic
process (as opposed to the upper 1 percent reshaping that process in its own favor).

Mill was a progressive in his day; he just happened to think
that the greedy masses had to be kept in check. He even
advocated giving the educated more than one vote, not see-
ing that the privileged might be as prone to making selfish
choices as the great unwashed. But in any case, elections allow freedom, which also means the freedom to discriminate
(under cover of anonymity) among candidates;[34] no candidate can complain that they would have won had citizens
not discriminated against them (whereas a candidate can
complain that she couldn't make her case, for instance, in an
ostensibly democratic regime that has systematically clamped
down on media pluralism).[35]

Representation *or* Democracy?

In a representative democracy, we remain free to choose our
own criteria for who is "best" and must respect the choices
other citizens make in this regard. This is obviously not the
same as self-rule, or taking turns in ruling and being ruled,
as Aristotle told us we should. Rather, we elect representatives
to rule us, and of course plenty of the politicians we choose

actually end up in opposition (or do not get into parliament or Congress at all), with the result that many citizens cannot even say that they somehow rule indirectly.

For those thinking along lines suggested by Jean-Jacques Rousseau, this would be the end of the story—and it's obviously not a happy ending: delegating people power to representatives is incompatible with a proper understanding of what democracy is supposed to be about. As Rousseau put it, mocking the English pretension to self-rule, "The English people thinks it is free: it is greatly mistaken, it is free only during the election of Members of Parliament; as soon as they are elected it is enslaved, it is nothing."[36] Rousseau held that in a proper polity one would obey only laws that one had authored oneself; everything else is servitude. As he put it starkly, either one lived in an "association that will defend and protect the person and goods of each associate with the full common force, and by means of which each, uniting with all, nevertheless obey only himself and remain as free as before," or one was enslaved.[37] Note how representation is doubly bad: it means unfreedom, but also fundamental inequality; clearly, as mere electors, we are not equal to representatives who actually set the course of the polity.

Rousseau's dismal diagnosis rests on two assumptions: representation as such is always undemocratic; and freedom in public life requires unanimity. If I don't feel that I can go along with the law decided by everyone else, either I will be forced to obey another will and become unfree, or I somehow have to take myself out of the polity altogether. (There is a third possibility: I change my feelings, perhaps with a little help from my fellow citizens. This is the ominous scenario of people in Rousseau's polity being "forced to be free.")

A conventional response to the first assumption would be this: the modern world simply doesn't allow continuous participation by everyone; indeed, representation by elected politicians is just one aspect of the modern division of labor. The Athenians could rule and be ruled in turn only because they were relieved of all kinds of day-to-day burdens; citizens in the democratic polis could do politics more or less non-stop, but only because slaves and women (and resident aliens) did the work, and also because the poorer ones, during some periods of democratic Athens's history, were paid to attend to politics and, in particular, to sit on the courts.[38] We do not have such possibilities (actually, some countries where resident aliens do all the work might, but as of now the citizens of the Gulf states appear to exhibit little desire to emulate ancient democracy).[39]

While this image of Athens isn't completely wrong, it's also not really right: Athenian citizens actually did work (plenty of the poor, whom Plato and other enemies of democracy feared, were laborers and artisans, not an uneducated mob of loafers waiting to be roused by a demagogue).[40] People were paid to attend the assembly and sit on the people's court precisely because they couldn't easily forgo a day's work or a day's wages (to be sure, some people did always turn up early in the morning each day in the hope of being selected in the lottery; for them politics had become a job). The price of democratic politics in Athens was not slavery; it was the actual money needed to finance widespread participation (in combination with the citizens' willingness to make the effort and put in the time). Politics was for most Athenian men an important but still part-time activity; historians have estimated that the number of those who were really devoted to it might have been as low as a thousand (out of a citizenry of thirty thousand).[41] For all our obvious differences with the ancient world, this is a practice from which we can still learn, without having to abandon the idea of representation or assuming, implausibly, that governing doesn't require special knowledge and skills; indeed, I'll spell out a compelling lesson from Athens in the last chapter of this book.

The obvious objection to Rousseau's second assumption is that complex modern life doesn't allow for unanimity. Again, the contrast of past and present isn't completely wrong, but it's also not quite right: premodern life was hardly ruled by perfect consensus; the Athenians fought over politics all the time and were an extremely litigious lot; they agreed on basic rules—as in simple majority decides—but hardly on substantive political questions. In the eyes of the critics, conflict made for inconstancy—I mentioned in the preface that the Athenians were seen by contemporaries as capricious—but disagreement also brought out different perspectives and, less obviously, different pieces of knowledge and information. Hence, for its defenders, the fact that Athens allowed for fierce internal competition actually constituted an advantage; it contributed to the polis's remarkable capacity for innovation and, ultimately, its surprising success in a world of city-states and empires, which, as a whole, also happened to be extremely competitive.[42]

Still, is representative democracy based on elections, then, at most a kind of second best (causing political theorists, if not most modern citizens, endless polis envy)? Is it not an uneasy compromise between principles that are ultimately in deep tension with each other? That is obviously what the American founders thought. They considered representation a distinct alternative to democracy, which for them meant continuous, direct participation by the people. James Madison held that representation served "to refine and enlarge the public views by passing them through the medium of a chosen body of citizens, whose wisdom may best discern the true interest of society."

Such views have strengthened the impression that "representative democracy" is in fact a contradiction in terms. It's representation *or* democracy. As a result, plenty of thinkers, often inspired by Rousseau, have concluded that representation has in fact served to keep the people at bay in the modern world; some have even held that representation is actually repression. But that conclusion is hasty: representation as such is neither as such democratic nor antidemocratic. The same holds for elections. It depends on how exactly they are understood and on what happens before and, especially, *after* votes for representatives are cast.

Democracy for Losers

Elections are a procedure to generate collectively binding decisions for a polity. Of course, there are other ways of producing such decisions: "only the dictator decides" is also a rule; and if the goal is just some de facto settlement of who has power and who doesn't, the outcome of a protracted civil war will also do. By contrast, democracy makes the promise of arriving at decisions peacefully *and* on the basis of every citizen's having an equal opportunity to participate, which is in turn grounded in the notion that all have, in principle, an equal capacity for political judgment that needs to be respected.

But by definition not everyone can win in an election. And even the winners might not feel at ease as a result of a victory; they might have things like this tweeted at them: "The losers all want what you have, don't give it to them. Be strong & prosper, be weak & die!" Even without Trumpian background noise designed to make winners anxious, one can be puzzled by the apparent need for losers to be at least somewhat schizophrenic politically: they do not agree with election winners' ideas, *and yet* at the same time they agree that these ideas should be put into laws binding everyone; the vanquished, as another self-consciously realist observer of politics, Walter Lippmann, put it, are supposed to "endure with good humor policies which they did not approve."[43] According to Rousseau, this seeming contradiction points to a loss of freedom. Does it?

It hasn't always been appreciated that losing is complicated business in a democracy. The point is not about manners and civility, as in graciously accepting defeat, the way the southern gentleman Al Gore did when he not only conceded to George W. Bush in December 2000 but also, with a somewhat artificial smile (to be sure, for some people everything about Gore seemed artificial), announced, "It's time for me to go."

The point is that certain forms of losing actively undermine democracy, while others can strengthen it. Most noticeable in our age is that populists often—not always—opt for a strategy that makes perfect sense for them but in fact harms the political process (even if such populist parties never actually come to power). The particular phenomenon I am referring to is this. Populist parties that do not do so well at the polls have to face an obvious contradiction: How can it be the case that the populists are the people's only morally legitimate representatives and yet fail to gain overwhelming majorities at the ballot box?[44]

Populists do not all choose what might seem the easiest way out of this contradiction. But plenty do, when, in effect, they suggest that one should take another look at one of their favorite terms, "the silent majority." By definition, if the silent majority has spoken, populists will always already be in power. If they're not holding office, that's because we are looking not so much at a silent majority as at a *silenced* majority. Someone or something must have prevented the majority from making its voice heard. Thus, populists often insinuate that they did not really lose an election at all but that corrupt elites must have been manipulating things behind the scenes. Trump is an obvious recent example: when, in the fall of 2016, he left it open whether he would accept an election victory by Hillary Clinton, he effectively called into question the integrity of the U.S. electoral system. Plenty of supporters understood well enough what he really meant: according to one survey, 70 percent of his followers thought that if Clinton became president, the outcome must have been "rigged" (the good news was that only 40 percent of Trump voters in Florida also held the view that Clinton was literally a demon; in other words, a clear majority still at least recognized her humanity).[45]

In 2020, we witnessed a chronicle of a fraud foretold: Trump had again announced that he might not accept an unfavorable outcome; this time, he actively sought to steal the election by accusing his political opponents of stealing the election. The underlying logic was once more inspired by the core populist claim: only a vote for the people's uniquely authentic representative is legitimate (and legal); and it could not really come as a surprise that Trump called the January 6 crowd assembled on the Mall "the real people"—professing his "love" for them and then giving them marching orders to overturn the election results.

To be sure, anyone can criticize, for instance, the U.S. electoral system; in fact, there's clearly plenty to criticize. And, to say it once again, such criticisms can be a sign of good democratic engagement. What is not compatible with democracy is the populists' claim that comes down to saying, "Simply because we did not win, our system must be corrupted and rotten." Thus, populists systematically undermine the trust of citizens in their institutions, and they thereby damage the political culture, even if they never get anywhere close to the actual levers of power.

Apart from these more or less symbolic ways of being a bad loser, there is a much more concrete way for incumbents to be defeated and yet not live with the consequences of defeat. Think of Erdoğan's AKP losing the municipal elections in Istanbul in 2019. Initially, the authoritarian leader kept complaining that the victory of an opposition candidate from the main secular social democratic party had been the result of "irregularities" or outright "theft at the ballot box." Eventually, his side lost a repeat election by even wider margins. While this result was celebrated as evidence that even in Turkey elections cannot be completely manipulated, what happened next was hardly noticed by newly optimistic international audiences: Ankara systematically reduced the Istanbul mayor's control over resources and access to financing.

A similar dynamic unfolded in Budapest in the fall of 2019. The local opposition had desperately hoped for the arrival of the "Istanbul Express" in Hungary. And, in the end, it did make a stop: in a significant blow to Viktor Orbán, a left-liberal alliance of parties won in the capital. But the national government then, in effect, sabotaged the local administration by instituting proceedings to take away funds and powers (in a country in which authority is heavily centralized already).

Or think of the way Republican legislators in a number of U.S. states have stripped offices that their party lost—primarily governorships—of specific powers: the rules of the game are changed so as to effectively turn winners into losers, or at the very least into actors who will be forced to play a different game from the one they thought they'd get to play after winning.

Of course, one doesn't have to wait until after a vote. Plenty of observers of degraded democracies such as the United States, or of de facto autocracies like Hungary, rightly find fault with the fact that incumbents gerrymander or use the state machinery for partisan purposes—for instance, by conflating advertisements for government policies with propaganda for a particular party. In other words, they try to tilt what should ideally be a "level playing field."[46] Sometimes political players also make it clear that they seek to keep certain citizens off the field altogether, because their inconvenient presence makes winning more difficult. Paul Weyrich, one of the founders of the conservative movement in the United States, said it out loud: "I don't want everybody to vote. Elections are not won by a majority of people. As a matter of fact our leverage in the elections quite candidly goes up as the voting populace goes down."[47] Politicians choosing the people, as opposed to the people choosing the politicians—this gesture would seem to confirm the worry inspired by Rousseau: losers will do anything to resist an impending form of unfreedom.

Yet maybe losing isn't always simply unfreedom or plain powerlessness. There's such a thing as willing sacrifice, an acceptance of loss for the sake of keeping the game going and keeping the polity together.[48] True, a loss can render one vulnerable, but it does not have to mean being disempowered (especially if one's presence in political institutions is assured; there's evidence that losers in systems of proportional representation feel less sore than in majoritarian ones). More specifically, the assumption that losing results in unfreedom doesn't take proper account of the freedoms an opposition should enjoy in a democracy. Less obviously, losing in the right way can pave the path to winning and set new terms for life in the polity as a whole.

One fairly self-evident way for losers to at least partially succeed is to force the winners into major concessions, either during an election campaign or as a result of a strong showing at the polls.[49] Another, less obvious one is to force the winners at least to listen, or even to embarrass them in front of a significant audience—on the record and for the record. Think of how Tony Blair, after having won his constituency of Sedgefield in the 2005 British election, stood expressionless as he had to absorb the speech of Reg Keys, father of a soldier killed in Iraq; Keys had decided after his son's death to stand as an independent antiwar candidate (he won a little over 10 percent of the vote).

Another, still less obvious lesson involves the art of turning a loss into a demonstration of integrity. Barry Goldwater got trounced by Lyndon B. Johnson in the 1964 presidential elections; he carried only the Deep South and his home state of Arizona. And yet, as the political scientists Jeffrey Tulis and Nicole Mellow have pointed out, he lost with *integrity*: he kept his political principles intact and built a platform for the conservative movement such that a Ronald Reagan—masking some of the crueler parts of its platform with sheer charm—could eventually succeed.[50] True, on one level it's all about winning. But just as it matters *how* you win, it also matters *how* you lose. Even devastating losses—if one loses in the right way—can turn into long-run victories.

There is an unambiguously democratic art of losing: when democratic losers concede by saying that because everyone had the chance of a roughly *equal say*—a meaningful opportunity to make their case in a fair process—defeat is acceptable.[51] A democratic election is not a one-off aggregation of preferences but the end point of an extended process of citizens' engaging one another, as a result of which losers can also understand themselves at least somewhat as the authors of the collective outcome.[52] Otherwise one would in effect claim to be superior to one's fellow citizens who happened to be in the majority at the polls.

Concretely, one demonstrates one's commitment to democracy by forming a *loyal opposition*: loyal, that is, to the procedures of democracy, as in "we don't denigrate the system just because we lost"; and loyal to the outcome of the political process, as in "we obey the laws, even if our opponents crafted them and we are convinced that our political program remains far superior to theirs, and we'll try harder next time to make the case for it."

One of the major innovations in modern democracy, in contrast to the ancient Athenian type, is precisely the notion of such a loyal opposition. When John Cam Hobhouse, a reform politician and friend of Byron's, first referred to himself as a member of "His Majesty's Opposition" in 1826, it was meant as a joke (and the proceedings of the House of Commons duly recorded laughter).[53] But, eventually, the idea gained serious recognition: democracy needs a more or less coherent grouping that is, for partisan reasons, against the government but *not*, for principled reasons, against the political system.[54] A group, in other words, that criticizes the government, even very harshly if necessary, but that does not deny the government's legitimacy. And a group that, according to an astute observation by Alexis de Tocqueville, can also develop consistent ideas in a way that rulers, consumed by what Max Weber called "the demands of the day," might not.[55] And, not least, a group that does all its opposition work *openly* and engages in a principled conflict. The alternative to a loyal opposition is not consensus but behind-the-scenes intrigue or chaotic issue-by-issue fights.

A governing party, in turn, must recognize the opposition's special role.[56] When Theresa May kept repeating, with increasing exasperation in the face of loss after loss in Parliament, the seeming tautology "Brexit is Brexit," she was in effect saying that the opposition must shut up until the next elections—a profoundly undemocratic intuition in obvious violation of the need for an opposition to question a government's approach from day to day and to provide a systematic, coherent, but precisely not anti-system alternative. Silvio Berlusconi, exhibiting a similar sentiment, would decree smilingly, "Since you have chosen me in a free electoral competition, you must now be quiet, and let me do my job."[57] George Washington, an avowed enemy of "self-created societies"—that is, political party pluralism—and a believer in democracy as unanimity, was positively offended by people's criticizing him in the period between elections.[58]

The opposition's loyal role can be institutionalized in many different ways that in turn allow winners to demonstrate *their* loyalty to the political system: there may be immediate replies by opposition leaders to ministers' speeches in a legislative chamber, thereby giving the opposition a chance to dramatize differences and demonstrate other policy ideas; low thresholds for establishing committees of inquiry; opposition days, where the losers of an election set the agenda of a parliament's business; giving the opposition what in the U.K. is known as Short Money to finance its parliamentary work (including what one might call opposition research);[59] even installing opposition figures as the chairs of important committees (where, after all, much of the real work of a parliament gets done). Government and opposition are thus forced into engaging with each other; the more that engagement can be understood as fair (and as ultimately a collaborative enterprise, despite all the necessarily adversarial aspects), the better; this contrasts with a crude view of democratic rules as simply "hydraulic mechanisms designed to move society in the direction of the greater force."[60]

Still, while an opposition must have its say, a majority must ultimately get its way.[61] That's important to underline because a creative opposition can turn opportunities to have its say into means of effectively getting its way: obstructing the legislative program of the winners, in all likelihood by insinuating that the government lacks legitimacy. The U.S. Senate leader Mitch McConnell's tactics are legendary in this respect: after announcing that his overriding goal was to make Barack Obama a one-term president, he created a whole playbook on how to use legislative procedures—violating their very spirit—to prevent a national leader from getting anything done (a kindred spirit, Steve Bannon, announced that if the wrong person won the 2016 election, "our back-up strategy is to fuck her up so badly that she can't govern").[62] McConnell was a bad loser in two senses: not accepting defeat, *and* damaging the political system in his ruthless pursuit of partisan, or quite possibly just personal, goals (even though—this is often forgotten by those in awe of McConnell's supposed mastery of the dark arts of obstruction—he didn't succeed in making Obama a one-term president).

In a proper representative democracy, an opposition is not enslaved, *pace* Rousseau, just because it does not control the levers of power. Contrary to McConnell's observation that the winners get to make laws and the losers get to go home, losers get to sit on the opposition benches, from which they can prominently keep making the case against the government; they retain the freedom to campaign for their alternatives nonstop. Ideally there is a running discussion between majority and minority, in parliament and beyond, with arguments circling in an ongoing (yet also contained) political conflict—the very thing that Washington thought was beneath him as a republican quasi-monarch.[63]

"Running discussion" might sound a tad too nice here—something like the ongoing confrontation between a British prime minister and the leader of the opposition is more like a running fight. There is nothing wrong with that, except when rough play turns into clearly unfair play, with power holders systematically trying to shut the opposition out, or preventing proper confrontations. Think of how, in parliamentary systems like Hungary's, the ruling party often has a member of parliament who doesn't belong to the cabinet introduce major legislation in the middle of the night, thereby avoiding the extended periods of debate necessary if the government itself put forward its drafts.

One might think that when the play becomes unfair, it is still best for the opposition to sacrifice for the sake of keeping the greater democratic whole together. But there's a danger, then, of democracy becoming divided up between suckers and scoundrels, as the political scientist Andreas Schedler puts it.[64] Game theorists tell us that we can reestablish proper rule following by answering every tat with a tit—except that responding to unfairness with unfairness might lead to a downward spiral of norm violations; fighting fire with fire could burn down the house as a whole (a scenario I'll say more about in the final chapter of this book).

It's crucial to realize that when it comes to political conflict, not all norm violations are the same. Not every invention of an insulting nickname on Twitter must be answered with the same childishness (of which even Trumpists may have tired at a point). The best answer to voter suppression is not somehow keeping out partisans of the other side. Mechanical tit-for-tat retaliation—even if sometimes emotionally satisfying—should be resisted in favor of what can be called democracy-preserving or even democracy-enhancing reciprocity: measures the other side won't like but that can be justified with genuine democratic principles.[65] In the U.S. context, think of giving statehood to the District of Columbia and Puerto Rico (in whose cases the injustice of "taxation without representation" should make sense to all American citizens). Obviously, an opposition might not have the power to plausibly make such threats, but the point stands that a legitimate opposition may on occasion prove its pro-system credentials by answering unfairness with drastic, even norm-breaking measures—as long as these measures can be clearly tied back to basic principles of freedom and equality: a kind of *riduzione verso il principio* by political actors.

One consequence of the rise of populist parties, or other, broadly speaking, anti-system groups, can be the de facto disappearance of the institution of a loyal opposition.[66] If other parties are committed to keeping the anti-system party out, they might eventually *all* have to join a government. A case in point is the German federal state of Thuringia: in the fall of 2019, the far-right populist Alternative for Germany had done very well at the polls; as a result, parties with deeply opposed programs, such as center-right Christian Democrats and the postcommunist left, effectively had to cooperate. This all-against-one, one-against-all situation has a pernicious side effect: it appears to confirm the rhetoric that populist politicians have long served to their supporters: the other parties are simply in it to preserve their illegitimate privileges and ill-gotten gains; they form a cartel to keep the only authentic representatives of the people out.

There's a further, less obvious side effect: large coalitions can reinforce the perception that there are no clear political choices. Populist leaders will remind their supporters: We always explained to you that, despite ostensibly different political programs, the "establishment parties" in the end care only about all together plundering the state. Indeed, who would have thought that in Italy, for instance, the nominally left-wing prime minister Matteo Renzi, who had promised *rottamazione*, literally "scrapping" the old system, would eventually make a deal with Silvio Berlusconi to push through changes in the election law? He appeared to perfectly validate the populist Beppe Grillo's fulminations about the corrupt *casta* of traditional politicians.

If all parties other than anti-system parties are in government, there is by definition no loyal opposition left, only an anti-system opposition. The National Socialists called their opponents *Systemparteien*—a derogatory term also used by today's far-right Alternative for Germany.[67] Thus a crucial element of representative democracy—the idea that a systematic but not anti-system alternative is always available—vanishes.[68] That's not so much a loss for individual parties; it spells damage to a democracy as such.

What about the reverse scenario—an opposition in a regime practicing the populist art of governance, or a government bent on undermining the rules of democracy (but that has not yet established a full-scale populist regime)? One would think that under an actual populist regime an opposition *has to be* disloyal and explicitly anti-system.[69] But things are not so simple, especially when an opposition is fragmented among many smaller parties (sometimes such "diversity" has been cleverly engineered by a populist regime; Hungary would be an example). Here it is important that partisans stick with their regular commitments, under the assumption that citizens can disagree about policy without signaling disrespect; one has to acknowledge that not everything a consolidated or aspiring populist regime does is authoritarian. Conversely, when basic political principles are at stake, an opposition absolutely must unite and clearly signal to citizens that some matters are not the stuff of run-of-the-mill political disagreement. For example, the abolition of the Patient Protection and Affordable Care Act (a.k.a. Obamacare) is a cruel and in many ways incoherent policy decision, but it's what any Republican president will try, and were it to happen, it wouldn't be the end of democracy. By contrast, defying any oversight by Congress (let alone having one's supporters storm Congress) is not a matter of ordinary political disagreement; it's an attack on the system as such. And it would warrant a distinctive democratic form of *disobedience* (about which I'll say more in chapter 4). Marking such distinctions is an art; if it's done convincingly, it may limit the spread of a resigned and cynical view along the lines of "whatever the government does, the opposition never likes it, so who cares what they say."

Clearly, highly fragmented oppositions might have a harder time presenting a coherent political alternative to a populist regime. Such a situation can also pose a particular dilemma. In Hungary, liberal and left-wing opposition leaders had to decide whether to cooperate with the far-right Jobbik party. The most plausible answer is that an opposition can unite—for instance, by proposing a common slate of technocrats as candidates—while still underlining crucial internal differences. Less obviously, it can also push for situations in which agreement on a government program is not required. As explained in the last chapter, populists in power do not actually implement direct democracy; opposition groups, however, can do well by demanding referenda: after all, the latter have a binary structure—yes or no—and if the question is suitably posed to embarrass a government (by demonstrating that the supposedly unique representatives of the people in fact don't even reflect majority opinion), it can do damage to a regime without the opposition's having to converge ideologically. Contrary to conventional wisdom, referenda are not necessarily the populists' best institutional friend; in fact, they can become a powerful and precisely targeted weapon against them in their own game. No wonder the Hungarian government, for instance, has done everything possible to prevent referenda initiated by individual citizens.

Finally, in autocratic (or autocratizing—alas, a very necessary neologism in our time) regimes, not all the burden of providing coherent alternatives is on opposition parties. When institutions such as a constitutional court have been captured by ruling populists, retired judges can form a parallel, independent institution. They may take on the same cases as the hijacked judiciary and issue judgments that demonstrate what a truly autonomous body would have decided. This has been attempted in Poland, where the Constitutional Tribunal had been captured by the ruling party.[70] Here a kind of dual state is not an imposition from above but a bottom-up construction to oppose the power of argument to the arbitrariness of power.[71]

Expect the Unexpected?

Note what a fine balance representative democracy requires in practice. There's got to be a reasonable chance that our side can win again; we need to be certain that this is at least somewhat of a possibility, for otherwise why not quit the game altogether? At the same time, if we were always assured of winning, we might well like that outcome, but observers would rightly suspect that democracy has disappeared. That is why Adam Przeworski has defined democracy as a form of "institutionalized uncertainty."[72] This unwieldy formula contains a profound truth: political outcomes—elections, above all—have to be uncertain. If one prefers the notion that everything is crystal clear in advance, then there are more or less attractive alternatives: North Korea, where official candidates literally receive 100 percent of the vote; or other dictatorships such as Azerbaijan, where election results were accidentally released on an iPhone app the day before the vote in 2013; or, for that matter, Trump announcing victory when he happened to be ahead and ordering the count to be stopped (bringing to mind Tom Stoppard's line "It's not the voting that's democracy, it's the counting").[73] Przeworski put his key insight more plainly, with a seemingly banal but in fact brilliant observation: democracy can be defined as a political system in which parties lose elections (and, one might add, to drive home the point, it's not a system where the *same* parties always lose elections).[74]

Uncertainty isn't the same as chaos or randomness, for it is necessarily institutionalized (after all, the outcome of civil wars can also be uncertain, but such wars are not institutionalized). Rules must both enable *and* contain conflict, but, I repeat the point, an emphasis on rules does not mean we have to reduce democracy to a tag team of elites.[75] Procedures have to enable losers to have their say, and winners to have their way, and allow not just for losers and winners to switch places but for new winners and losers to enter the game over time.

True, it's hard to imagine pro-democracy demonstrators with posters proclaiming, "We want institutionalized uncertainty now!" (especially in the wake of a pandemic characterized by often unbearable levels of uncertainty and a U.S. election after which results were uncertain for long, long days). But uncertainty for winners is the same as hope for losers. That's why Peter Thiel is quite right to say that competition is for losers (even if what he meant to flag was actually the idea that a real winner in business will find ways of establishing monopolistic power). And, not least, if there's no uncertainty, there's also little reason for citizens to become engaged politically.

Of course, it does not follow that the more unpredictability or even randomness, the better, or the more democracy.

But it's important to emphasize that on a very basic level democracy makes no sense without the possibility of people at least sometimes changing their minds, and that includes changing their minds about democracy and how it's realized through particular rules at any given point. That is the reason why the truly shocking word in Hillary Clinton's infamous speech about the "deplorables" was not "deplorables." What her opponent in the 2016 presidential election and some of his followers were saying simply *was* (and is) deplorable. Rather, it was her casual remark that some citizens were simply "irredeemable"; in other words, it just wasn't worth trying to talk to them, engage them, perhaps make them reconsider. Similar in spirit, but by now less well remembered, is Mitt Romney's version of such antidemocratic determinism: in 2012, he drew a not-too-subtle distinction between the makers and the takers; the latter—47 percent, according to the Republican's estimate—would vote for Obama "no matter what."

Most consequential may be the kind of demographic determinism that is often shared by a left and a right that otherwise can't agree on much. In the United States, some Democrats still seem convinced that the emergence of a majority-minority democracy ensures their long-term electoral prospects; conversely, a figure like McConnell can condemn the proposal of statehood for Washington, D.C., and Puerto Rico as a left-wing "power grab," as he simply assumes that minorities will be voting against his party.

Of course, we know that in practice plenty of people do not change their minds all that often, and that particular groups are historically loyal to a specific party. But we cannot always know in advance who they will be; we cannot give up on the notion that democracy is based on the expectation that some people will at least sometimes develop different views—and that ascriptive identity is not political destiny.

Taking the uncertainty out of democracy not only harms losers or, put differently, the minority; proper democracy also protects members of a onetime majority who might want to change their mind.

To accept this picture, one doesn't have to adopt lofty ideas about citizens carefully considering different policy menus put forward by parties at every election and then, after careful, rational deliberation, opting for what they consider the party most attuned to the common good.[76] For decades, the profession of political science in the United States appears to have been dedicated wholeheartedly to destroying civics textbook wisdom about the politically attentive citizen with consistent views; in fact, some of my colleagues seem to positively relish hammering home point after point about just how unbelievably irrational and ill-informed most people are (about politics, that is; they are fairly well-informed about *American Idol*, *Big Brother*, and so on). Hence the view—increasingly popular among liberals in despair on account of political disasters such as Brexit and Trump—that we must let go of the "folk theory of democracy"; according to that theory, citizens form a coherent popular will that governments, responsive to "the will of the people," then implement.[77]

Some scholars don't shy away from casting doubt on what many consider the absolute minimum of what can be said in favor of democracy: it is the only peaceful way to get rid of bad rulers. Even this might be based on too starry-eyed a view of our fellow citizens. For what is colloquially known as "throwing the bums out" presumes that people comprehend who's a bum and who isn't. A favorite story to make the point— part of the folk wisdom of political realism, one might say—is one about sharks. Four months before the 1916 presidential elections, residents and visitors at the Jersey Shore were terrified by a string of shark attacks. A shark (that would serve as inspiration for a Hollywood blockbuster six decades later) supposedly even swam up a creek and tore apart two youngsters.[78] What came to be known as the "twelve days of terror" is said to have led to a drop in support for the incumbent, Woodrow Wilson, of between nine and eleven points in the shark-infested townships, when the president obviously had absolutely nothing to do with the horror on the beaches.[79] Bad experiences—maybe as innocuous as the local sports team losing—make people irrationally turn against their rulers. Retrospective voting, so it seems, is blind; it's not blind rage, for there's rage for a reason, but the reasons have nothing to do with democratic politics.

It's a great story, cherished by liberals fond of cultivating skepticism about ordinary folks, but it might not entirely hold up. Wilson lost other, shark-less states in the Northeast in the 1916 election, while in the township where the shark swam up the creek, his share of the vote in fact increased. Most important, the shark attacks devastated the tourism industry of the affected coastal towns. The government did virtually nothing to mitigate the economic effects, despite desperate citizens firing off letters to Congress pleading for help.[80] It may well be anachronistic to think that Washington could have helped substantially in a pre–New Deal era—but even so, citizens might still not have been completely irrational to turn against Wilson for failing to express sympathy or particular concern about a state he had governed for two years.[81] After all, what could appear as merely symbolic gestures still sends an important message about a politician—be it his capacity for the right rhetoric in the face of unexpected circumstances, or, more important, setting a tone that encourages Congress to take particular individuals' interests seriously. Trump failed disastrously at not only managing the federal bureaucracy during the 2020 pandemic but also managing the mood of the country: he was singularly unable to articulate any kind of empathy or collective mourning (let alone apologize for any mistakes). That rightly counted against him, irrespective of how well he performed as a chief executive in a more technical sense.

It's easy enough to demonstrate that individuals lack all kinds of politically relevant knowledge or have inconsistent views. But it does not follow that politics as a whole becomes arbitrary, let alone that political prizes will always go to the greatest demagogue. Citizens do have a good enough sense of their interests; they pick up cues from other individuals and institutions (parties, the media, and organizations such as trade unions); as in so many other areas of life, taking a shortcut is not a sign of irrationality.[82] If anything, the problem is not with the psychology of individual citizens but with the state of what I've been calling democracy's critical infrastructure, which indeed is in dire need of repair in the United States and a number of other countries.

When citizens appear to vote against what might be construed as their purely material interests, they often do so not because they've been deceived by the great demagogue or suffer from false consciousness; rather, it's that they deem other interests—having to do with so-called moral or cultural issues, for instance, or even "emotional self-interests"—more important.[83] As E. E. Schattschneider once put it, people don't just have interests; they have ideas about interests.[84] And ideas—and values—are not a simple matter of rationality versus irrationality.

It's a mistake to think that politics was easier when, supposedly, it was just about groups bargaining over material interests. For one thing, on closer historical inspection, no such golden age will be found. Workers didn't just fight for wages and better working conditions; they also struggled for dignity and recognition of their way of life—all "cultural values" and questions of identity. And, as Lawrence Lessig has pointed out, "the right to vote was the first fight of identity politics," because the struggle throughout American history—and other national histories—has been to overcome franchise exclusions based on identity.[85]

Conversely, what is today often derided as "identity politics" is not just about some abstract demand for validation of a particular group's experience; it aims at a very concrete redistribution, or sometimes just the actual enforcement, of basic rights. Contrary to what critics often allege, "identity politics" does not ask for the recognition of obscure cultural particularities or preferences, which others might simply be unable to comprehend; rather, it is about claiming that basic rights have to be made effective: for instance, the right not to be groped (let alone raped) by powerful males, or the right not to be constantly harassed (let alone shot) by the police. The notion that conflicts could be settled more easily when they supposedly just concerned dividing material products—as opposed to dealing with personal identity—misses just how much interests, identities, and ideas about interests and identities have always been mixed with one another.

Still, what if the party defending my interests—however conceived—always loses? Or what if parties in power change often enough—Przeworski's minimal criterion for democracy seemingly satisfied—and yet my interests appear *never* to be taken care of? This is precisely the scenario political scientists have diagnosed for a range of democratic systems, the phenomenon that at least partly explains one of the secessions I discussed in the first chapter. Especially, but not only, in the United States the evidence appears shockingly unambiguous: where the well-to-do and the rest of the population (not just the poor) have diverging preferences, the well-to-do win out. This is not because only the well-to-do have rational, or even just realistic, ideas about policy; it's because in the United States, on many issues, the political system is de facto unresponsive to the entire *bottom two-thirds* of the citizenry.[86] "Democracy" here is a by-product of the views of those at the top contingently aligning with those of numerical majorities (but without the latter actually *saying* or *doing* anything). An obvious conclusion is this: it's not just that in a democracy parties lose elections; it's also that in a real democracy, at least sometimes, powerful interests *must* lose in elections.

That is all a long-winded way of saying that a regular turnover of parties isn't enough to show that either political equality or political freedom is real. And we can't assume political equality is in place just because we don't hear right-wing populists openly denigrating parts of the population or suggesting that some citizens are not "real" or are at best second-rate, and so on. The existence of robust antidiscrimination legislation might be perfectly compatible with political disempowerment of large parts of the citizenry. So, there's got to be more.

In Praise of "Demagogues"

If exact equality of influence is not a plausible aim, what else might political equality mean concretely? One answer is this: a roughly equal likelihood of getting the policy that serves one's interests. If one loses, it is not because one's interests are systematically neglected (let alone that one's standing in the polity is systematically undermined); rather, it was tough luck that one lost this round.[87] In other words, loss does not equal evidence of systematic disadvantage or of lack of standing.

How loss is viewed (or feels) depends not least on the answer to a crucial question: How easy or difficult is it to become engaged in politics? Can citizens exercise their basic political rights in a way that gives them a voice and not just a vote? In practice, that often comes down to the question, How many voices are already audible? How many choruses are there that you might choose to join (in particular ones that don't sing with an upper-class accent)? How many representations of different ideas, interests, and, for that matter, identities?

Ancient Athenians enjoyed the freedom of voting in the assembly, and they had an equal chance to serve in office through lottery, especially on the people's courts, which were crucial for keeping the wealthy in check. But ancient democracy didn't do entirely without the principle of representation. In fact, it prominently featured a figure called *demagogos*. This wasn't the demagogue in our contemporary sense; rather, he acted as a kind of leader, or *instigator*, bringing up issues and appealing to people in light of particular ideas and interests. These were not party leaders, for, as we saw, there simply were no political parties, but in the absence of standing associations and informational leaders—in our language, media— their function was very similar, and in fact indispensable for Athenian democracy to work at all.[88]

Representation has traditionally been conceived in two ways. You choose a representative who will advance your substantive interests, or you choose a representative who has important traits that match your own, as in women should represent women (whereas a purely substantive conception can produce something like the Party of the Brazilian Woman, which at one point had no female deputies in parliament, because the substantive interest of "the Brazilian Woman" was taken to be outlawing abortion).

Yet there is another, more dynamic and creative understanding of representation. Here representation is not conceived as substantively or descriptively reproducing something that already exists. It is not a matter of mechanical reproduction. Rather, it is a process in which individuals offer to a possible constituency an image of themselves based on so far unrecognized ideas, interests, or aspects of their identities. As a result, citizens might perceive themselves and the politics they need in a novel light. A constituency is not so much reproduced, or even revealed, as talked into existence and, as a result, uses its political freedoms in novel ways.

This isn't something new, or something that only started with "identity politics": workers know that they are workers, but they don't spontaneously discover that they form part of the working class; neither identities nor, for that matter, interests naturally suggest themselves to us; they have to be organized to result in something like political solidarity.[89] Private Willis in Gilbert and Sullivan's *Iolanthe* assumes exactly the opposite when he sings,

> I am an intellectual chap,
> And think of things that would astonish you.
> I often think it's comical—Fal, lal, la!
> How Nature always does contrive—Fal, lal, la!
> That every boy and every gal
> That's born into the world alive
> Is either a little Liberal
> Or else a little Conservative!

By contrast, the London *Times* recognized the creative and dynamic element of representation when it praised Disraeli (a.k.a. the first Earl of Beaconsfield):

> What distinguished Lord Beaconsfield from the ordi-
> nary Tory leaders was his readiness to trust the En-

glish people whom they did not trust, and his total indifference to the barriers of caste, which for them were the be-all and end-all of politics. In the inarticulate mass of the English populace which they held at arm's length he discerned the Conservative working man, as the sculptor perceives the angel prisoned in a block of marble. He understood that the common Englishman, even when he personally has nothing to guard beyond a narrow income and a frugal home, has yet Conservative instincts as strong as those of the wealthiest peer.[90]

In theory, *anyone* can make a "representative claim"—that is to say, articulate an idea about a group that might be said not to have been represented properly, or perhaps not represented at all.[91] Walter Lippmann, arguably the most influential twentieth-century American journalist (and a deeply disenchanted democrat), was not wrong to observe that the "public does not select the candidate, write the platform, outline the policy any more than it builds the automobile or acts the play. It aligns itself for or against somebody who has offered himself." But that somebody might have discovered something new about different publics, or made them conscious of parts of their lived experience so far unrepresented, or created an entirely new image of themselves for them. This can but doesn't have to be a top-down affair; #MeToo, for instance, spread horizontally, not as an imposition from above; the same goes for the astonishing fact that a hitherto-unknown teenager, Emma González, one of the survivors of the Parkland school shooting, within a few days had more followers on Twitter than the mighty National Rifle Association.

Or think of Black Lives Matter. The facts of police violence were hardly unknown before 2013. But it took a particular appeal by three female activists—and a particular hashtag!—to generate both an effective representation of a particular group and a particular claim about what was happening to them and why: those subject to harassment by law enforcement simply didn't seem to count, their lives appeared to have no value (another way of putting this would be: they had no real standing in the polity; in this sense, BLM sought to enforce what I have been calling the hard border). So, it's not that anything was made up here; nor did drawing attention to a particular experience ask non-Black citizens to pretend that they could truly understand that experience as if it were their own. As the mass protests in the wake of the murder of George Floyd showed, people of very different backgrounds could come together based on a shared principle.

BLM did not "reveal" anything, for "reveal" would suggest there's a fully formed political subject already there that just has to be uncovered. The same could be said of early Pride parades, or the protests against the Belarussian dictator Alexander Lukashenko in 2020: as an observer put it, "something repressed is coming out, surprised and delighted to recognize itself."[92] But the coming-out—be it out of the closet, or out of homes onto the squares to face off against a brutal police force—itself changes the way people think of themselves and relate to others. Identities don't preexist their proper politicization; they are partly formed in it.

This point underlines why the demographic determinism to which politicians across the spectrum often subscribe is so mistaken: what partisan loyalties folks develop will very much depend on how they are being addressed. *Pace* McConnell's defeatism, it is by no means obvious that, for instance, Puerto Rico's culturally rather conservative inhabitants would never find anything to like in a Republican program (as long as they forget how a Republican president tossed paper towels at them after a hurricane, foreshadowing his carelessness and cruelty in dealing with the pandemic a few years later). Elections are based on a census, but they are not like a census; a dynamic political process might lead citizens to prioritize aspects of their identity in surprising ways. That's also the reason why Isaac Asimov's short story "Franchise," from 1955, is so dystopian: instead of all citizens voting, a single, supposedly "most representative" American is selected by a supercomputer, Multivac, to decide the November 4, 2008, election. On Election Day, the machine poses questions to Norman Muller, the "Voter of the Year," and in the world's "first and greatest Electronic Democracy," his answers (only men can "vote") then determine election results across the entire country.

Representations are best thought of not as neutral descriptions of some obvious, let alone objective, social reality, but as calls to battle. Drawing lines around a group that hasn't really been represented at all, or in the proper way, also means drawing the lines of conflict. These lines are not somehow naturally given: whether peasant families in eastern Poland feel closer to the right-wing Law and Justice party or to a credible left-wing alternative that cares just as much about providing child allowances is an open question; it's the craft and creativity of politicians that will at least partly decide the answer. Or think of another example farther west: it seemed as if power in Ireland would forever change hands between two center-right parties whose archaic names show just how much they still live off the credit of the fight for independence—Fianna Fáil, the "Warriors of Destiny," and Fine Gael, the "Tribe of the Gaels." In the 2020 election, Sinn Féin ("We Ourselves"), while not free from historical baggage itself, changed the nature of the game when it picked up on people's urgent concerns about housing and health care, finally creating a proper left-right split in Irish politics.[93]

As Schattschneider, one of the most astute thinkers about the role of conflict in creating both division and cohesion in a democracy, observed in the mid-twentieth century, the art of describing conflicts requires skill in defining to one's political advantage the scope of a conflict; it's "about who can get into the fight and who is excluded" (or, as he also put it, "*Whoever decides what the game is about decides who can get into the game*").[94] Schattschneider went on to explain,

> Competitiveness is the mechanism for the expansion of the scope of conflict. It is the *loser* who calls in outside help. (Jefferson, defeated within the Washington administration, went to the country for support.) The expansion of the electorate resulted from party competition for votes. As soon as it becomes likely that a new social group will get to vote, both parties favor the extension. *This is the expanding universe of politics.* On the other hand, any attempt to monopolize politics is almost by definition an attempt to limit the scope of conflict.[95]

The easier it is to enter the game of offering oneself and particular representations of shared interests to groups in society, the more likely it is that citizens will experience their political system as free and open to change. They will find out what others think and what concrete concerns people might have in common. And the more representations are out there, and the more we can say that access to the means of making representative claims is equal, the higher the worth of one's voice and one's vote.

I keep belaboring the point about the creative and dynamic aspect of representation partly because observers of contemporary politics so often ignore it. They tend to think that success at the polls reveals an objective truth about society. When right-wing populists do well, the previous judgment that they're all lying demagogues or at least *terribles simplificateurs* is quickly replaced with the notion that they have unveiled ultimate sociological verities, long ignored by "mainstream parties." Trump demonstrated the discontent of "the white working class" (never mind that crucial support came from citizens who are clearly much better-off than "worker" suggests, and never mind that it wasn't the workers who came out to vote for Trump who cost Clinton the election, but the workers who stayed home); or, by another, similarly misguided reading of the objective lessons of 2016, the man showed conclusively that there are sixty-three million racists in the United States (in fact even more, once the results of the 2020 election started to become clear). Meanwhile, Boris Johnson proved to us that Brexit had been people's deepest desire all along. Of course, it's not the case that politicians can just conjure up anything; they must have something to work with, and in the first chapter I analyzed the larger political and socioeconomic developments that have facilitated the nefarious work of right-wing populists. The point is that claims about conflicts in a society can be presented in different ways; there is a creative element in how major political choices are put together and offered to voters. And every such presentation of conflict has a cost—not just in the obvious sense of a loss for losers, but also because some citizens might feel that the conflict isn't about or for them; they have nothing at stake and ultimately might feel completely alienated from politics as a result. A democracy will want to minimize such costs.

Why Not Replace Representation with Random Selection?

Representation's dynamic and creative element is simply missing in systems that use lotteries to fill offices—what some philosophers advocating the revival of ancient Athenian practices have called "lottocracy."[96] Citizens selected by lot, according to such schemes, should address particular policy challenges and receive advice from experts in doing so. Lobbying or outright bribery is ruled out not just legally but because the randomness of who's going to end up serving in a lottocracy makes it impossible to target the powerful, even indirectly; one simply could not tell in advance who will be selected (that's why the Athenians drew lots in the morning; they worried that if it were done the evening before, there might be attempts at bribery during the night).[97] In this specific sense, then, institutionalized uncertainty about officeholders is guaranteed.

Lottocracy thus combines equal chances with institutionalized uncertainty. Is that not superior to elections, which might fail to deliver one or both of these? The trouble is that proposals for lottocracy betray what can only be called a technocratic mind-set: politics is understood as a series of problems to be sorted out; what matters is finding the correct solution. It's unclear, however, who defines what counts as a problem to begin with, and it's especially unclear whether novel cries about injustices, triggered by new self-perceptions and resulting in demands for novel forms of representation, will be heard in such rarefied, expert-driven institutions: the messy streets and the lottocratic-technocratic *isoloir* in which randomly chosen citizens meet might remain completely separate worlds. Representative democracy is not always the best at finding solutions, but it's probably best at producing—as in identifying—problems.

What could at first sight seem like the exact opposite of lottocracy, namely meritocracy, suffers from the same shortcoming. A meritocratic system—even if one ignores all the obvious problems with gaming such a system—relies on a more or less fixed notion of who is best equipped to address particular challenges; it assumes what Thomas Jefferson called a "natural aristocracy." Rather than randomly selected ordinary people advised (or perhaps reeducated) by experts, here the experts get to do the job themselves. Again, the expectation appears to be one of a uniquely correct solution to a problem; the idea that problems become visible only in messy struggles for democratic representation, and that different solutions might be more or less plausible in light of one's commitments to different values, is left out, or in fact doesn't even really make sense. In both lottocracy and meritocracy, once the lucky winners of the lottery and the most competent figures filtered out by exams get going, we, the rest of the citizenry, will effectively have to shut up. Thus, ironically, both lottocracy and meritocracy also end up doing what populists propose: they shrink the demos; not all citizens will be the decision-making public (even if that happens for completely different reasons here).

For all its advantages in specific contexts, then, lottocracy (no less than meritocracy) lacks important virtues of representative democracy based on regular elections: its dynamic and creative elements. Lottocracy and meritocracy also do not help to preserve peace in the way elections do: they fail to measure the strength of different groups in society; they also leave no way for losers to mobilize in order to win the next time around.[98]

Representation is not necessarily democratic: the pope is a representative, but that doesn't make him a democratic figure.

And yet democracy and representation are also not necessarily opposed to each other: choosing representatives is a discrete act, but representation constitutes an ongoing process. Citizens do not ignore what happens in representative institutions until the next election; they can participate through voicing their opinions and considered judgments.[99] Representatives in turn don't just diligently check off election promises they have fulfilled; they also anticipate what voters might care about at the voting booth next time; and—without necessarily being manipulative—they can try to convince constituents that they deserve reelection even if they didn't make good on a range of promises; something else, let's say a national challenge such as a pandemic, turned out to be much more important to address, and politicians would want to be judged on the record of how they dealt with it.[100] Nobody ever gets to vote twice; the citizen who has to choose whether to reelect particular representatives is a different person from the one who helped them into power in the past.

The running discussion between majority and minority happens not only in representative assemblies but also between the assembly and the citizenry, and among the citizenry itself, especially if well-functioning intermediary institutions can facilitate this process.[101] True, on one level, representatives have more power—and more freedom—than we mere voters do; Rousseau's specter will not just go away.[102] But all this does not mean they can simply ignore citizens. And the latter also can't be told, May-style or Washington-style, to just shut up.

Representation and participation should not be understood as opposites; the antithesis of representation is exclusion, and the opposite of participation is abstention or some form of secession from shared political life.[103] This, then, might be the best thing to say to the losers: they remain at liberty to make their case; they are not excluded or systematically disadvantaged (as they are under the rule of authoritarian populists). And the best that can be said to anyone who fears they're not in the democratic game at all is this: if equal liberty is real, then it should allow them to disrupt the status quo and start a conflict about which conflicts matter most. Whether equal liberty is real will depend not just on abstract commitments in a constitutional document but on the state of democracy's critical infrastructure: parties, movements, the media—all of which are indispensable for the work of representation and dealing with conflicts in such a way that democracy as a whole does not perish. It's to a closer examination of such institutions that I now turn.

3. CRITICAL INFRASTRUCTURE

A people is not just a political entity, as was once hoped.
Parties, organized campaigns, and leaders make
up the reality.

—JUDITH SHKLAR

The public which generated political forms is passing
away, but the power and lust of possession remains
in the hands of the officers and agencies which
the dying public instituted.

—JOHN DEWEY

Democracy is unthinkable without basic political rights—to speak up freely, to assemble, and to associate. The worth of those rights is greatly increased if their use is facilitated by other actors, namely intermediary powers.[1] I can demonstrate on the street all by myself, and tirelessly tweet, send out all my unpublished op-eds to family and friends, or spam strangers with them, but, obviously, associations, political parties, and so-called legacy media can do wonders in multiplying my message. Political equality is best understood as equality of opportunity to participate politically. Concretely, that requires reasonably easy-to-access intermediary powers, as well as reasonable chances of creating new ones.[2]

Of course, not everyone agrees with this bright picture.

A darker view suggests that intermediary powers entrench or even exacerbate inequalities. In fact, intermediaries have sometimes been interpreted as inherently conservative, if not outright aristocratic. The call for *corps intermédiaires*—familiar from nineteenth-century liberals such as Tocqueville who lauded their moderating effect—seems to be a polite attempt to *reduce* political equality: these institutions appear to *divide* the people and to create *distance* between the people and the state. And, most damning of all, they are said to alter the people's voice: to mediate is potentially always to *distort*. These were exactly the reasons Rousseau was so adamantly opposed to intermediaries, so much so, in fact, that he did not even want the citizens of his ideal polity to talk about collective choices, lest these debates lead toward the formation of anything like political parties. He wasn't worried about silenced majorities; he positively wanted everyone to be quiet, resulting in a perfectly silent unity of the entire people (this thought, incidentally, left a lasting legacy in France: intermediary bodies were prohibited during the French Revolution, and mass political parties did not become properly legal until 1901).

But in a society that doesn't look like Rousseau's idealized—small and isolated—mountain community, the question arises: How can citizens become active and exert any power at all if no organizations exist to help them shape and spread their views? The alternative to what the French theorist Pierre Rosanvallon has called "structured democracy" is not unstructured democracy; it's no democracy at all. Democracy requires a critical infrastructure; like physical infrastructure (and like the post office), it facilitates the reaching of people and being reached by them; not for nothing was the first weekly German-language paper, published out of Strassburg in the early seventeenth century, called *Relation*.[3] And like the built environment that allows citizens to connect, such an infrastructure can be of higher or lower quality. The question is how we would know.

What Matters About Intermediary Institutions

We hear ever more cries to get rid of intermediaries altogether; often enough, this call is based on the insinuation that to mediate means by itself to manipulate. A Texas Republican advised that it was "better to get your news directly from the president. In fact, it might be the only way to get the unvarnished truth."[4] Trump's preferred instrument of spreading the unvarnished truth was of course Twitter, which he described variously as a newspaper without the costs and losses, as a literary medium (with himself as the "Ernest Hemingway of 140 characters" going, in his own words, "bing-bing-bing"), and—somewhat closer to the "unvarnished truth"—as a "megaphone" (until it was taken away in January 2021):

> This is my megaphone. This is the way that I speak directly to the people without any filter. Cut through the noise. Cut through the fake news. That's the only way I have to communicate. I have tens of millions of followers. This is bigger than cable news. I go out and give a speech and it's covered by CNN and nobody's watching, nobody cares. I tweet something and it's my megaphone to the world.[5]

Beppe Grillo, one of the founders of the Five Star Movement in Italy, told his followers to connect with him directly via his blog, bypassing political parties—*la casta* of corrupt politicians, in his words—and professional journalists, who were all said to be in bed with the politicians. Ordinary people were supposed to know what was really going on, and he promised to be their "amplifier." Five Star, and other up-start parties, such as Podemos in Spain, claimed to offer a new model. Rather than inserting themselves between citizens and the state, they would provide something like a "platform" (a digital platform, above all); that platform would connect members, dispensing with the kind of bureaucratic apparatus typical of the mass parties that started to form in the late nineteenth century. Whereas the latter were characterized by what the sociologist Robert Michels called "the iron law of oligarchy"—bureaucracy meant rule by a few insiders—such "platform parties" would be much more egalitarian and somehow "horizontal."

False advertising? Before we get to an answer, we need a better sense of the specific functions of intermediary insti-tutions, beyond the multiplication of individual voices. We also need to understand why, ever since the nineteenth cen-tury, two particular types of mediating institutions were seen as indispensable for making representative democracy work: political parties and a professional press (and later professional broadcasting).

Both are routinely declared to be in crisis today. Here's a typical sample of observations about the media: "The pres-ent crisis of western democracy is a crisis in journalism"; "the public, in the sense of a great consensus of separate and dis-tinct viewpoints, is finished." Except that the first sentence was written by Walter Lippmann in 1920, and the second statement comes from a 1967 volume authored by Marshall McLuhan and Quentin Fiore.[6] It's easy to gesture at a golden age, but evidently none ever existed; the more interesting question is whether intermediary institutions were once able to preserve their core functions in the face of what observers even then feared were fundamental threats to them.

Let's once again go back to something basic, another *riduzione verso il principio*: democracy has a dual nature, or, put differently, two crucial sites. First, it requires a designated locus (and specific times) for collectively binding decision making—for the expression of political will through lawmaking: a majority getting its way, after the opposition has had its say. On the other hand, it is in need of a place for the continuous formation of opinions and political judgments in society at large: anybody can have a say, at more or less any time.[7]

Decision making requires procedures, which always means clearly segmented time frames; elections—Whitman's "powerfulest scene and show"—are supposed to be held at regular intervals. Hence the first site of democracy is characterized by a certain predictability, even if the predictable procedures are ultimately to enable uncertainty.[8] By contrast, the realm of opinion formation can, as the German social philosopher Jürgen Habermas once put it, be a space for "wild cacophonies." And that's a good thing, too: multiple voices clash, opinions get tweaked and fine-tuned; people pick up cues as to what they should think, even if they can't spend hours on the finer details of policy. Prima facie, there's no pattern here, no end point; the public is a never-ending film, not a snapshot, or, rather, it's many films and plots all at once. To use an image that would have made no sense before the second decade of the twenty-first century: it's a mass Zoom meeting, with some people talking at us, unsure whether anyone is listening, others off in group chats on the side, and some engaged in private one-on-one exchanges.

Now, the two sites of democracy are always connected. As

John Stuart Mill observed about the relationship between the British Parliament and society at large,

> The Parliament has an office . . . to be at once the nation's Committee of Grievances, and its Congress of Opinions; an arena in which not only the general opinion of the nation, but that of every section of it, and as far as possible of every eminent individual whom it contains, can produce itself in full light and challenge discussion; where every person in the country may count upon finding somebody who speaks his mind, as well or better than he could speak it himself—not to friends and partisans exclusively, but in the face of opponents, to be tested by adverse controversy; where those whose opinion is overruled, feel satisfied that it is heard, and set aside not by a mere act of will, but for what are thought superior reasons . . . ; where every party or opinion in the country can muster its strength, and be cured of any illusion concerning the number or power of its adherents.[9]

The public sphere depends neither on a specific location nor on particular advances in media technologies. It certainly can be a special place. The agora in ancient democratic Athens was a site of people's courts, commerce, religious rites, and chance encounters where the oligarchs rubbed shoulders with slaves (while the nearby hill known as the Pnyx featured the actual assembly, the body issuing decrees).[10] In the eighteenth century, coffeehouses and salons became the venues, and newspapers the means, for the formation of opinions. Over coffee, gentlemen debated the merits of the latest novels. Eventually, conversations turned to matters of state, literary criticism became political criticism, and in both enterprises, at least according to Habermas's idealized image, only the better argument (or at least the sharper witticism) counted, not higher social status. The coffeehouse was not a wild place, but the conversation had no boundaries. And politics talk eventually built up into pressure on regimes not simply to represent themselves *before* the people but to submit themselves to the judgment *of* the people and be their proper representative.[11] Until 1771, it was an offense to report on debates in the House of Commons; deliberation held in camera had precisely been meant to keep public pressure away (and prevent preening and grandstanding in front of the people).

Opinion publique—an expression dating back to Montaigne but increasingly used in a political context in the eighteenth century—was supposed to supervise governments. The philosopher Jeremy Bentham praised the "super-intendence of the public," which had adopted a "habit of reasoning and discussion." The public did not rule, but it did speak up. This was a far cry from Rousseau's vision of a unified sovereign public: first silent and then speaking with one voice, based on a consensus of the heart, rather than a continuous critical engagement of minds.[12]

By 1840, Balzac could matter-of-factly observe, "Public opinion is manufactured in Paris; it is made with ink and paper." Yet the media were not the only critical institution in this new "regime of publicity." In the eighteenth and especially the nineteenth centuries, they were joined by political parties, even though many political thinkers, no less than many politicians themselves, found what George Washington had derided as "the spirit of party" wholly and utterly undesirable, with Jefferson even claiming melodramatically, "If I could not go to heaven but with a party, I would not go there at all."[13] These politicians identified parties not just with Washington's "self-created societies" but with pernicious "factions"—akin to conspiracies—bound to destroy the civic cohesion of the polity. As James Madison put it, they had to be feared as "a number of citizens, whether amounting to a majority or a minority of the whole, united and actuated by some common impulse of passion, or of interest, adverse to the rights of other citizens, or to the permanent and aggregate interests of the community"[14] (note how Madison makes room both for an oppressive majority guided by selfish interests—conventional enough—and for something like a tyranny of the minority, akin to what the U.S. Republicans have been exercising in recent years).

And yet Madison himself, together with Thomas Jefferson, became a party founder (of the Democratic-Republican Party, that is). Eventually, he even declared that "no free country has ever been without parties, which are a natural offspring of freedom" (even the hyper-anti-partisan John Adams conceded in letters to Jefferson, "All countries under the sun must have parties," but he added, "The great secret is to control them"[15]). Martin Van Buren, president from 1837 to 1841, crafted the first real American party system, in which two centrist parties were supposed to engage in ordered competition for office and moderate ideological strife; what's often forgotten is that he also advocated the creation of new parties in case the main existing ones came to resemble each other too much (and he was as good as his word: he ended up running for president in 1848 as the candidate of the Free Soil Party).

It's similarly forgotten that parties and newspapers were often tightly fused during this era. As Tocqueville observed,

> In democratic countries . . . large numbers of men
> who feel the desire and need to associate may often

find themselves unable to do so, because all are insignificant and none stands out from the crowd, so that they cannot identify one another and have no idea how to meet. But let a newspaper come and give visibility to the feeling or idea that has occurred simultaneously but separately to each of them, and all will immediately rush toward this light. Wandering spirits that had long sought one another in darkness will meet at last and join forces.

The newspaper brings them together, and they continue to need the newspaper in order to stay together.[16]

In other words, free press and free association were dependent on each other, and in the America Tocqueville witnessed, both served the ends of partisanship. Of course, we might find the idea of an unashamedly partisan press objectionable, but this erstwhile fusion points to an important function that both parties and professional media fulfill: parties are not just what Edmund Burke described as "a body of men united for promoting by their joint endeavours the national interest upon some particular principle in which they are all agreed";[17] they also, just like the media, offer representations *of* society, and in particular, of its political conflicts, *to* society. They present what the social theorist Pierre Bourdieu called a "vision of divisions." By this, he didn't mean idle speculations about social trends; he was referring to real power, namely "the power of imposing a vision of divisions, that is, the power of making visible and explicit social divisions that are implicit, is the political power *par excellence*: it is the power to make groups, to manipulate the objective structure of society."[18] Of course, parties do this with a view to motivating and mobilizing their actual and potential followers; media, in general, do not appear to have such a mobilizing agenda (though some contemporary counterexamples—newspapers starting campaigns and TV channels riling up their viewers—will come to mind immediately; we'll get to these soon).

Parties do not just mechanically reproduce given conflicts; they consciously structure them, and sometimes they even create them. The media, for the most part, have no choice but to follow major parties in how they present conflicts, for instance, by accepting a basic left-right schema. But media can also suggest different ways of looking at conflicts through investigative reporting that uncovers hitherto not so obvious forms of social and political discontent, or scandals that suggest collusion of nominally opposed parties and hence prompt the formation of protest movements or even entirely novel political parties: think of Spain or Greece, where both the major left-wing and the major right-wing parties were deeply entangled in corruption.

The point is that intermediary institutions have a choice in how they present and structure conflicts. They obviously might have reasons that are not directly related to the overall health of democracy as such: to put it bluntly, parties want to win elections; media owners (for the most part) want to make money. But these more particular goals are not incompatible with the requirement to stage political battles in such a way that the political system can cope with them, or, if you prefer, process them peacefully, or, even more bluntly, so that losers can live with the outcome.

Representative claims by parties that set up conflicts are *not* primarily claims about truth. As Hannah Arendt opined, opinions ought to be constrained by facts, but they are clearly *partisan* perspectives, and that's a fine thing, too.[19] Under conditions of pluralism, as already mentioned, citizens come to different judgments depending on different life experiences, a different sense of how to weigh various facts, and different subjective dispositions (I am risk averse; you're not).[20] Hence, democracy cannot be a project of instantiating a single whole truth in politics; in fact, as Arendt insisted, *the* truth in politics is bound to be despotic.[21]

The point can easily be misunderstood, but the Austrian legal theorist Hans Kelsen, arguably the twentieth century's greatest jurist, was right to argue that democracy has a deep philosophical affinity with relativism: different people see the world in different ways, and pursue different ends; when they differ, it's not necessarily because they are selfish or stupid, or just ignorant of the facts; by contrast, according to Kelsen, forms of philosophical absolutism—the opposite of uncertainty, one might say—are bound to legitimate autocratic forms of rule.[22] Elections are not about finding the truth; if they were, there couldn't be such a thing as a loyal and legitimate opposition. Instead, we would have to assume that losers who persist with their positions are simply liars.

Representative claims—and election choices—should of course be constrained by what we can plausibly call facts. The *Protocols of the Elders of Zion* is also a particular "representation" of society and "conflict," in fact about as clear-cut a "vision of divisions" as one can imagine, but it is obviously not a legitimate part of democratic politics. Things are different when, for instance, all sides agree about the basic scientific consensus on global warming but then come to conflicting judgments as to how important the fate of our children and grandchildren is (the Let's-Just-All-Have-a-Good-Time-Now Party will have a distinct view on this), or how optimistic we should be about the probability of technological breakthroughs that would save large parts of the planet, or whether preventing climate catastrophe is at all possible under a capitalist economic system, and so on.

The philosopher John Dewey called for nothing less than government's "alignment with science." Lest governments *informed* by scientists turn into governments *formed* or even *run* by scientists, Dewey insisted that "no government by experts in which the masses do not have the chance to inform the experts as to their needs can be anything but an oligarchy managed in the interests of the few." And what counts as "needs" not only can be but must be fought over in ordinary democratic politics. After all, needs can be debated, and opinions about who should win and who should lose can be fought over, but they must be based on something plausibly understood as *accurate* facts. The latter are of course, as Arendt also argued, very fragile indeed: once facts are forgotten—or have been successfully attacked by authoritarian powers—they are unlikely, though not impossible, to recover.

Wanting conflicts to be constrained by facts—for facts to be another *hard border* of democratic politics—does not mean that establishing all the facts is a precondition for public argument. As Christopher Lasch shrewdly observed,

> What democracy requires is public debate, not information. Of course it needs information too, but the kind of information it needs can be generated only by vigorous popular debate. We do not know what we need to know until we ask the right questions, and we can identify the right questions only by subjecting our own ideas about the world to the test of public controversy. Information, usually seen as the precondition of debate, is better understood as its byproduct. When we get into arguments that focus and

fully engage our attention, we become avid seekers of
relevant information. Otherwise we take in information passively—if we take it in at all.[23]

Intermediary institutions don't mechanically replicate
particular realities (let alone dictate the truth). Ideally, they
should offer choices, which means not that everyone gets to
choose their own reality but that everyone, ideally, finds a perspective on particular realities informed by different value
commitments. That is another way of saying that they ought
to enable both *external* and *internal* pluralism.

External pluralism refers to a significant range of both political parties and professional media: entities that are not
just in competition but also in significant opposition to each
other, such that citizens (and, for that matter, consumers)
have clear-cut options differing in substance. The point here
is not the conventional one that a competitive "marketplace
of ideas" will make the truth win out; on many political
questions, disagreement is not about the fact of the matter as
such. Rather, at issue is the multiplication of creative representations of groups in society; those who have new ideas about
interests and identities ought to be able to test them out freely
and get to see if there are any takers.

Internal pluralism is less obvious. What I mean is that it's
desirable to have a diversity of viewpoints also *within* individual intermediary institutions. Concretely, this implies
that political parties ought to have proper democratic processes on the inside such as primaries or extensive debates
preceding the election of party officers. This practice is in fact
prescribed in a number of constitutions, the thought being
that parties which lack internal democracy are likely to pose
a danger to democracy as a whole.[24] Professional media generally do not have internal democracy; in fact, a number of

countries exempt them from standard labor laws that are supposed to enable employees to be involved in decision making. In Germany and Austria, they fall under the category of *Tendenzunternehmen*—literally "tendentious corporations," meaning organizations with an orientation to ideals, which, rather obviously, also include churches. But media can of course still present a variety of views—the kind of imperative that, in the United States, was once codified in the Fairness Doctrine. The latter obliged broadcasters to present opposing views on controversial issues of public importance (and to grant those who felt misrepresented a right to reply).[25]

Such demands on intermediary institutions are not uncontentious, of course. Even if a state does not abuse its regulatory powers to tilt the democratic playing field, one might wonder how such prescriptions go together with rights of free association and free speech. In fact, one can ask whether such regulations might not misunderstand what particular institutions are really supposed to be about: After all, are internal pluralism and partisanship not on one level incompatible? Parties aren't debating clubs, and maximal "openness" could allow market libertarians to join social democratic parties and completely change their direction (which is one reason "blanket" and "open" primaries in the United States have been opposed by parties: their "brand" could be seriously undermined by partisans with entirely different agendas who would also be utterly unaccountable for the outcome; they worry as well that their own followers could start voting in primaries of minor parties and—God forbid—develop an attachment to them).[26] While Kelsen was right about the affinity between relativism and democracy as a whole, those who join political parties obviously don't do so because they think that everything is relative. Rather, they are precisely committed to certain political principles, and they wish to associate with others to promote the realization of those principles by passing laws. Parties are supposed to make that sort of sustained commitment possible, and the freedom of association from which they benefit includes the freedom *not* to associate with citizens who have very different principles.[27] Parties might even come as close as is possible under modern conditions to an Aristotelian ideal of civic friendship, based not so much on personal sentiment as on shared pursuit of principles. It requires loyalty and patience and even forgiveness up to a point—giving one another some slack—as well as a memory of past struggles, and it's not just about trying to stand for principles but also standing with others trying to realize them.[28] Obviously, one cares about the particulars of one's actual friends, not about maximizing the diversity of people one claims to be friends with (which is not to deny that some people acquire token friends).[29]

Partisans are by definition committed to particular principles, and sooner or later their precise meaning will become contentious. Lyndon Johnson, not a pol with philosophical pretensions, once opined, "What the man on the street wants is not a big debate on fundamental issues; he wants a little medical care, a rug on the floor, a picture on the wall." But, as his party has learned the hard way, even "a little medical care" will eventually become a matter of principled conflict. In any case, principles do not implement themselves, nor do they magically generate actual political strategies. Moreover, hardly anyone is ever committed to one principle only, and if they are, others will probably get tired of their going on and on about it fairly quickly. So, even beyond the question of practical implementation, there is a question of how principles coherently connect with one another. To test such matters, parties must be, among other things, as Antonio Gramsci put it, "laboratories."

What follows? Arguments have to take place, and a properly pluralist internal party democracy allows partisans to have them. There's also a potential learning effect: more views will be on the table, and the pressure to justify them and, ideally, make them mutually acceptable for partisans will render them more refined. But there's also a less obvious side effect: internal debate habituates partisans to the notion that others might just *possibly* be right and that those who lost the debate or at the ballot box can remain in loyal opposition (members whose side lost a mass plebiscite within a party are much more likely to head for the exits; those who could make their case in discussion and then lost tend to stick around).[30]

Against this background, it is highly problematic that the world's largest democracy has a so-called anti-defection provision. In India, the 1950 constitution said absolutely nothing about political parties; an amendment introduced in the mid-1980s stipulated that deputies who want to leave their party or just refuse to toe the line must lose their seats. The amendment responded to politicians selling their votes to the highest bidder for cash or government office; one politician infamously switched parties three times in a single day (this problem also notoriously plagues another large democracy, Brazil). However, effectively outlawing not just defection but dissent within a party makes it impossible for politicians to follow their conscience and convictions in how they interpret their party's principles—hence nothing like an internal loyal and legitimate opposition can be established.[31] Yet it is precisely such internal pluralism that might strengthen the idea that democracy as a whole depends on the existence of legitimate disagreement and loyal opposition. And that, in turn, is maybe as close as we can get to Aristotle's ideal that citizens experience themselves as both ruling and being ruled. For one presumably only accepts being ruled by someone who just possibly might be right.[32]

True, this vision of internal party debate is still highly idealized. Not least, there's the problem not often articulated in the polite company of sophisticated democratic theorists, but never put more elegantly than in Oscar Wilde's quip: the problem with socialism is that it takes too many evenings (those who've attended the party branch meetings of socialist parties know exactly why that is). As usual, there's a serious point behind Wilde's seemingly frivolous remark: social scientists find that a large number of "amateurs" and "hobbyists," that is to say, folks who love endlessly debating big ideas, but who cannot be bothered to do the humdrum work of canvassing, stuffing envelopes, or whatever other boring practical tasks might need to get done, might indeed become a problem for a party. Such aficionados are usually educated and economically fairly well-off; for them the party really is a kind of party—a fun thing to do in the evening and on weekends. By contrast, citizens who really have a lot at stake and an urgent sense of a shared political fate—let's say the prospect of having their health insurance taken away—will care about principles no less, but also have their minds focused on winning the battle for power here and now.[33]

There is something inherently problematic about parties that have only one member—an example being Geert Wilders's right-wing populist party in the Netherlands (in fact, there are two members: Wilders and a foundation of which—one might have guessed it—Wilders is the only member). A vast improvement in pluralistic democracy appears to be the Brexit Party, which boasts about being a "people's party" with more than a hundred thousand "supporters." Except that the party is actually a limited liability company, with only four officers and only *one* person registered as having "significant" control: Nigel Farage. The supposed people's party is thus another one-man party. Such forms of intraparty autocracy (autocracy is in effect autonomy, if it's just you there) arguably signal a profound aversion to the idea that the other side could *possibly* be right, for no other side is admitted to begin with.[34] In some countries, such autocracy would even be plainly illegal: Germany and Spain have constitutions and special legislation on political parties that make a minimum level of pluralism obligatory.[35]

In common-law countries, by contrast, such a norm appears inherently illiberal: parties are the result of people associating freely with one another, and that freedom extends to the question of how to regulate the inner life of parties.[36] Yet political parties aren't like private clubs in which individuals can contract with each other as they see fit; they exist in the hope that at least some of their members, as a result of free and fair elections, get hold of the legitimate means of coercion, that is to say, the levers of the state.[37] And, indeed, a for-whites-only party is illegal even in common-law countries: the British National Party, for instance, was ordered to open itself to British citizens of whatever descent, as opposed to only "Indigenous Caucasians"; in the United States in 1944, Democrats in Texas were told they could not hold a whites-only primary.[38]

Of course, that's just saying that what's illegal outside a party is also illegal inside a party. But parties can have internal hierarchies; just as representatives have more power than ordinary citizens, party committees may have special control over party affairs. That is a concern because parties have a particular vulnerability that doesn't apply to states: a massive entry of people into a party might change its character completely, subverting its original partisan commitments. This peril is often referred to as "entryism," following the concerted efforts by Trotskyists to enter social democratic parties and turn them in a revolutionary direction.

This peril underlines the need for intermediary powers

within intermediary powers: at least sometimes, those who have spent time working their way up the party's ladder will have good reasons to exclude new entrants, or, for that matter, presidential hopefuls who seem primarily interested in building their own commercial brand. Party elders can serve an important function of *peer review*; it's a function that should not be outsourced to consultants or TV stations, whose rationale will be ratings, as opposed to keeping faith with core partisan commitments. As Les Moonves, then CEO of CBS, infamously acknowledged, Trump was bad for America but damn good for CBS.

Intraparty democracy can be open, but it can't be open-ended; parties must be able to reach conclusive, binding decisions (and members have to be willing to be a loyal opposition, something that British Euroskeptics in the Conservative Party spectacularly failed to do). As the Labour Party leader Lord Bevan once put it bluntly, "We do not want to be in the position of having to listen to our own people."[39] But that can only be the case once "our own people" have had a chance to say something and then are bound by something like a common program. The problem in so many countries today is precisely that citizens are highly partisan—and feel they haven't been listened to—while parties are hollow and weak and unable to serve as laboratories for a coherent conception of the world, to pick up Gramsci's term again.

Obviously, professional media are not primarily dedicated to the promotion of political commitments or the fostering of political friendship. Here it's much more straightforward to argue that both external and internal pluralism are important; we want a wider range of views across the media, and within any given institution (though, as said above, a "tendency" can also legitimately limit internal media pluralism). The trouble is rather that sound criteria for media pluralism are hard to come by (nobody is ever officially against media pluralism, but that stance is facilitated by the fact that nobody can really say what it is). As is so often the case, we might see it more clearly when it's gone: the staffing of public service media with pure loyalists, as has happened in Hungary and Poland; the concentration of ownership among the bosses of what is sometimes called the "construction bourgeoisie" in Turkey (that is, the beneficiaries of the building boom, who, as a thank-you to the president, used their resources to acquire what had been critical or even just broadly neutral newspapers); and the total withdrawal of state advertising—crucial for struggling newspapers in particular—if journalists don't toe the line.

There's still something else: beyond staging the battle of democratic politics, and beyond providing pluralism, there is the role of intermediary powers in structuring political time. Parties hold primary elections at particular intervals; newspapers and broadcasters offer news and opinion on a given schedule. Here again, they bring—as James Bryce put it when describing the role of parties—"order out of chaos to a multitude of voters," and here we also find yet again something of an analogy with a democratic political system as a whole. After all, elections concentrate citizens' minds; they establish relations of accountability, because candidates make promises during election campaigns to which voters will return. Not least, they serve as a ritual affirmation of the importance of democracy as a whole, partly by creating a simultaneous experience for all citizens, where possible (in the United States, citizens all voted on the same day for the first time in 1848). Simultaneity appears impossible in the world's largest democracy, as voting is stretched out over a month in India; it also became impossible in many countries during the pandemic, when the possibility of voting by mail could be a matter of life or death.[40]

Again, there is no point in idealizing any of this. In the nineteenth-century United States, Election Day was not a moment of solemnly practicing civic mindfulness; it was a time to get free whiskey and possibly have a good time fistfighting; people didn't study pamphlets, as idealized visions of the public sphere would suggest, but rather joined raucous parades that usually ended up at the houses of the richest citizens—which bluntly reaffirmed that the latter had most of the power.[41]

Yet these periodic events also give a rhythm to democratic life; they provide common reference points around which partisans can coordinate.[42] And they furnish not just winners but also—once again, this is crucial—losers with resources: the victors get to implement their political projects more or less independently of changes in opinion, but the losers get to prepare for a distinct moment when they will have another chance.[43] This was and is true of democracy inside political parties as well. And it used to be the case with professional media, and not just for the reason that the media were mostly in sync with the larger pattern of political time; rather, there were rituals such as the proverbial six thirty or eight o'clock news that brought significant parts of the country together around the TV set. Hegel, a comfortable inhabitant of the early nineteenth-century bourgeois public sphere, remarked that reading the morning newspaper constituted the daily prayer of the bourgeois; Marshall McLuhan, a provocateur in and of the twentieth-century mass public sphere, described the ritual a bit differently: "People don't actually read newspapers. They step into them every morning like a hot bath."

It is easy to underestimate, or even ridicule, this point: rhythm and ritual might just be dismissed as stilted bourgeois norms. But think about how the twenty-four-hour news cycle, the sheer nonstop bombardment with supposed "information" online, has made it harder to form political judgments. Constant distraction is the opposite, obviously, of predetermined moments of political focus. The direct and instant address (or so it feels) by tweeting presidents and over-politicized friends potentially does away with the work that used to be done by well-functioning intermediary institutions.

Planning (and Paying for) Infrastructure

Intermediary institutions do not fulfill their roles spontaneously, and they obviously do not operate in a vacuum; they are part of systems: parties form party systems; media make up media systems.[44] The shape of these can differ dramatically from country to country; what kinds of systems are formed depends crucially on what the American sociologist Paul Starr calls constitutive choices.[45] This is fairly evident in the cases of parties: the United States settled on "first past the post" as the rule for electing members of Congress—that is to say, winner takes all; loser loses all—in 1842; in combination with the direct election of the president, this choice made an overall two-party system virtually inevitable (but note that the rule has no special constitutional standing; in theory, Congress could introduce proportional representation tomorrow).

The loser-loses-all logic has meant that those pressing for political ideas that are currently not taken up by either of the two major parties are well advised to get to work inside the more or less big tents of those parties, in the hope that the tents become even larger or perhaps as a whole are shifted more rightward or leftward, as the case might be. A somewhat different logic (and more colorful metaphor) suggests that the pain of a loss inflicted by a third party can make a party jump; third parties, according to Richard Hofstadter's image, are like bees: once they've stung, they die. Think of how Nigel Farage's UK Independence Party, and then subsequently his Brexit Party, succeeded in making the Conservative Party effectively into the Brexit Party; consequently, the actual Brexit Party LLC could become history.

Constitutive choices are never neutral. They are not necessarily irreversible, but they do become entrenched, and those benefiting from the rules as they are will try to find ways of re-legitimating them if they come under pressure. An example is David Cameron outplaying his Liberal Democratic coalition partners roughly a decade ago. The latter had succeeded in obtaining a binding referendum on changing the election system as part of the coalition deal with the Conservatives—which they went on to lose decisively (this victory, together with the defeat of a vote for Scottish independence, and the impression that in referenda citizens break late for the status quo, probably contributed to a false sense of certainty that Cameron had figured out the direct democracy game and would prevail on Brexit, too).[46]

Constitutive choices also shape media systems. The adoption of one kind of distribution network or another makes particular media more or less expensive, and thus helps or hinders the emergence of a mass circulation press quite apart from basic decisions about how to regulate content. A European country that did not have a mass readership for newspapers in the late nineteenth or early twentieth century—be it for commercial reasons or because too few people could read—would never develop one later, even if states converged economically and in their literacy rates.[47] This still explains the comparative weakness of newspaper markets—and perhaps the public sphere more broadly—in the south of the Continent.

Starting conditions plus political choices open some pathways of development and close off others. This perhaps pedantic-sounding observation has two important implications: First, proponents of whatever kind of reform must take a larger—that is to say, systemic—view. What works perfectly well in one context might turn out to make things considerably worse in another: presidentialism seemed particularly democratic at a time when the United States was seen as the world's leading democracy; it turned out that it worked only because parties were not highly polarized, and, *surprise!*, in other contexts it proved disastrous. Second, especially with regard to the media, technology matters, but technology is not destiny. The invention of the telegraph in and of itself decided nothing about whether it was going to be owned by private business; the creation of radio obviously didn't mandate the creation of the BBC. Technology determines neither the legal conditions of its own application nor, for that matter, the self-understanding of those using the technology, such as journalists—in particular their widely varying views on the question of how their "professionalism" (whatever that might mean exactly) relates to politics.

As Starr has shown, for instance, it was not technology as such but "architectural" choices informed by particular values that made for distinct trajectories of the media in the United States and Britain. The development of a relatively decentralized newspaper industry in the United States was massively helped not just by high literacy rates; what mattered enormously in comparison with European countries was the federal government's decision to subsidize papers through low postal rates for periodicals. In the 1790s, as much as 70 percent of the mail was newspapers; the number rose to 95 percent in the 1830s.[48] Tocqueville, traveling in Kentucky and Michigan, marveled at the "astonishing circulation of letters and newspapers among those savage woods"; he also remarked that an American would only ever plunge into the "wilds of the New World" with "his Bible, ax, and newspapers."[49]

That wasn't an accident, or the sheer genius of American capitalism; it was part of the founders' program for a functioning republic: Jefferson had emphasized the need to give the people "full information of their affairs through the channel of the public papers, and to contrive that those papers should penetrate the whole mass of the people. The basis of our government being the opinion of the people, the first object should be to keep that right." (Jefferson was as good as his word: he ran and funded an opposition newspaper while serving in Washington's cabinet.)[50] Madison, in turn, stated categorically that "a popular Government, without popular information, or the means of acquiring it, is but a Prologue to a Farce or a Tragedy; or perhaps both" (Fox News and Trump proved that it could indeed be both).

To be fair, none of these high-minded pronouncements by eminent political architects meant that American papers would necessarily provide accurate information: as said above, the press was highly partisan; up to 80 percent of newspapers were linked to parties in mid-nineteenth-century America.[51] Tocqueville concluded that decentralization of political power, large numbers of associations, and a proliferation of newspapers all went together. In the Frenchman's view, newspapers, since they produced associations and were in turn sustained by them, necessarily had to take sides politically: "A newspaper cannot survive unless it reproduces a doctrine or sentiment shared by a great many people."[52] Utterly unable to curb what for the usually skeptical aristocrat was genuine enthusiasm, he celebrated the fact that the newspaper causes political life to circulate through all the parts of that vast territory. Its eye is constantly open to detect the secret springs of political designs and to summon the leaders of all parties in turn to the bar of public opinion. It rallies the interests of the community round certain principles and draws up the creed of every party; for it affords a means of intercourse between those who hear and address each other without ever coming into immediate contact.

Eventually, newspapers cut loose from parties, relying on private profit rather than party coffers. The nineteenth-century "penny press" proved to cultural pessimists that civilization was going to hell. But sensationalism sold, and as a result newspapers could do without the patronage of powerful politicians: the reader was now primarily a consumer, not a voter.[53] Today still, the penny press provokes admiration among progressive American political and legal theorists, for they equate its triumph with a broad process of democratization.[54] As the Yale jurist Robert Post has put it, "The responsiveness of newspapers to consumer demand was ultimately a political question. The broader the public to which newspapers responded, the more democratic the public sphere which they created."[55] A less rosy estimation would add that these papers often lied shamelessly, could not care less about privacy, and frequently stole content from their competitors.

Such practices eventually provoked a push for professionalism. The latter could easily be read as a sign of disdain for unruly mass democracy. U.S. progressives sought to codify special roles for journalists to generate "objective" reporting. They also demanded particular training in proper journalism schools: the École Supérieure de Journalisme in Paris and the University of Missouri compete for the title of oldest journalism school in the world (1899 and 1908, respectively, or 1910 and 1908, depending on different criteria—there's apparently no objectivity here).

A profession, by definition, has to be able to restrict access, usually through credentials obtained on the basis of education. To this day, Italian journalists can practice their craft only if they are members of the Order of Journalists, for which they have to pass an exam (none of which means that Italian journalists are generally considered particularly professional).[56]

For critics, professionalism has always just been elitism. But, at least in theory, professional standards are also a way of shielding institutions from economic and political power. Reformers had the ambition, as Lippmann (one of the great protagonists of professionalization) put it, of bringing the "publishing business under greater social control"—that is to say, exerting legal power over private interests in the name of a conception of the common good. Lippmann had witnessed how government propaganda in support of World War I had poisoned the American public sphere, but he resisted the conclusion that the only options were state control or shameless commercialism, which left what he called the "manufacturing of consent" to unregulated private actors. Professionalism promised autonomy without losing accountability; if one failed to observe professional standards, one could be judged, perhaps even be condemned accordingly, by professional peers.

After World War II, various commissions of wise elders suggested that newspapers follow a model of "social responsibility" in how they handle information and opinion. Like the push for "objectivity," this amounted to a call for self-regulation in accordance with public, and not in any narrow sense technical, standards. As a result, major American media concentrated almost entirely on information, in contrast to interpretation, let alone advocacy (*The New York Times* did not have a designated op-ed page until 1970).[57] Newspapers "reported" mainly on what various government figures had said and done; there was not much explaining what it meant, let alone judging whether it amounted to anything positive.[58] As a journalist covering the witch hunts of Joe McCarthy confessed, "My own impression was that Joe was a demagogue. But what could I do? I had to report—and quote— McCarthy . . . The press is supposedly neutral. You write what the man says."[59]

Many U.S. journalists eventually changed course; mere information was complemented by interpretation; in addition to "who," "where," "when," there was now "why." Asking that question turned out to be highly profitable: in the 1980s and into the 1990s some U.S. newspapers still had larger profit margins than Google has today (partly because savvy interpretation could be nicely bundled with ads for luxury brands and upper-middle-class jobs).[60] In the eyes of conservative critics, however, interpretation was merely partisanship.[61]

In newly democratized European countries such as West Germany, journalists also assumed an explicitly political role, but less as interpreters than guardians of democracy; they claimed to protect the latter from overreaching or secretive executives. Such self-conceptions as a Fourth Estate were reinforced by the official ethos of public service broadcasting or, in the United States, the small number of major networks (and also a still relatively small number of radio stations). All of them remained subject to the Fairness Doctrine, which had been instituted in 1949 and drew the ire of conservatives for decades. The doctrine was finally abolished in 1987 by a Reaganite deregulator who dismissed TV as "just another appliance . . . a toaster with pictures."

From today's vantage point, the period of the Cold War might appear a golden age when the media were a fourth power supporting or even furthering democracy. But it could also be seen as a period when new claims for representation were very hard to advance. Only 10 percent of heads of households in U.S. sitcoms were working-class (not to speak of skin color and gender; women were portrayed as very capable only when they could serve as contrasting with buffoonish working-class dads).[62] Older white male gatekeepers decided what was newsworthy and how it should be interpreted; when the longtime anchor Walter Cronkite closed news programs by announcing "and that's the way it is," who among the thirty million who watched him could disagree, and who, among those who disagreed, was to get a hearing? As feminists charged, "objectivity" was just male subjectivity.

To maximize audiences, broadcasters invariably decided to offer what an NBC executive called the "Least Objectionable Program."[63] Except that it was of course highly objectionable from the perspective not just of conservatives obsessed with "liberal bias" but also of left-wing critics. Journalism that depended on profits from advertising, in the eyes of radical dissenters, had a distinctly ideological function: as Upton Sinclair claimed, "Journalism is one of the devices whereby industrial autocracy keeps its control over political democracy."[64]

The postwar period might not have been golden, then, but it certainly was exceptional in one respect. What in France is referred to as the *trente glorieuses*—the thirty glorious years of rapid and virtually uninterrupted economic growth—took the edge off much political conflict. Many parties transformed into what political scientists at the time called "catch-all parties." They ditched distinctive and what could often be seen as sectarian ideological commitments. German Social Democrats, for instance, expunged the last remainders of Marxist language at the end of the 1950s; instead, they aimed to be electable by all (at least in theory).[65] These were sometimes called people's parties, but unlike populists they did not claim that only they represented the people; rather, the populace was imagined as divided, but with citizens on different sides of various conflicts able in principle to change allegiances. While becoming blander, parties also became much more professional; for critics, this proved once more the truth of Michels's iron law of oligarchy: power inside a party inevitably falls into the hands of the few. There was little by way of internal pluralism; reason giving in democratic debate was replaced by responsiveness to opinion polls.

So there goes another notion of a golden age . . . Although this in and of itself is not, of course, a conclusive reason to deny that intermediary institutions are in deep crisis today.

Expect the Expected?

It's commonplace to observe that opinion about the impact of the internet has swung from one extreme to the other: from the view that the Web would finally realize democracy to something like "Facebook means fascism."[66] What the diametrically opposed opinions have in common is an unspoken commitment to technological determinism, as well as a tendency to overestimate change. We see few articles with headlines such as THINGS HAVEN'T CHANGED AS MUCH AS WE THINK, as opposed to HOW TECHNOLOGY DISRUPTED THE TRUTH (an actual headline from *The Guardian*), and nobody remembers that a British reactionary such as Carlyle claimed in the nineteenth century, "Invent the printing press and democracy is inevitable."[67]

No technology determines the conditions of its own implementation.[68] True, the internet creates a new kind of infrastructure, but the shape of that infrastructure will depend a great deal on the infrastructure we have already inherited, that is to say, the party systems and, above all, public spheres that have been formed by basic regulatory (and often deregulatory) decisions over the past two centuries.

The United States is a case in point. In a brilliant analysis of the 2016 presidential election, three Harvard-based social scientists identified what they call a distinct right-wing media ecosphere. Within that largely self-enclosed sphere, "news" serves primarily as a form of political self-validation; disinformation (or even just misinformation) goes largely uncorrected, because the audience of a kind of right-wing political "entertainment complex" has hardly any contact with even center-right sources of news and opinion, such as *The Wall Street Journal*.[69] The result is that misinformation and especially disinformation—divorced from any fact-checking whatsoever—can travel fast and far, a process for which Lippmann's condescending expression "contagion of unreason" seems fairly accurate.

The crucial insight of the Harvard scholars is that the emergence of this right-wing ecosphere—which has no symmetrical counterpart on the left—significantly predates the internet. The rise of AM radio as a channel of conservative talk and of highly partisan cable news after the end of the Fairness Doctrine in 1987 proved crucial (in fact, even today, the medium that Americans spend most time with is radio).[70] The introduction of Fox News increased the vote share of Republicans by between 0.4 and 0.7 percent (not much, one might conclude, but remember that George W. Bush "won" Florida by fewer than five hundred votes; Fox, according to this calculation, gave the Republicans an additional ten

thousand supporters at the ballot box).[71] The regulatory decisions that enabled cable TV and other mediums to flour-
ish as they did were political choices; they were shaped only
to a limited degree by technological innovation. In turn,
those decisions enabled a form of polarization that, it just so
happens, turned out to be very, very big business, especially
for self-declared "advocacy journalists" or "opinion journalists" on the right. And rather than the party controlling
the paper, as had been the case in Tocqueville's day, it now
seems that the electronic media are ideologically policing
the party (though, possibly, as an unintended side effect of
maximizing profit).[72]

None of this is to say that reregulation would magically
make polarization and disinformation disappear. But it is
to claim that a new technology is often fitted into an already
existing infrastructure—possibly exacerbating, but not necessarily creating from scratch, challenges for democracy.[73]

Still, recent economic and technological changes may have
an unintended side effect on the infrastructure of democracy.
Both misinformation and disinformation have become easier
to spread—partly because it's simpler to obscure where stories
originated, partly because there's now a well-developed art
(if not quite a science) to making stories go "viral." During
the 2018 presidential election in Brazil, WhatsApp served as
the (free) messenger of choice for a massive disinformation
campaign funded by corporations pushing for the far-right
candidate Jair Bolsonaro.[74] WhatsApp is used by 120 million
out of 210 million citizens in a country where internet access
is very expensive for households and where mobile plans tend
not to include unlimited data: the result is that Brazilians
use messaging apps heavily but do not necessarily have any
link to the World Wide Web as such, let alone media that
could serve as a check on disinformation. Because WhatsApp

(which is owned by Facebook) primarily connects friends and family, "information" shared on it seems automatically more credible, since those who transmit it are more trusted.[75]

This was not a spontaneous outcome: corporations supporting the far-right candidate paid huge sums to push a pro-Bolsonaro message. Ironically, a recent campaign finance reform measure worked well enough in limiting donations to politicians but left the social media loophole open: Bolsonaro and other candidates and the media had actually signed a pact not to spread "fake news." The reality turned out to be that 98.1 percent of Bolsonaro voters had been confronted with pieces of false information; 89.77 percent gave them credence.[76] It was perfectly justified for the far-right president's fans to shout "Facebook, Facebook, Facebook" at his inauguration. Once more, the creation of a closed system is not due to the medium as such being authoritarian or to people being just gullible or inevitably tending toward tribalism; it's because of basic regulatory and economic decisions.

Meanwhile, in India, the NaMo app has been presented as a way to keep up with government announcements; users are not aware that it is privately owned by Narendra Modi and employed to harvest data. As Freedom House observes, the app "was secretly routing users' personal information to a behavioral analytics company with offices in the United States and India."[77]

These cheap ways to create new publics through misinformation or outright disinformation can be weaponized against professional journalists. The latter regularly get accused of bias and of ignoring "ordinary citizens" and their legitimate political self-expressions. Some succumb to the incessant pressure to prove their innocence. Studiously mindful of traditional norms of objectivity and balance, they retreat from interpretation back to what seems mere uncontentious information:

the old "you write what the man says." But symmetrical coverage in situations of asymmetrical polarization—where only one party has turned against fundamental democratic rules or is misleading the public systematically about basic facts—turns into distortion.[78] The effects of a self-consciously neutral stance are not neutral. An alternative—about which I say more in the next chapter—is to hold on to objectivity, in the sense of providing accurate information that can be checked (and double-checked), but also to interpret events based on a clear commitment to democratic principles, or, for that matter, even partisan principles, as long as everyone knows that that's what's happening.

Quite apart from the enormous financial pressures under which practitioners now labor, professional journalism had already become more fragile through what we might as well, on this occasion, refer to as neoliberalism. What I mean specifically is the suspicion that professionals—be they academics, doctors, or indeed journalists—run a kind of closed shop through requiring specialized education and training (even if many countries differ from Italy in that there is no formal certification as such for journalists).[79] Once inside their self-created system, they can relax; unlike those engaged in business, who are mercilessly exposed to the punishments meted out by objective market mechanisms, they can get away with a lax attitude toward their own products. Margaret Thatcher evidently assumed that most professors, other than in the hard sciences, were just wasting taxpayers' money by sitting around drinking tea and spouting leftist nonsense. The turn toward simulating markets inside universities and the National Health Service—through a relentless "audit culture" that would have given central planners in the Soviet Union the pleasure of instant recognition—was to make professionals compete, work properly, and, above all, become accountable to society at large (that is, taxpayers). The latter were assumed to think that the whole game of professionalism was probably always rigged, that "liberal elites" simply reproduce themselves in a world where in fact there are no real standards.

When Donald Trump revealed his cabinet appointments, some observers pointed with glee to what they thought was an obvious contradiction: How could a supposed "populist" surround himself with corporate bosses and Wall Street figures with a combined worth of 4.3 billion dollars—all epitomizing the elite, after all? What such critics failed to see was precisely that these exceptional human beings weren't for the most part professionals: their success (and "hard work") could be measured objectively, in dollars;[80] they were obviously competent and capable of implementing the real people's will—unlike professionals who would always end up distorting it while lecturing everyone on how they simply knew better because, after all, they had more education.

Right-wing authoritarian populists are not simply "anti-elite"; they target a particular elite, including journalists who are accused of being unfair und unbalanced. With Trump, this was always obvious, but there are more subtle ways of denying that professionals are anything special: during the pandemic, Boris Johnson, shifting to a more and more presidential style of press conferences, insisted on first taking a question from "Michelle in Cornwall," making it plain that any citizen would be as capable as journalists of asking the important questions (the question Michelle, a hotel owner, ended up asking was, "Please can we ask how tourism within the UK will be managed in the coming weeks?").[81]

The denigration of professionalism preceded the internet; these are political strategies, not inevitable outcomes somehow generated by technology. Still, there remain two clear-cut arguments for how the unintended consequences of the internet may prove detrimental for democracy; one is very concrete, the other somewhat abstract and speculative.

First, local journalism in particular has suffered from the restructuring of the economy in the past two decades. Advertising used to sustain serious reporting; as Clay Shirky famously put it, Walmart might not have any interest in the Baghdad bureau, but they de facto subsidized its staff.[82] As advertising revenue was hoovered up by Google and Facebook, local papers in particular saw their newsroom staff cut dramatically. One in five local newspapers has disappeared in the United States since 2004; five million Americans have no local newspaper at all; sixty million have only one.[83]

The growth of such "news deserts" has had profound political effects.[84] Corruption increases, as no journalist reports on town council meetings, public procurement decisions in particular. Political interest declines: the shuttering of local papers has been associated with lower turnout in elections, fewer candidates running for office, and more incumbents winning. Citizens also have less effective representation at the national level. As local and regional papers cannot afford a correspondent in the capital, it becomes more difficult to understand what exactly congressmen or members of Parliament are doing, making it harder to hold them accountable.

Less obviously, the shrinking of proper local news reinforces pernicious trends of polarization. In their neighborhoods, citizens can often agree on diagnosing concrete problems and discuss practical solutions—all without getting into extended culture wars.[85] But as local news—and hence local debates—disappear, national news fills the void.[86] And national debates often contain much more partisan posturing and the re-coding of conflicts as questions of cultural identity.

Here is the second challenge: as by now everybody knows, corporations that provide services which are "free" for consumers (or, with the usual euphemisms, "users," "the community," and so on) monetize their consumers. These corporations gather data about consumers and sell them to advertisers; they make the consumer herself into the product they sell. As David Runciman has observed about Google, "To search is to be searched," a variation on the adage "If the product is free, you are the product."[87]

In one sense this mechanism is hardly novel; political parties have always "microtargeted": the Communist Party of France did not hand out party materials in the richest parts of Paris. Newspapers sold advertising space to businesses based on information about who their readers were; they made the advertisers pay for eyeballs, while the owners of the eyeballs had to pay, too, as Paul Starr has put it. While every reader paid the same for the paper, not all readers were worth the same. The more reliably one could identify wealthy consumers and sell them to advertisers, the better for the balance sheet.

But, of course, these ads were visible to all. Microtargeted "dark posts" are not.[88] They deprive parties, and citizens more broadly, of the chance to counter them with different information and, in the language of the Fairness Doctrine, "contrasting points of view." It also allows for an endless reinforcement of political identifications in a system that Shoshana Zuboff, with a seminal concept, has called "surveillance capitalism."[89] Zuboff notes Google made a conscious choice to build its business model on profiting from the "behavioral surplus" generated through its searches. Data about individual behavior not only permits tech companies to improve the "user experience"; it can also be sold to advertisers who can then target individuals with ever more precision.

The internet giant, Zuboff warns, ends up claiming ever more "human experience as free raw material for hidden commercial practices of extraction, prediction, and sales"—a kind of colonization of ordinary life made all the easier the more individuals become dependent on an internet of things that can comprehensively surveil them at all times.

Constant surveillance goes together with a tendency to give us ever more of the same. It may lead to manipulating us to only ever want more of the same, or to always behave the same (or to having no choice at all, because only some things show up on screens). Algorithms generate predictions premised on the notion that our future behavior will be a lot like our past behavior, and also prompt actions that make those predictions more likely to be true. This runs counter to one of the core features of democracy discussed earlier: democracy as institutionalized uncertainty. If democratic politics is only the systematic activation of seemingly given identities—based on ever more precise profiles generated through surveillance—its dynamic character, its open-endedness, and even its beneficial randomness are lost: only ever expect the expected.

To be sure, democracy's open-endedness can be exaggerated: modern democracy has also been about mobilizing groups that had coalesced around particular self-conceptions, and these self-conceptions were not remade with every election; on the contrary, parties tried to reinforce them by getting their supporters to turn up at the polls. Echo chambers appeared as soon as there were any chambers in which those with "common sympathies"—to quote Mill again—could meet. The evidence as to whether citizens today are really trapped in politically homogeneous spaces is mixed; if anything, there are reasons to think that their off-line social world is politically more uniform than their online existence (and that, for the most part, politics matters little to them overall).[90]

Still, the potential level of closure is new, because the ability to make money, or profit politically, from cognitive biases is becoming much more refined. Previous media serving politics also weren't nearly as addictive as social media.[91] They also did not, on the basis of algorithms designed to maximize "engagement" (and hence revenue), steer their consumers to ever more radical ideas for essentially commercial reasons.[92]

In the end, then, our online profile becomes a self-fulfilling prophecy, so to speak; past behavior is the best predictor of future behavior in any case, but with the right incentives or "nudges," or through making us systematically feel insecure and in search of validation (am I being liked?), past behavior can even more easily be reproduced. Facebook has already demonstrated that its users' moods can be changed with a few simple signals; it also appears to sit on conclusive evidence that its algorithms increase the engagement of the people by dividing the people.

The problem is not that this machinery is necessarily being used for nefarious purposes at the moment, but that it could be so used. Think back to the portrayal of the oligarch developed in the first chapter: one characteristic related to personality ("grab and grab and grab"), the other to the power to shape political structures—including intermediaries—at will. Concentrated power means that unaccountable individuals could influence elections, but it could also permit governments to exert pressure on individuals who will tweak their politics so as to preserve the platforms' profits. A Trump and a Zuckerberg are individually perilous for democracy; all the ways they might use each other significantly compound the dangers.

Is the Party Really Over?

One great anxiety today is partisans replacing professionals in the media—another kind of "Fox effect." However, in many political parties the opposite seems to have happened: the number of partisans—as in party members—has been dwindling, while what is sometimes derided as a "blob" of consultants, pollsters, and spin doctors has been expanding. This is not necessarily proof of Michels's iron law all over again; rather, mass bureaucratic parties have begun to resemble the firms that outsource many of what used to be thought of as their core activities. They also resemble firms in another, even less savory way: when they can, they form cartels. Members are no longer needed for their money or their legwork, when the time arrives for door-to-door canvassing; financing can be obtained from states, and instead of having activists go door to door, the party can always already appear on the screen of someone microtargeted for mobilization (especially in democracies in which getting potential supporters out to vote has become more important than persuading the undecided—the reality, according to many observers, in the United States since about 2004 or so). Cartel parties lose elections, too. But they make sure opposition is fairly cushy; what matters to them most—as with any cartel—is that no new players enter the game and compete to claim state resources.[93]

This picture, painted by political scientists studying Europe in particular, is a caricature, but like with all good caricatures the overall likeness is clearly there. Citizens are not wrong to think that somehow parties have become disconnected from society; less obviously, they are also not wrong to suspect that what can look like attempts to reconnect are just more sophisticated ways to create political firms that can "produce" more power for their founders. Think of an entity like Silvio Berlusconi's Forza Italia: nominally a party, but created by marketing experts, and, as lived experience, more like a soccer fan club (in fact, at European Union summits, Berlusconi often wanted to talk about soccer and women, rather than boring policy stuff); devotion to a personality, rather than sustained commitment to anything recognizable as partisan principles; and, obviously, no internal pluralism, given the founder's treatment of the party as an instrument for getting into power and staying out of prison. TV crucially enabled the *Cavaliere* to dispense with a traditional bureaucratic apparatus that would have connected to civil society; Berlusconi could reach *la gente* directly and, not least, sell governing as yet another nightly show.

What some observers have called the "TV party" characterized an era that might already have passed. In the last decade or so, yet another novel institution emerged with the digital or "platform party." Social media have renewed a promise of political participation that is not reducible to fandom, and bucking the trend, a number of parties have increased their membership massively: Momentum, the association of mostly young left-wing citizens enthused by Jeremy Corbyn, a self-described "people-powered, vibrant movement," brought tens of thousands of new people into the British Labour Party. After the party had shrunk to fewer than 200,000 members under Tony Blair, Labour today boasts more than half a million members (making it the largest political party in Europe, according to some estimates). Jean-Luc Mélenchon's left-wing La France Insoumise also claims to have more than half a million *adhérents*, and the number of *personas inscritas* of the Spanish left-wing Podemos is around 540,000 (Podemos's degree of "openness" in this regard is remarkable: you can subscribe and still be a member of another party). Italy's Five Star Movement is today the largest political party in Italy.

As the social scientist Paolo Gerbaudo has observed, many of these new parties function somewhat like the business model of digital corporations: it's free to sign up; there is no traditional fee-paying membership at all; one joins by leaving one's email address and clicking something like *je soutiens* (in the case of La France Insoumise). There are almost zero marginal costs of communicating online; maximizing "engagement" with supporters constantly generates more data that in turn can help with what two senior advisers to Bernie Sanders's campaign in 2016 called "distributed organizing"—that is to say, microtargeting the people most likely to go out there and do some actual legwork when needed.[94] Like social media in general, this kind of participation can take too many evenings, but unlike Michels's bureaucratic and therefore inevitably hierarchical parties of yesteryear, the promise is of equality. Among the Five Star Movement's mottoes is *ognuno vale uno*, "everyone is worth one," or what in the old days would simply have been "one person, one vote" (even if this commitment to equality is obviously undercut by the movement's rule that candidates under forty are to be preferred to older ones, even if the latter obtained more votes—exactly the opposite of the ancient Athenians' rule that certain magistrates had to be *at least* forty).

Enthusiasts for these platform parties have suggested that direct, permanent participation can usher in an era of genuinely post-representative politics: rather than delegating decisions to professionals, committed partisans, with minimal efforts, can make choices themselves via online consultations; or, as in the Pirate Parties' "liquid democracy"—which in many ways pioneered the approach of today's platform parties—they can flexibly delegate their vote to a friend they find particularly competent.

The stories these new parties tell about themselves are that they emerged seamlessly from mass protests on the streets and squares. They've assiduously presented themselves as movements as opposed to traditional parties (which Grillo simply declared "evil").

But this story is misleading, especially for the Five Star Movement, which at the time of writing is busy transforming itself into a traditional party (representatives are now allowed to serve more than two terms in office, and preelection alliances with parties of the dreaded *la casta* are permissible). In Spain, the major protests—under the slogan "They do not represent us," with the "they" referring to the political class and business elites—took place in 2011. Podemos—literally "we can"—was not formed until 2014. Its founders were political scientists who thought the main lesson from protests on the squares was that left-wing concepts no longer resonated with citizens. Instead of left-right, they held, the main political dividing line should be *la casta*—the caste of professional politicians—versus *el pueblo*, or simply *arriba* versus *abajo*, top versus bottom (or, with a zoological metaphor, the elites as cats and the people as mice). They also concluded, "If you want to get it right, don't do what the left would do"—even if their actual policy ideas about housing and employment, for instance, were close to what traditional Social Democrats would have offered. This self-consciously post-ideological stance was shared by Grillo, who proclaimed that "the days of ideology are over . . . the M5S is neither left—nor right—wing. It is above and beyond."

Something else united the new southern European platform parties: an unabashed emphasis on strong (mostly male) leadership. The reason is not that southerners are more prone to machismo but that charismatic personalities helped establish a brand: at the beginning, Podemos would just put a headshot of its leader, Pablo Iglesias, originally a political science professor from Madrid, with his trademark ponytail, on the ballot. Iglesias was in due course accused by critics inside his party of *hiperliderazgo* and "online Leninism." He responded, alluding to a famous passage in Marx, that one could not storm the heavens by consensus.

Iglesias had come to prominence through his own talk show on a cable channel, later described as a "training camp for politics." Podemos leaders held that TV had become for politics what gunpowder had been for war and that "TV studios have become the real parliaments"—a view later modified in favor of arguing that online participation was the real means of "hacking democracy." By contrast, Grillo had been banned from Italian TV after irreverent jokes about politicians' corruption. Instead, with the help of the internet-guru-cum-businessman Gianroberto Casaleggio, he created his enormously influential and popular blog, where strong opinions went together with what Grillo praised as investigative journalism and fact-based expertise. M5S promoted itself as an "antiparty"; it promised the advent of direct democracy and the unleashing of "collective intelligence" through continuous online participation by ordinary citizens (after all, everyone must be an expert on something). Casaleggio Associates, the company in charge of M5S's operations, established the movement's online system for participation, now not so subtly named Rousseau (Casaleggio had also claimed that the internet "makes us equal in being smart" and that it was "like Athens"—not a crazy thought if one thinks back to the fact that ancient sortition, selection by lot, assumed roughly equal capacity among citizens). It was telling that Grillo would never criticize just *la casta* of full-time politicians; he equally denounced professional journalists. One of his V-Days—short for *Vaffanculo*—was dedicated to protesting against the public financing of newspapers; it also called for abolishing the journalists' professional association.

Bernie Sanders's senior advisers once declared that the "revolution will not be staffed." But, as with Facebook's sentimental, and self-serving, proclamations about community building, the reality has been rather different. While seemingly doing away with traditional intermediary powers and making direct participation an ongoing reality, these new cloud-like or swarm-like associations, such as Five Star and the Sanders campaign, still rely on mediation, after all: the platform itself is the medium. And the medium is not neutral. Like Facebook, the revolution is not only staffed but staffed with a small number of exceptionally powerful insiders; an enormous number of members who appear horizontally equal on the one hand is combined with a barely visible but very steep hierarchy on the other.[95] Grillo kept the copyright of the M5S symbols and denied their use to anyone he deemed to have broken the movement's rules; he also resisted Italian legislation mandating democracy inside political parties by arguing that M5S was not a party: it allegedly had no members; there were only people using its "franchise."[96]

Davide Casaleggio, son of Gianroberto and inheritor of the movement's online infrastructure, once declared, "One should not settle for representation when one can achieve *participation*."[97] But participation has been systematically oversold. As Gerbaudo has noted, the reality of participation has often been online mass plebiscites; the positions of the *hiperlider* are endorsed by majorities that would have pleased Stalin. The reality of Rousseau—the online system—confirms the premonitions of Rousseau the thinker: representatives do not engage with ordinary members and don't give reasons for their positions; there is not even a pretense of equality.[98]

The attempt to disempower party elites—intermediaries within intermediaries, so to speak—has been justified with the argument that regional barons are a thing for established parties (a claim also prominently made by Emmanuel Macron). But the result has been a vacuum between leaders and ordinary members; no middle management and hence also no personnel with experience in politics. Instead of being on experience, the emphasis has been on expertise of a certain technical kind. For instance, more than half the candidates fielded by Macron's LREM party for the 2017 legislative elections had never held political office before (90 percent of LREM's candidates were professionals or business leaders—who together represent roughly 13 percent of French society).

The new parties have pushed an ideology of "participationism," to use Gerbaudo's expression. The reality has not matched the promise of constant engagement. But we should not forget the argument developed in the previous chapter: representation does not have to be understood as the opposite of participation. Whatever else they have accomplished, it is beyond doubt that these platform parties offered new visions of division; in southern Europe, they crafted collective representations for people whom Gerbaudo describes as "young, connected, broke." What Podemos, M5S, and the left-wing Syriza party in Greece achieved is that the main conflict in southern Europe—for shorthand, economic austerity versus anti-austerity—could be plausibly represented inside the political system.

The mere fact of representing a conflict, of having drawn a battle line, is not much, radical critics would insist, pointing to the fact that all these parties had to abandon their promise to end austerity once they entered office. But it is much when compared with the impression that especially young southerners had when they looked at the party systems as they existed before: the pattern consisted of two large political formations alternating in power but almost always ending in corruption and, in practice, not implementing very different policies—a classic cartel. Podemos and M5S managed to get well-educated young people who were either unemployed or stuck in jobs for which they were overqualified back to the voting booths. It is not a given that young people whose opportunities in life have been heavily damaged by the Eurocrisis would first demonstrate on squares and then vote for new parties and then go home and resolve to try again, once those parties had failed to gain majorities (young people in the 1970s, for instance, sometimes had rather different ideas—terrorism in the name of left-wing ideals being one of them).

True, many of these parties failed by their own standards: they did not truly craft a vision beyond left and right. Podemos, the *partido de profesores*, described themselves as "artisans with words." In the end, however, the political language they developed didn't sound all that different from old-style leftism; the same was to some degree true for Grillo and his successor, Luigi Di Maio. What distinguished them was the creation of what one might call, with a paradoxical-sounding term, "techno-populism."[99] Loud proclamations of faith in ordinary people went hand in hand with the empowerment of nonpartisan technocrats, starting with the Italian prime minister, a professor of civil law. Grillo had once referred to M5S deputies in parliament as "technicians," even as he promised that instead of an economics professor he would put a housewife with three kids in charge of the Finance Ministry.

Yet the contradiction is in appearance only. Technocracy

and populism, rather than being extremes entirely opposed to each other, actually resemble each other in one respect: the technocrat holds that there is a single rational solution to any policy problem; the populist claims that there is a unique authentic will of the people and that such a will cannot fail to aim at the common good. Once the two were put together, something like the extremely odd and yet strangely coherent 2018 Italian government resulted. It was led by two university dropouts—Matteo Salvini of the far-right Northern League and Luigi Di Maio—who have lived their entire lives for (and off) politics. In office, they claimed to champion the people and put nominally apolitical, highly educated experts in charge of key ministries. Technocracy and populism are both anti-pluralist or even antipolitical, if one takes politics to mean that the solutions are never just given by either expertise or the fiction of a completely uniform popular will.

TO SUM UP, then: parties and media provide the essential infrastructure of democracy; they help citizens associate with one another. Social media have been helpful for "platform parties" while at the same time posing a mortal threat to at least some forms of professional journalism. Social media are not like a newspaper—there is no content produced by professionals—nor are they comparable to a more or less neutral telephone network; they allow individuals to offer collective representations that are reminiscent of the fusion of party and papers prevalent in nineteenth-century United States; they can also, ideally, facilitate conversation (though one would hesitate to call Twitter an online salon).[100]

Contrary to the devotees of technological determinism, it is not the technology per se that creates dangers for democracy. It is the fact that a technology which allows individuals to reach others is at the same time a component of an ever more fine-tuned surveillance machine aimed at predicting behavior, or even at *making* behavior predictable (or, worse still, reinforcing polarization and resentment, because those, too, can be monetized). That is not a given. It's also not a given that we are faced with so few choices of social media. We can organize our parties and our sources of information and opinion differently from how we do. But to say that does not answer the question of what one should want, ideally.

4. REOPENING

The problem is not how 180 million Aristotles can run a
democracy, but how we can organize a political community
of 180 million people so that it remains sensitive to
their needs. This is a problem of leadership, organization,
alternatives, and systems of responsibility and confidence.
— E. E. SCHATTSCHNEIDER

Political parties may rule, but they do not govern. The
public is so confused and eclipsed that it cannot even
use the organs through which it is supposed to mediate
political action and polity.
— JOHN DEWEY

We need, in every community, a group of
angelic troublemakers.
— BAYARD RUSTIN

What do we need from intermediary institutions in a democracy, parties and the media in particular? They should be
widely accessible; access should not turn into a privilege for
those already advantaged. They should be accurate; that is to
say, political judgments and opinions, as Hannah Arendt held,
must be constrained by facts, even if, as Arendt also observed,
facts are always fragile. They should also be autonomous—
that is to say, not depend on more or less hidden actors in a

corrupt way. They must be assessable by citizens. And, as a result of all of the above, they can be accountable. What do these abstractions mean concretely?

TO START WITH access, which has an institutional and an individual dimension: How easy should it be for a party to establish itself in a party system, and how easy should it be for individuals to enter or, for that matter, start a party? Many countries require a minimum number of members to demonstrate serious intent to engage in elections, but the figures differ dramatically: in Australia it's five hundred, whereas in the U.K. one can register a party with two (!) officers and a 150-pound nonrefundable application fee. How one creates a party legally isn't the only question, because parties and electoral systems interact. Even if it's easy to form a party, it might be impossible to get on the ballot, as access requires fielding candidates everywhere or requires costly litigation (on which independents in the United States sometimes spend most of their campaign funds), and even if one gets on the ballot, the rules of representation might leave smaller contenders in the wilderness: think how, again in the United States, voters are often allowed to participate in only one primary, which makes them more likely to stick with the large parties, lest they lose their influence on the overall outcome.[1]

If one takes seriously the idea that democracy must be open to new claims of representation, then one would want the political process to be as accessible as possible. That idea is not uncontroversial, though, for access for everyone might mean structure for no one: too many actors, too much noise, and, potentially, the powerful finding ways of—in Stephen Bannon's words—"flood[ing] the zone with shit" to maximize confusion. For confusion would always seem to work in favor of the most powerful.

The most harmless version of this worry is that easy access will result in a proliferation of frivolous parties tricking citizens into wasting their votes: clown candidates tend to degrade a political process as a whole. Except that, if one looks at actually successful clown candidates, they usually have a dead serious point. Tiririca, a Brazilian comedian, ran for Congress in 2010; his disarming slogan was "It can't get any worse" (little did he know about Bolsonaro). Tiririca also courted voters with the message "What does a federal deputy do? Truly, I don't know. But vote for me and I will find out for you."[2] It seems people did want to know: he ended up receiving more support than any other candidate in the election.

Rather than condemning him as a precursor of what critics see as a far-right horror clown—that is to say, Bolsonaro—one should see satire as legitimate representation for despairing citizens (one of Tiririca's other election promises was that he would support all Brazilian families, especially his own). Iceland's Best Party, which won the municipal election in Reykjavík in 2010, campaigned with the slogan that whereas all other parties were secretly corrupt, they would be openly corrupt (a comedian actually became mayor and, by most accounts, did a more than decent job). One of the longest-standing and probably best-known joke parties—the U.K.'s Monster Raving Loony Party—was founded by the musician David Sutch (a.k.a. Screaming Lord Sutch), who had started to develop provocative campaign antics when he stood for his National Teenage Party in the 1960s; the party advocated for the lowering of the voting age to eighteen, the argument being that if teenagers were old enough to be drafted and die in war, they should also be able to vote. Like all good satire, satirical parties' platforms point to a truth, or at the very least make people think; or, as one lower U.S. court once put it, the right to vote for Donald Duck must be constitutionally protected, for it could be intended as a "serious satirical criticism of the powers that be." Joke parties need not be a joke; the worry that people could completely misunderstand their nature grossly underestimates citizens' judgment.

Even more patronizing is the view that people could become all confused if there are too many parties.[3] This notion has served as a reason for U.S. courts to allow the two main parties to make the registering of new parties exceedingly onerous. It's simply assumed that there is no other way than the alternation of two moderate parties with established and easy-to-understand "brands"; everything else could result in "irresponsible government" or factionalism. In theory, such an approach is premised on the Martin Van Buren ideal of two stable, centrist parties absorbing all political demands from society; in practice, it has allowed the beneficiaries of the "two parties as responsible government" view effectively to "lock down political markets."[4]

To be sure, the manufacture of confusion is a tried-and-tested tactic of authoritarians: in 1998, the ruling party in St. Petersburg managed to find a pensioner and a plumber with exactly the same name as the main opposition candidate; placing them on the ballot split the vote sufficiently for the incumbents to succeed (this is not a Russian innovation: a janitor named Joseph Russo was once placed on the ballot in a House primary, as one of the contenders had the same name, while another one was called John F. Kennedy, and it was the father of the latter who had paid the janitor to come forward as a candidate).[5] In rural Hungary, three parties appeared out of nowhere; they happened to be registered to the mother, father, and son of the same family. Such phony parties are the real joke parties, and the joke is obviously on the electorate.

Arguments against wider access ride on the notion that citizens need to be able to properly assess the options in front of them. That intuition also applies to the media: the problem is not that particular views are spread by Russian bots or sock puppets; the problem is that people don't understand that they're looking at bots and sock puppets (or, as Trump once put it, "the whole age of computer has made it where nobody knows what's going on"). According to one study, half of Twitter accounts discussing "reopening America" in the spring of 2020 might have been bots—a potentially massive influence operation of which very few citizens will be aware.[6] And having fake followers—and pointing to them as evidence of popular support—is akin to publishing opinion polls falsified in your own favor.[7]

True, transparency is a bit like education: everyone's in favor of it, and it always happens to be the solution to everything. But with parties and media, the concern is justified. What we see is not always what we get in politics, and what we see really should be what we see. Citizens need some assurance about the autonomy of what they're opting for, be it a political formation or a source of news and opinion. This call for autonomy is not the same as a demand for impartiality: by definition, parties are not impartial, but media can also legitimately place their reporting in a frame of values they pursue—*as long as* that frame is clearly acknowledged and assessable. Timothy Garton Ash has coined the term "transparent partiality." An example would be Orwell, who made it absolutely clear to the readers of *Homage to Catalonia* that his reporting on the Spanish Civil War was presented from a particular point of view, an engaged partisan; there was no pretense of a "view from nowhere."[8] As Garton Ash observes, we believe him precisely because he does not claim to be "fair and balanced."[9]

What does autonomy mean more concretely? Most

intermediary institutions do not pay for themselves: in general, parties cannot survive just on membership fees; all large-scale newspapers and TV channels need more than individual subscriptions to be financially viable (not to speak of being profitable). It would seem therefore that autonomy necessarily has to be compromised: there will be financial dependence on something or someone; the only question is whether it'll be the market or the state (or oligarchs, for that matter). Obviously, these options are not all equally bad; as we saw in the first chapter, the particular problem with oligarchy is that wealthy individuals use parties and partisan media to reshape regulation, in an opaque manner, so as to advance their business interests. The dependence of British and Australian politicians (including nominally left-wing ones such as Tony Blair) on Rupert Murdoch, who has systematically used political influence for financial gain, trading publicity for policy, is only the most obvious example in the West.[10]

If powerful private actors can use intermediaries to increase their power further, a distinctly public approach promoting equality of opportunity would seem the obvious solution: some democracies understand parties and broadcasters as something like "public utilities," and they finance and regulate them accordingly.[11] Parties and reliable news sources are clearly acknowledged as part of the necessary infrastructure of democracy: after all, they're producing "public goods," and the nature of public goods is that nobody can be excluded from them (think of national defense or roads in most countries). That also means, though, that such goods will never be provided sufficiently by anyone observing solely the imperative to make a profit.[12]

The obvious drawback of public provision is that "public" here means the state and the state effectively means the government and that ultimately means the parties themselves. The object of regulation happens to be the subject of regulation, and the danger is precisely the formation of party cartels, for which keeping newcomers out completely is more important than getting into office oneself in a given contest.

But what if the public actually meant the people? What if the care for democracy's infrastructure did not rest exclusively with its constitutive parts, such as parties, and instead we asked citizens themselves to maintain it?

Democracy is not free. It was never free: the Athenians had to construct the complicated sortition machines and build an amphitheater for the assembly; moreover, they held that it was okay to pay people for participating (much to the outrage of antidemocratic philosophers, who deemed democracy the most expensive constitution, even if the annual expenditure for the assembly was roughly the same as that required to feed the horses of the thousand-strong cavalry).[13] Democracy today also costs substantial amounts of money, from the actual machinery of voting (shockingly outdated in parts of the United States) to the transportation of mail-in ballots (shockingly underfunded in parts of the United States) to parties and actual campaigns (shockingly overfunded in the United States).[14] The question is, who pays? In the United States, public funding has effectively stopped at the federal level (even a self-declared socialist like Bernie Sanders rejected it); it is owners of concentrated wealth—as well as some citizens making small contributions—who today bankroll campaigns.

While everyone knows that the costs of such campaigns are mind-boggling, citizens of other democracies are not necessarily entitled to turn up their noses at the crazy Americans. In western Europe, donations are also highly concentrated among the wealthiest (as well as large companies, in countries where corporate donations are permissible: for instance, the German car industry and Philip Morris, the cigarette maker, spend lavishly on the two largest left-wing and right-wing parties, with the tobacco giant also sponsoring party conventions and "summer parties" in Berlin—expenditures that, needless to say, are easy to hide).[15] For the British Labour Party, large private donations eventually became more important than membership fees (but dried up under the leadership of Jeremy Corbyn).

True, many countries offer public funding of parties, but those same countries often set very weak limits on private contributions.[16] Less obviously, where states seemingly put funding directly into the hands of the people in a more democratic manner—offering tax deductions for spending on our system of self-rule, so to speak—the effect is highly skewed: as the wealthier pay much higher taxes, they also disproportionately benefit from such schemes. As the French economist Julia Cagé points out in her important study *The Price of Democracy*, the poor end up subsidizing the political preferences of the rich (who tend to be much more conservative in economic matters, of course). In France, according to Cagé, the average donation of the bottom 10 percent of French citizens was twenty-three euros; meanwhile, the wealthiest 10 percent received twenty-nine million euros in tax relief.[17] It's as if democracies had returned to a version of property qualifications for political participation: you get one vote at the ballot box, but some get to vote again (and again) with their wallets (which is reminiscent of the 1820 French election law, whereby the richest literally could vote twice).[18]

Cagé, as well as a number of U.S. constitutional lawyers (and even a few congressmen on the Democratic side), has proposed an alternative for funding democracy's infrastructure:[19] individual vouchers that citizens can distribute incrementally (or all at once) to parties and candidates of their choice, with the possibility of contributing cash up to a strict limit in addition (a commonly cited figure is 250 dollars);[20] all larger donations—and corporations buying themselves a political voice—are to be outlawed. There would be an initial hurdle to qualify for receiving such vouchers: new parties should be able to raise funds from a sufficient number of citizens or demonstrate nontrivial support in polls. Unused vouchers could be distributed according to the last election outcome (in the same way that funding in many countries is already decided at the moment).

There are several advantages to such a scheme. It would be a significant, if hardly perfect, check on the political uses of concentrated wealth—in short, what I have been describing as the oligarchic tendencies in today's democracies. Less obviously, it would strengthen the open and dynamic character of at least some existing democracies, in which, currently, the funding of political parties is determined on the basis of previous election results. Newcomers could get real support even in the middle of an election cycle. Losers—let's say, traditional parties—would lose less if their supporters wanted to punish them at an election but not see them wiped from the political map (think of left-leaning French citizens who wanted to sanction the Socialist Party for Hollande's less-than-glorious presidency, but still maintain an effective alternative to Emmanuel Macron). Last, while the numbers might seem tiny, being able to contribute something might give individuals a sense of efficacy in a democracy ("I can give and shape something, just like Gates and Soros!").[21] This would be even more the case, of course, if this scheme forced politicians to engage with a wider range of voters than is the case in a country such as the United States, where currently congresspeople are said to spend four or more hours every day on soliciting donations from the affluent, making them into telemarketers for a particular segment of the population more than representatives of all their constituents.[22]

Let's talk numbers. Cagé's suggestion is a seven-euro voucher for every voter; this doesn't add up to an outrageous total number; it's roughly what the German state spends annually just on the foundations close to political parties that, among other things, develop policy and engage in "political education." In the United States, there has been the suggestion of "democracy coupons" worth a hundred dollars, in twenty-dollar increments, or "democracy dollars" of fifty dollars, stored on a special credit card account, according to the scheme developed by the Yale Law School professor Bruce Ackerman and Congressman Ro Khanna.

There is a serious question of whether individuals' spending decisions should be made public; corporations might not respond well when their workers are on record giving funds to an anticapitalist party (or company leaders might just pressure their employees to donate to a particular candidate). Cagé would stick with the idea of funding candidates or parties by using tax returns to deploy one's democracy vouchers, possibly giving special credits to the millions who earn so little that they don't pay income tax (which means concretely at least half of eligible voters in many countries). This would prevent anyone from buying up vouchers at a premium or even just at face value—in the way that privatization vouchers were amassed by savvy investors in central Europe in the 1990s. Also, there'd be ways to erase the information after a short period, thereby providing a kind of de facto online *isoloir*.

These aren't just fantasies. One such scheme was actually implemented in Seattle for local elections. Citizens received vouchers in the mail; alas, plenty thought the envelopes contained junk; others left them lying around but forgot actually to contribute their "democracy dollars."[23] Pessimists about the capacities of ordinary people will feel good about the fact that in the end only 3.3 percent of Seattle residents who had received vouchers ended up using them. On the positive side, the overall number of small contributions increased, and there is some evidence that candidates without access to wealthy donors benefited from the system.

Schemes to give citizens direct financial control of democracy's infrastructure might increase their sense that elections have integrity.[24] It could counter the widespread (and often correct) impression that votes count but hidden resources decide (in the formulation of the Norwegian political scientist Stein Rokkan). The conclusion for many citizens today is not only that dependence of this kind corrupts the process but also that there's no point in getting engaged in politics, and this passivity in turn gives the resource-rich yet more leverage.

Of course, some vouchers might go to waste, as citizens can't devote attention to politics or somehow find it too burdensome to actually distribute their vouchers: just as people fail to exercise their vote, they might fail to use what in effect is "free money." A less demanding alternative would be simply to base funding on something like an annual poll.[25] Such a poll might lend a new rhythm to democracy beyond elections. But it could also turn into the functional equivalent of an election, with an added side effect of making parties campaign annually (instead of focusing on policy), which in turn would require more resources . . .

Such schemes can look as if they get us close to an ideal of equal influence; after all, we have only seven euros each. But those with more time to devote to politics, those in elite functions as heads of companies or trade unions, will still have better access to the political arena and hence more influence. What George W. Bush, with his charming offensiveness (almost innocence), called "the have-mores" will still be in a different position from what Bush termed the simple "haves."[26] But they won't be in a different world or able to secede and live according to different rules entirely, and the have-nots will have something in addition to their vote (whereas now they really have no resources at all to, for instance, make small donations to political campaigns). None of this promises better political outcomes as such, but it holds the possibility of opening up democracy to new representatives, and more particularly such new claim-makers can be given a boost even before ever doing well in an actual election. Less obviously, this scheme also sends a signal that the responsibility for maintaining democracy's critical infrastructure rests not with what in the United States is nowadays often called "the donor class" (in effect, critics would say, the *taker* class—see the 2017 tax cut). Rather, it is firmly placed in the hands of all citizens.

In principle, there is nothing wrong with having a parallel voucher scheme for the media—except for the worry that venerable public service institutions such as the BBC might all of a sudden be starved of funds, if citizens could somehow be manipulated to distribute all resources to private competitors (who would have every reason to turn people against public broadcasters as "liberal elitists," and so on). For what it's worth, as evidence, a Swiss initiative aimed at radically reducing the financing of public service broadcasters—derided as supposedly left-leaning "state TV"—failed decisively in 2018: 71.6 percent voted against abolishing the yearly fee of 450 Swiss francs (a not-so-trivial indirect tax for many citizens).[27] And, as we saw in the first chapter, radical right populists in power have generally preferred capturing, rather than abolishing, public media.

As with parties, a voucher scheme might give a much-needed boost to journalistic upstarts; and a large percentage of such vouchers could also be set aside specifically for local journalism. It is the same Julia Cagé who has suggested the creation of "nonprofit media organizations" that would combine the advantages of joint-stock companies and private foundations.[28] Both large and small donors could "buy into" such a nonprofit and receive tax deductions; they could also distribute their "media vouchers" as they see fit. The obvious danger is the capture of such media by wealthy individuals who donate to dominate (and again, the poor would end up subsidizing the political preferences of the rich through tax deductions). After all, the problem with private foundations in general is that they exert largely unaccountable political influence and receive tax breaks for doing so (quite apart from employing the ne'er-do-well relatives of the founder, and the children of the friends of the founder, and so on).

Cagé's ingenuous suggestion is to *decrease* voting power in line with tax-deductible contributions, so large donors would receive significant tax benefits (and the sense of satisfaction that might be associated with helping a cause), but they would not automatically dominate. In other words, unlike with regular joint-stock companies, minorities—in particular small donors who might join forces in what Cagé calls "readers' societies"—could exert significant control. This would make media accessible: anyone could become a member of a nonprofit media organization. And it would be perfectly fine to have such organizations operate according to the principle of "transparent partiality": in fact, that partiality might be the very reason why someone passionate about social justice (or the latest news about Catholic natural law, for that matter) might want to become a member in the first place.

Such a convergence of transparently partisan media and political parties will ring alarm bells: Aren't the media supposed to hold politicians accountable? Do we want to politicize yet another institution from which one would expect an impartial framing of democratic politics? That's a real worry, but it overlooks that parties and press were often mixed in the past, and not always in a nefarious manner. Many leaders of socialist parties started out as journalists, or even actively combined the roles of parliamentarian, agitator, theorist, and journalist. In fact, some historians have argued that the very idea of revolutionary socialist parties emerged from radical journalism (rather than trade unions and the labor movement): Karl Marx was a journalist before he ever led a party (and the *Communist Manifesto* was written at a time when there was no Communist Party whatsoever; Marx and Engels wrote, and reported, it into existence).[29] In 1920, a U.S. presidential election pitted two newspaper editors (who both happened to be from Ohio) against each other. There is nothing inherently wrong with a party emerging from a talk show (Podemos) or a blog (Five Star) as long as what it says is accurate and what it does is autonomous. That logic also goes the other way: there is nothing wrong with a paper being produced by a party; the problem with a number of small-town publications in rural America, for instance, was not the partisanship but the fact that financing and partisan orientation were hidden on purpose.[30]

To be sure, the setup of nonprofit media, with its structural empowerment of individual members, is no panacea. Under Cagé's scheme, a well-organized minority with a peculiar agenda could change the orientation of a particular media organization, and more moderate large donors—who have their tax-deductible contributions locked in—couldn't do anything about it. Except that such a captured nonprofit medium might turn off citizens, once that capture has become clearly visible.

Citizens might not necessarily find partisanship the most attractive selling point for their investment or distribution of media vouchers, if there were such a thing. Some of the hopes placed in "citizen journalism" have been disappointed, but in principle those dissatisfied with the existing state of local news could finance outlets that give room for nonprofessionals in a not-too-amateurish way. The same is true of "public journalism," which orients itself toward—as the name suggests—the public.[31] For instance, instead of the typical horse-race coverage of elections—in which there's always a suspenseful story and journalists can maintain neutrality (after all, it's all about objective poll numbers)—practitioners of public journalism would proceed differently: they would engage with citizens first, find out more about the issues that concern them, and then press politicians to engage with precisely these issues (this is what the media critic Jay Rosen has called a "citizens' agenda approach"). And when democracy itself is at stake—as politicians make it a habit to cross the hard borders suggested in this book—there is also nothing wrong with journalists presenting themselves as partisans of democracy. Obviously, there are risks here: the reporter as romantic resistance fighter who forgets that not all their pet policy preferences are democracy as such, or the clever maneuvering, Bannon-style, of the media into the role of the opposition, such that anything journalists claim can immediately be discredited as purely political. But if journalists can explain their case—that they are not living recording devices, but that their work depends crucially on basic democratic freedoms which they ought to protect—citizens might just about see the crucial difference. They might also recognize that seemingly asymmetrical judgments are not evidence of bias but reflect political realities when authoritarian populist parties—but not their competitors—have crossed the border into political fiction or hate-mongering (as an American observer put it, "a balanced treatment of an unbalanced phenomenon distorts reality").[32]

This last point shows yet again that in the end all possible improvements of the infrastructure of democracy depend on

one thing: that intermediary institutions be not only accessible and autonomous but also *assessable*, as the British philosopher Onora O'Neill has put it.[33] If they are to contribute
to citizens' judgments, it matters that citizens can also judge
them: How are they financed (who owns them, in the case of
media)? What agendas do they have? Might it be the case that
a party is just the instrument of an individual with nefarious
interests (think back to Berlusconi's TV party)? Might the
real power behind a party's candidate be what in the United
States has been called "shadow parties" or "para-parties"—for
instance, campaign committees pushing a candidate without
limits on spending, injecting unaccountable "dark money"
into the political process?[34] Or maybe even foreign parties,
as in the case of the Five Star Movement, whose Rousseau
platform acknowledges openly that it is financed by "foreign parties"—which remain unnamed—alongside plenty of
anonymous donors?

In turn, a "para-media" organization might appear impartial but not truly independent (it's at the whim of an oligarch); conversely, it might be independent without being
impartial, a state of affairs that could be perfectly acceptable
as long as there is no pretense otherwise. The problem with a
station like Fox is not that it tries to speak from a "conservative
working-class perspective" (according to the former presenter
Bill O'Reilly)—whether or not that's the case, the working
class can very well decide on its own—but that it presents
matters in a way that, charitably put, is inaccurate (claiming,
for instance, that an unspecified "they" had dead people vote
in U.S. elections, thus backing up Trump's long-debunked as-
sertions about widespread voter fraud).

A media company might also say one thing while doing another, and, alas, it's again one particular TV station that comes

to mind: in the spring of 2020, Fox anchormen clamored for "opening the economy" and for people to mingle in the middle of a pandemic; meanwhile, Fox's own offices were closed, and employees were instructed to stay at home. To judge the former public claim, it helps to know about the latter, private one.

The internal workings of both media organizations and parties have to be assessable: there has to be a clear enough sense of who ultimately makes decisions about the direction of an institution as a whole.[35] Ostensible democratization—"let the members decide!"—can be meaningless if party elites tightly control short lists, in line with the famous observation of Boss Tweed, the nineteenth-century U.S. machine politician: "I don't care who does the electing, as long as I get to do the nominating."[36]

So far, I have stressed the importance of access and autonomy as political standards, standards that in turn are rooted in democracy's basic principles. Such standards should help us decide what we want from particular institutions and how well those institutions conform to a particular standard. But standards should also inform actual legal regulation. Just as with voucher schemes, it would be technocratic solutionism to pretend that there is a uniquely correct way of doing things here; citizens themselves should debate what precise regulations they wish to see. Lest that be thought of as avoiding the difficult part: such a debate is more likely to succeed if one comes to it with an understanding of why those who benefit from existing systems would ever allow change; for instance, parties benefiting from financing systems as they are will not clamor to open up democracy to "the little man, walking to the candidate with his little voucher" (to paraphrase Churchill). So we need to consider how structural change might become a reality.

As to the first question, think back to an institution we already encountered in chapter 2, lottocracy. Back then, placing decision-making power in the hands of randomly selected individuals was dismissed as a plausible replacement for representative democracy as we know it, at least when it comes to continuous policy making. But there is an important qualification to this judgment: sortition can have a limited role in breaking deadlocks over reforming the democratic process itself (its advocates are also right in suggesting that it can occasionally help decide fundamental moral questions, such as abortion). In both cases, however, whatever randomly chosen citizens decide should be submitted to the electorate as a whole in a referendum.

Campaign finance, the size of legislatures, term limits—these are questions that might require representatives to deprive themselves of obvious benefits. At the same time, one might say—without falling back into demophobia—that these are not issues easily subject to a one-off yes-no vote: it's easy to see politicians cozy with the donor class campaigning against the public financing of politics with slogans like "Not my money for those wasteful pols!"

That is where the more or less corruption-proof device of sortition can come in: randomly chosen citizens could be presented with various procedural changes and then issue a recommendation to the electorate at large as to which might be best. This isn't a fanciful idea; it's more or less what happened with the constitutional convention in Ireland that ran from 2012 to 2014. And in the United States, this combination of a representative sample's political choice (informed by expertise) with a subsequent referendum has long been known as the Oregon model. Such a scheme does not disempower most citizens in the way that strict lottocracy would (though it does get us the benefit the Athenians already valued: the randomly chosen are much harder to bribe).

The Oregon experiment—officially Citizens' Initiative Review—has been ongoing since 2008: twenty to twenty-five voters are chosen in a process of blind but representative sampling; they listen to advocates for and against a particular ballot measure such as criminal justice or school reforms; they also hear out experts; and then they put down in simple language what they regard as the major arguments for and against the proposal to be decided (they're also paid the average wage during this exercise; again, democracy is not free).[37] What ends up being mailed to all households is a short document with these arguments—information *by* ordinary voters *for* ordinary voters, officially presented as "citizens' statements for" and "citizens' statements against." The people themselves end up making the final decision, but with the help of thoughts put down by people "just like them." They don't always follow what some democratic theorists would regard as representatives of their "better-informed selves," but there is plenty of evidence that the information on which they base their judgments is more accurate than what they'd encounter otherwise.[38] And that—as we saw in the discussion of Mill above—is all we can ask in cases of highly controversial questions on which reasonable citizens will disagree.

Note that *demagogoi*—in the neutral sense—will in all likelihood be fully involved in actual referendum campaigns: parties and media commentators will take and often actively push particular positions. For some in the democracy innovation industry, that's precisely the problem: whatever rational solutions randomly chosen citizens—understood as the representatives of our better, that is, fully informed, selves—have selected will be torpedoed and sunk by professionals with vested interests in a different outcome.[39] To be sure, this can happen, and there is some evidence that parties and also, less obviously, media have on occasion been hostile to Oregon-style experiments, because the latter undermines their traditional power. Moreover, skeptics might say that parties would never allow anything of this sort—sortition, that is—in the first place. The best answer is that social pressure can be sufficient to at least enable the initial institution of randomly chosen assemblies: Ireland and Iceland are examples. Of course, the initial pressure resulted from the financial crisis, when the political class in both countries had thoroughly discredited itself (the creation of Iceland's Best Party was another consequence).

There is another benefit of such schemes, which might be attractive for at least some parties: just as with vouchers, the experience of one's vote possibly making a difference in a referendum starts a virtuous cycle of political engagement.[40] This seems to have happened in Ireland after the abortion and same-sex marriage referenda: especially young people— usually the least likely to vote—appeared at last to take a stronger interest in elections to the Oireachtas Éireann, the regular legislature.[41]

Closing Democracy to Save Democracy?

One might wonder whether the story told about democratic politics so far is not all too Panglossian. Openness and accessibility—who's against them in theory? But who in practice wants to live with increasingly fragmented party systems and the uncertainty, for instance, of not having a proper government for 589 days (as happened in Belgium in 2010–2011)? The fracturing of party systems has been a major development of our era. And it is in and of itself a sign of democracy's crisis for an astute analyst such as Adam Przeworski.[42]

Now, it's true that politics was indeed somewhat more predictable when citizens were basically born into more or less
stable political identities: a worker voted socialist, period.
But that age is gone, and any transition to something more
fluid (and necessarily uncertain) is bound to be confusing.
Schattschneider, in analogy with Clausewitz's famous observation about the "fog of war," wrote of the inevitable fog of
political conflict. As societies change, the fog thickens. That
makes political judgment harder, but it is not necessarily a sign
of crisis or an indication that access and openness are intrin-
sically problematic goals; in fact, the real problem would appear to be "stability" in the form of a complete inability of
party systems to respond to new challenges.

Still, there's a quite different, graver worry one might have
about access and openness. What about—for shorthand—
bad actors bent on undermining democracy, on playing the
democratic game in bad faith? A response might be that even
if such antidemocratic figures come to power, bad laws will
not stand, as long as courts get to check what comes out of
the legislature in a process of judicial review. And if they
aren't in power, such politicians can be subject to the criminal
law; witness the prosecution of the Dutch right-wing populist Geert Wilders for inciting hatred of citizens of Moroccan
descent (Wilders had asked an excited crowd, "Do you want
fewer Moroccans?" and responded to shouts of "Fewer, fewer"
with "We're going to take care of that").[43]

That comforting response is a little too quick. It fails
to see that elections aren't just moments of aggregating the
preferences of citizens and determining who gets to be in
government; they are also extended periods of political mobilization.[44] The argument about representation—that politics
doesn't just reflect but can create people's self-perceptions—is
again crucial. In early 2016, there was no Trumpist movement;

years later, plenty of Americans see themselves as Trumpists in the depths of their souls (and will probably do so long after Trump has departed the national stage for good; for them, the attack on the Capitol will not be evidence that Trump's claim to dominance failed in the end; instead, it will signify martyrdom and be fodder for a myth centered on betrayal by elites, all holding together a community based on shared victimhood and outrage).

That is the reason why some states have established what is often referred to as "militant democracy"—the idea being that a democracy should restrict rights for the sake of defending its existence against parties (and particular individuals) bent on undermining the political system.[45] This is not just a matter of clamping down on actors who turn to violence or other forms of conduct already covered by criminal law; rather, militant democracies erect a set of special, *political* prohibitions. Alternative terms—which help to clarify the underlying aspiration—are "a democracy willing to fight," as it is called in Germany, or what in Israel is known as the "defending-democracy paradigm." The idea as such is hardly new: the Athenians had ostracism, the banning of powerful individuals who threatened the democracy. Contrary to the cliché of mobs ganging up on innocent people, the evidence suggests that it was figures well-endowed with both financial resources and rhetorical abilities who were seen to pose a peril. Oligarchs sometimes had to leave for a decade or so. Perhaps surprising from our vantage point: no stigma was attached to them (and they could eventually return). By contrast, *atimia*—a punishment for crimes against the polity—spelled the permanent loss of political rights.

Closer to our age, the case of Weimar Germany dramatizes the issue, which is in many ways reducible to the conundrum of whether to tolerate the intolerant. The NSDAP stood for elections. Once in power, it proceeded to abolish democracy—an abolition that had been foretold in no uncertain terms by Joseph Goebbels and other Nazis: Goebbels had announced in 1928 that the Nazis sought to arm themselves "with weapons from the arsenal of democracy"; he later gloated, "It will always remain one of the best jokes of democracy that it provided its mortal enemies itself with the means through which it was annihilated."[46] He also freely admitted in 1940, "One could have arrested a few of us in 1925, and everything would have been finished and over."

After World War II, the lesson seemed clear enough: democracies should have legal instruments to deal with existential threats by antidemocratic actors abusing the "arsenal of democracy." More particularly, they should be able to restrict rights. In practice, this has primarily meant the banning of parties—limiting rights to association—even if there is also the possibility of prohibitions applying directly to particular individuals: for instance, Article 18 of the German Basic Law specifies that citizens can lose their basic political rights. Four attempts have been made to use that article; all have been unsuccessful, either because courts decided that the individuals in question didn't pose a grave enough threat or because they'd already been taken out of political circulation, so to speak, due to conduct covered by criminal law.

Militant democracy has been developed most prominently in postwar Germany (the idea of including it in the constitution was probably suggested by a civil servant in the French occupation force in Baden).[47] It was seen as part and parcel of an antitotalitarian stance that explicitly refused Kelsen's association of democracy with relativism; instead, it sought to identify democracy with objective and substantial values, human dignity above all, and then defend those values firmly. One of the convenient side effects of developing the doctrine during the Cold War was that the spotlight was on the horrors of Communism, effectively sidelining the Nazi past. The de facto successor to the NSDAP was prohibited in 1953, but much more attention was focused on the Communist Party, which suffered the same fate three years later.

It would be wrong to view such militancy as a uniquely postwar European phenomenon (in the way American constitutional lawyers typically do). After all, in the aftermath of the Civil War, the North refused to seat southern Democrats in Congress unless they accepted Reconstruction; in effect, they restricted rights in the name of democracy.[48] When Franklin Delano Roosevelt asked Congress to investigate whether the Louisiana controlled by the demagogue Huey Long still adhered to basic democratic principles, he was contemplating a militant intervention (Long was assassinated before the inquiry could get anywhere; FDR had probably been concerned not just about democratic principles: the then senator Long was contemplating a presidential run that might have imperiled FDR's chances for reelection).[49] And when, from the mid-1960s onward, states in the Deep South were required to submit any changes in voting arrangements to the federal government for approval, the logic of the Voting Rights Act was a form of militant democracy: states' rights had to be restricted in order to protect the fundamental political liberties of African Americans. True, the much more common approach has been the outlawing of parties, and that has essentially never happened in the United States (even at the height of McCarthyism, the CPUSA was not effectively prohibited and, incidentally, still exists today).[50] The same is true of Britain, where in the 1930s fascists were beaten back politically, not taken out of the democratic game by the state itself.

Sometimes it's not just a party but the entire political game that gets shut down. This was infamously the case in Algeria, where an Islamic party was poised to win office after the second round of national elections. The party held that "Islam is light . . . darkness is in democracy." The military promptly proceeded to cancel the vote. The United States condoned the move, with the ambassador announcing that his country supported "one person, one vote," but not "one person, one vote, one time."[51] Could he have foreseen that this cancellation of democracy would be followed by a decade-long civil war?

Militancy is motivated by the thought that democracy is a form of politics uniquely at risk of self-abolition. It is, this line of reasoning suggests, the only political system that can decide to do away with itself in a way that's perfectly legal and legitimate. Except that's not really true. In theory, a monarch or a dictator could single-handedly determine that his domination must give way to a form of democracy. The ruled may or may not obey his wish, but that uncertainty also exists in a self-abolishing democracy. Less pedantic is the point—discussed at length in the second chapter of this book—that majorities must allow minorities to become majorities one day; a decision by 51 percent of the electorate to abolish the basic political rights that all had enjoyed hitherto isn't democratic in the first place. In fact, only a 100 percent endorsement of a transition to authoritarianism would vindicate the idea that there is something inherently paradoxical about democracy (whereas the abdicating monarch or dictator is not doing anything contradictory). And, strangely, we have not seen such legitimate transitions to authoritarianism.

Critics of militant democracy reject the idea that democracy requires special protections. A democracy that restricts fundamental political rights to defend itself might already cease to be a democracy; the very effort to save democracy will harm it; diminishing political pluralism for the sake of political pluralism makes no sense. It's an illusion that fire can be fought with fire; the result will be the whole house of democracy burning to the ground.

Hans Kelsen, employing a different metaphor, insisted that as a consistent democrat one had to accept a majority's wish to be done with democracy: in 1932, he stated that "one has to remain faithful to one's flag, even when the ship is sinking"; the jurist held that "popular rule cannot maintain itself against its own people . . . whoever is for democracy, cannot let himself be caught in the fateful contradiction of reaching for dictatorship to save democracy."

But perhaps dictatorship isn't the only option. It's generally courts that have decided on rights restrictions, and often with great caution because interfering in the political process is bound to endanger their own legitimacy. The reason is straightforward: courts are assumed to be impartial guardians of the rules of the democratic game as such.[52] That the reality is often different—courts are hardly entirely above politics; they tend broadly to follow long-term shifts in public opinion—is a point many defenders of courts as central actors in militant democracies would concede. But they would also remind us that the judiciary, for all its shortcomings, does not have the perverse incentives political parties would appear to have, namely to use militant measures to get rid of other players in the democratic game. They also would seem to have no reasons to score points with electorates by attacking vulnerable minorities or generally unpopular political views.

Consider Australia's 1950 Communist Party Dissolution Act, which was justified as being "necessary for the security and defence of Australia and for the execution and maintenance of the Constitution and of the laws of the Commonwealth."[53] The act received overwhelming support in opinion polls—some 80 percent—but was eventually invalidated by the High Court. The main reason was that the Parliament had exceeded its powers, yet the judgment also contained a general warning about the central paradox of militant democracy: "History, and not only ancient history, shows that in countries where democratic institutions have been unconstitutionally suppressed, it has been done not seldom by those holding the executive power. Forms of government may need protection from dangers likely to arise from within the institutions to be protected."[54]

And yet, in a number of militant democracies, political parties actually play a significant role, in what might be described as a process akin to peer review. Germany is the paradigmatic case. Only the government, the parliament, or the executives of federal states—all of which are occupied by *parties*—may initiate a process of banning a party in the name of defending democracy; the constitutional court cannot decide all by itself that it ought to investigate and possibly outlaw a party. This fact has something to do with the basic setup of militant democracy: the relevant article in the Basic Law holds that parties hostile to the constitution can be banned; it does not say that they *must* be banned. There is no agent, then, entirely disconnected from party politics—an independent commission of experts, for instance, or a figure like an autonomous political prosecutor—who could simply go after a political association. Parties in effect are asked to judge whether a peer suspected of undermining democracy is or is not sufficiently *like them*. Concretely, does a party subscribe to a consensus on basic democratic principles? Obviously, what we described earlier as cartel parties might take advantage of such a system and harass troublesome newcomers in party politics.

One obvious reason parties don't abuse militant democracy is that they have to worry about their own standing in the eyes of the public. This is not just a matter of being unable to outlaw parties that have already grown too large (a ban might spell the beginning of civil war). Even the frequent banning of smaller parties could be seen by citizens as a systematic attempt to close the political system to competition and to disingenuously defend pluralism by reducing pluralism.

Even if established parties don't act in bad faith, citizens might get the sense that they simply no longer have confidence in themselves to defeat what are seen as threatening competitors at the ballot box, with the possible effect that citizens' support for the democratic system as a whole is weakened. Defending democracy through rights restrictions thus comes across as a form of defeatism; the older parties are so convinced that new parties are bound to capture the political system that they can think only of repression as a response. And this defeatist conclusion could prove contagious for citizens. This problem is exacerbated if banned actors prove adept at presenting themselves as political martyrs (a role that Erdoğan played masterfully after the Welfare Party was prohibited in Turkey because of its supposed plan to undermine the rule of law). That's even more the case if they then find ways of returning to the electoral scene under new party names (as Erdoğan did with his Justice and Development Party).

Instead of automatically banning any party that may pose a threat to the system, one might see the value of something like party peer review, of a measure of *discretion*.[55] Rather than going after each possibly problematic association, one can wait and see how a party develops, and also make a call as to how large a threat to a political system as a whole it really poses. Such a level of discretion is actually built into the impeachment procedure in the United States (and other countries): there is no duty to impeach; it's the judgment of other politicians—not judges—whether a president has committed "high crimes and misdemeanors" and, crucially, whether there's a pattern of conduct that gives Congress reason to think that the chief executive (or even a former chief executive) will endanger the Republic in the future.[56]

One may also provide incentives for moderation. A democratic party might spell out its preconditions for a coalition with what is generally considered a left-wing or a right-wing extremist party. An example would be the Austrian Social Democrats, who developed a *Kriterienkatalog* (catalog of criteria); they argued that they would be open to talks with any party that fulfilled the criteria in question. This move was obviously undertaken with a view to nudging the radical-right populist Freedom Party toward the center (eventually, the Freedom Party joined a coalition with the Christian Democrats and, in the process, didn't really have to fulfill any criteria before entering government).

So, is there in the end a proper criterion for prohibitions? The most plausible answer is this: political associations that *systematically*, as a matter of political mobilization, deny the standing of other members of the polity as free and equal *are* candidates for banning.[57] Parties are different from individuals. Whether individuals ought to face penalties beyond social sanctions is something about which reasonable people can disagree.[58] It's one thing for someone on the proverbial soapbox, or Twitter, for that matter, to denigrate others. It's something else to form a party aimed at gaining state power to systematically put such denigration into practice; this is the *hard border* of conflicts about peoplehood proposed in the first two chapters of this book. The dangers of systematic or structured denigration go beyond the founding of parties. Think of the white supremacist who step by step bought up lots in Leith, a small town in North Dakota, aiming to make it a model village of racial purity.[59] The leader of the U.S. National Socialist Movement (*sic*!) paid a visit; citizens from other parts of the country protested; and eventually the planner of this venture in Nazi prefigurative politics was convicted for terrorizing the town. That wasn't the end of the matter, though: in apparent desperation, the mayor sought to dissolve his own government, fearful about future takeover attempts of the depopulating town.

This story points to the difficulties of assessing where a threat to democracy is really located. Neither in Germany, where a ban of a neo-Nazi party (NPD) was attempted in 2013, nor in the United States do *openly* racist parties appear to have realistic chances of occupying the federal government. That's why the German Constitutional Court declared the NPD "actively hostile to the Constitution," but too insignificant a danger to democracy as a whole to merit a ban (while also allowing for the possibility of excluding the party from public funding, which raises an interesting question—whether such a party could receive vouchers under the scheme outlined above).

But what if small parties manage to terrorize citizens locally? If nothing happens in response, because there's no problem at the national level, the message these citizens then actually receive from the democratic state seems to be this: "This, after all, is acceptable." To be sure, states can also talk back at anti-democrats without restricting their rights; there are options other than silence, both-sides-ism ("very fine people" on both sides), or banning: a government can engage in MLK or Juneteenth commemorations, more civic education, official endorsements of tolerance.[60] But, at least in countries where bans are permissible, those officially opposed by the democratic state in this manner can then charge the government with apparent hypocrisy; they might say something like "If we're really so bad, why don't you ban us? And if you're not going to ban us, don't betray your own principle of equal political chances for all contenders by employing public power to denigrate *us* in the eyes of the people."

These challenges are real. But one can be forgiven for thinking that some of them are also yesterday's—that is to say, the twentieth century's—battles. The expectation of the original theorists of militancy was that parties announce in their programs their wish to violate citizens' fundamental rights. Yet few parties do that today. We are not in Weimar anymore. True, right-wing populists insinuate that some citizens do not belong to the "real people," but these figures also carefully hedge their rhetoric (remember Trump's "and some, I assume, are good people"?). The threats democracies face today are not openly announced; rather, they are vulnerable to the stealthy capture of independent guardians of democracy, such as courts, watchdogs inside the bureaucracy, or election commissions, and the systematic reshaping of the political process such that institutionalized uncertainty is radically reduced.[61] Just think of Trump's de facto vendetta vis-à-vis any inspector general who might expose the corruption of his administration, or his break with the tradition of nominating experts to the Federal Election Commission in bipartisan pairs, thereby giving his party a majority on this crucial supervisory body.[62]

The oligarchic influence discussed in the first chapter can be both cause and consequence of such attempts to rig the democratic game. While oligarchy was not the original focus of militant democracy, courts, ombudsmen, and, for that matter, political parties are not powerless in such situations. While it is hardly ever justified to take away the rights of ordinary citizens, powerful actors—such as oligarchs—might plausibly be banned from the democratic game when they violate its rules. Think of how Berlusconi or Trump did not just make one-off mistakes but exhibited a consistent pattern of seeking to undermine the rules of the game as such (which eventually justified Trump's impeachment, a legitimately political approach that did not require proof of actual criminal conduct). By contrast, suspending such figures permanently—assuming they have not engaged in criminal activity—is more of a stretch. After all, as discussed at length earlier in this book, democracy is based on the notion that no one is politically irredeemable and that anyone can change their mind. Silvio Berlusconi, after many years in politics (thus benefiting from immunity) was eventually convicted for tax fraud; after doing community service, he was elected to the European Parliament. Trump, by contrast, showed no remorse after the violent attack on the Capitol, and was a much better candidate for permanent banning from political life.

Constitutional courts are often tasked with protecting the integrity of the political process. When a court strikes down a law on what seems to be substantive grounds, it may actually be trying to correct the failure of lawmakers to deliberate properly, give the opposition a say, and so on. Sometimes, such institutions also directly seek to rectify an imbalance of power. South Africa's Constitutional Court, for instance, systematically strengthened the National Assembly when it held President Jacob Zuma accountable for corruption.

Yet these appear to be exceptions rather than the rule. What really brought down Zuma were defections in the ANC (partly caused by the fact that his corruption was so blatant). Aspiring autocrats have become highly adept at actually following procedures and crafting laws that look formally correct (or are even modeled on those in democracies beyond reproach, such as Scandinavia's).[63] But their compounded—and intended—effect is precisely to take uncertainty out of the political game. Such strategies can work even in the face of popular opposition: when the Law and Justice party tried to take over the Polish Constitutional Tribunal (and then the Supreme Court), citizens came out and projected the words "Our Court" on the judges' building; they not only listened to Chopin piano pieces but sang the constitution (with fifty-five people intoning different articles) in addition to the national anthem.[64] In India, the preamble was read at protests against Modi's new exclusionary citizenship laws, and the recordings were shared on Twitter, YouTube, and TikTok. But neither chanting nor "TikToking the constitution" was of avail (or so it seems at the time of this writing).[65]

If even the people themselves cannot save democracy, who can? But then again, maybe we shouldn't give up on "ordinary citizens" quite so quickly.

If All Else Fails? Democratic Disobedience

Citizens (and, for that matter, private companies such as Twitter) can always try some of the things full-time politicians should do: push authoritarian populists to stay within the hard border of debates on peoplehood, or at least signal to audiences what is so dangerous about anti-pluralism in a democracy. So-called ordinary people might find ways to circumvent the barriers that have made the right-wing media sphere so isolated and engage other citizens directly: on streets, in squares, even in their homes. Obviously, one should not be starry-eyed about such encounters; social scientists have long been skeptical about the contact hypothesis (according to which actually meeting people about whom one has prejudices is likely to change one's mind).

What about something more drastic? In the face of rising authoritarianism around the world, there has been much talk of "resistance" (as well as a fair bit of what can only be called resistance kitsch), especially in the United States. "Resistance" is a broad term: it might encompass the regular work of mobilizing for opposition candidates, but it can also allude to the existential risks shouldered by those who went underground to sabotage Nazi occupations (and, needless to say, resistance is not the exclusive property of the left).[66]

Vagueness is helpful if one wants to appeal to as many citizens as possible, but it can cloud one's thinking about what one is actually doing or about what one is ultimately trying to achieve. A more precise alternative to "resistance" is civil disobedience. In theory, civil disobedience should be an effective weapon against authoritarian populists.[67] But there are two formidable problems. One has to do with a widespread misunderstanding of what civil disobedience entails; the other, much more serious one concerns structural changes we touched on already and that yet again haunt our discussion: distorted public spheres also affect the possibilities of political protest.

The classic definition of civil disobedience was formulated by the American philosopher John Rawls in the early 1970s: civil disobedience meant overt lawbreaking. But not just any, of course; it was supposed to be conscientious, nonviolent, and, above all, aimed at persuading fellow citizens that a law ought to be changed because it amounted to a serious injustice, a violation of fundamental rights in particular. Rawls also held that lawbreakers should be prepared to accept penalties for their acts; they ought actively to demonstrate "fidelity to the law" as a whole (provided a society and its institutions were what Rawls gingerly called "nearly just").

Today, even protest that does not amount to breaking laws is often criticized for being "uncivil" or deepening the fractures of already polarized societies. When citizens confronted politicians during the hearings for the Supreme Court nominee Brett Kavanaugh both inside and outside the Senate in Washington, D.C., in the fall of 2018, they were derided as a "mob." The Black Lives Matter movement has been admonished for being too aggressive and divisive. Noisy demonstrators against the government in Budapest have been labeled "liberal anarchists."

The danger is to confuse civil disobedience with civility in the sense of politeness or respectability. True, Rawls was echoing Martin Luther King Jr., who had insisted that civil disobedience, if done properly, expressed "the very highest respect for the law." In other words, one had to appeal to principles of justice underlying the law and break laws in such a way that future cooperation with one's fellow citizens would not become impossible. King even wrote of disobeying laws "lovingly."

There was absolutely nothing soft about such invocations of love, and no suggestion that disobedients could not be confrontational, or that lawbreaking was never allowed to upset anyone. In fact, not being angry under glaring circumstances of injustice can give an audience a false sense that there's nothing to be angry about. Anger is not a vehement passion beyond reasons but always based on a reason such as the impression that one is being treated unfairly in a democracy, that one is systematically denied one's say.[68]

A sanitized, sentimental version of the history of the U.S. civil rights movement suggests that in the 1950s and '60s, appeals to arch-American political principles of freedom and equality were sufficient to make whites come around to the idea of ending segregation once and for all. In fact, the movement acted in highly strategic ways and aimed at confrontations with police and defenders of white supremacy, which were bound to become violent. These clashes generated images of white brutality that made at least some citizens reconsider their unconditional defense of what they took to be legitimate Jim Crow rules and "law and order" in general.

As the social scientists Erica Chenoweth and Maria Stephan have shown, such nonviolent but still tough and confrontational strategies have been remarkably successful. In a study spanning more than a century, they show that what they call civil resistance has been twice as likely as violent alternatives to bring about its stated goals. According to their data, sustained participation by a mere 3.5 percent of a population can be enough to bring about fundamental political change.[69]

Yet the actual history of the civil rights movement in the United States also points to a novel problem in our age. Rawls, King, and other defenders of civil disobedience took it for granted that the appeal to principles of justice would reach a majority of citizens in a more or less undistorted way. But in some of the countries discussed at length in this book, publics have become so fragmented that one can hardly, like King, speak of one "national opinion." An appeal to what Rawls called a "public sense of justice" is not straightforward under such conditions. Where the populist-authoritarian art of governance is already practiced, such appeals are either silenced or, more likely, severely distorted, sidelined, or, to put it bluntly, drowned in info-feces—in line with Bannon's strategic advice to "flood the zone with shit."[70]

What are the lessons for potential practitioners of civil disobedience? They should not get caught in the trap of respectability. Controlled lawbreaking or even just ignoring regular rules is not the same as anarchy. When opposition politicians disrupted the proceedings of the Hungarian parliament through whistle blowing and blocking access to the speaker's podium (and trolling Orbán to his face), they were accused of attempting a putsch.[71] All they actually tried to do was make the point that their national assembly—characterized by many procedural irregularities and rule twisting in favor of the government—was no longer a regular representative body passing legitimate laws. They were pointing less at a specific injustice than a fundamental problem with the democratic process.[72] In fact, they could be understood as practitioners of militant democracy, stepping in as individuals after institutions charged with protecting uncertainty had been captured and disabled, or, in the words of Thoreau, providing "counter friction to stop the machine." That kind of resistance is obviously risky; it can always be portrayed as just being a bad loser. But it is explicitly encouraged in constitutions—such as the German one—that include a right to resistance in the name of defending democracy, a kind of last-ditch effort when all else has failed.[73]

Disobedients will have to find ways of dealing with the structural challenge of fragmented or—putting it less politely—highly polluted public spheres. Sometimes they might be able to work around the barriers: the revolution might not be televised, but disobedience can be livestreamed and possibly afford audiences an undistorted view (think of the independent media collective Unicorn Riot during the 2020 U.S. protests against police violence, or the Nexta channel on the messenger service Telegram—founded by a self-declared "digital nomad"—used in the 2020 demonstrations against Lukashenko in Belarus). But not always. We thus come full circle to the discussion of intermediary institutions: when they are not accessible, autonomous, and assessable, attempts at disruption are less likely to succeed. A vicious circle, apparently.

These difficulties also pose an answer to the question of why exactly laws might have to be broken. True, if it is to generate publicity, there are surely other ways: think of demonstrations against the far right whose motto was simply "There are more of us."[74] If your wish is to underline the credibility of your engagement and the urgency of rectifying the problems of the democratic process, it is not clear that a majority which might not agree with your substantive arguments would be swayed by the fact that you are prepared to go to jail as a result of your lawbreaking.

There is a particularly difficult challenge for those engaged in specifically *democratic disobedience*, that is to say, those who are not concerned with violations of fundamental rights as such but who want to signal that the political process has become stuck (or been blocked on purpose). Consider, for example, those protesters who did not deny that a democracy can declare war and draft young people, but nonetheless held that the Vietnam War had never been properly authorized (let alone debated). Of course, such blockages are more likely if a democratic infrastructure is in a state of disrepair; think back to cartel parties and the way they shut themselves off from society.

Such defenders of the democratic process need to ask themselves, under which conditions would they concede defeat on substantive policy questions and, for that matter, admit that their criticism of the democratic process fails to resonate with other citizens? The fact that I don't get the legislation I favor can't be sufficient reason for disobeying; there must be reasons why over time, because of systematic distortions of the political process and lack of proper mutual engagement of citizens, losers cannot in good conscience give their consent to political outcomes and understand themselves, at least indirectly, as authors of a collective decision (to return to the discussion in the second chapter).[75] If it's always the same people who sacrifice for the sake of keeping the polity together, that's a strong indication that something must be wrong. When Black Lives Matter was called "not your grand-father's civil rights movement," the point was to highlight that systemic racism evidently persists in the face of what by global comparison seems highly advanced antidiscrimination legislation in the United States.

This leaves a somewhat gray area where no lawbreaking is involved but where distinctly uncivil forms of confrontation aim at changing the minds of audiences witnessing an encounter between citizens and actors who in one way or another promote or sustain authoritarian populism. Think of instances when Trump administration officials were refused service, or yelled at, in restaurants. Or think of how a group of activists went to the home of the Fox News presenter Tucker Carlson (he wasn't there, but his family was) and chanted, "We know where you sleep at night!"[76] Or think of citizens admonishing Dominic Cummings, special adviser to Boris Johnson, outside his house in London for breaking the very rules he himself had authored to deal with the pandemic. Or think of someone stealing the clothes of the German far-right leader Alexander Gauland, generating images of the seventy-seven-year-old having to walk home in his bathing trunks; the thief supposedly shouted, "Kein Badespaß für Nazis!"—"No bathing fun for Nazis!"

Being confrontational does not automatically amount to disrespect for the standing of others in a polity. There is nothing wrong with being uncivil, as long as a number of conditions hold: First, the confrontation is directly with the person involved in the unjust practices to which one seeks to draw attention. That means no legitimacy for collateral damage; there is nothing admirable about scaring kids in a home that just happens to be that of a media superspreader of far-right messages. Second, confrontations have plausibly to communicate the actual injustice or the precise flaw with the democratic process. Yelling openly at a politician may or may not be a good way to appeal to majorities who do not yet agree with your view about an injustice; Pussy Riot's "Punk Prayer" at a Moscow cathedral might or might not have articulated an accurate criticism of Putin's autocracy, but it probably did little to convince many ordinary Russians; exposing an old man to ridicule on social media, by cruelly forcing him to exhibit his flabby body, has no discernible communicative content relating to an injustice. Third, it's okay to be "uncivil," as long as disobedience relates to the civic: the very basics of the polity, as opposed to ordinary policy disagreement. Put differently, disobedience is most plausible when it defends the hard border defined in the first chapter, the status of all members of a democracy as free and equal. In this case, it's not the disrupter who is truly "uncivil"; rather, it's those who attack the very foundations of citizenship, including the most soft-spoken ones sporting jackets and ties.[77]

Militant democracy proposes to fight fire with fire. That is risky, but as long as it enforces the hard border of democracy, it can be justified, especially because it does not deny citizens a continued role in politics (only the permanent restriction of individual rights would do so). When individual citizens disobey the law to defend the hard border, that can also be understood as fighting fire with fire, and that's also justified, as long as they don't burn bystanders' (or their own) house down in the process.

CODA: Five Reasons for Democratic Hope
(Not Optimism)

Millions of people around the world are evidently dissatisfied with their democracies. But they are not turning away from democracy as a set of ideas. The ranks of those disappointed by democracy, but not ready to ditch it, include millennials, who have been suspected of caring less about democracy than they should.[1] This is a reason for hope; it's also a real difference from the twentieth century, when citizens felt that institutions like parliaments were deeply discredited as such.

This is one reason why parties and movements bent on undermining democracy don't openly denounce democratic ideals, and why authoritarians put so much ingenuity (and resources) into faking democracy. On occasion, citizens might take them at their word that they are offering a successful mutation of democracy (such as "illiberal democracy"), or even an improved version of "self-rule"; they assume that they still live in democracies when in fact democracy is being degraded or disabled altogether. Hypocrisy can make us hopeful: many of today's authoritarians keep paying lip service to democratic ideals; that doesn't make them automatically vulnerable, but it provides an opening that different versions of autocracy would not.

Yet there's also a more uncomfortable truth. Not all voters who support authoritarian politicians are being duped; sometimes voters do engage in trade-offs: they accept rhetoric and conduct inimical to democracy for the sake of partisan interests. The tragedy is that everyone will have their own reasons for doing so (not least oligarchs).

This is particularly likely when authoritarian populists have managed to reshape a political landscape such that citizens feel they have no choice but to be on one side of a kind of internal frontier. Existing culture wars can facilitate the rise of such figures, but they don't determine them. In the end, culture is not the "cause" of democracy's weakening; if anything, the two secessions, and rising inequality more broadly, are the real culprits. Most important, what politics has created, politics can undo. Polarization and tribalism are not givens of human nature but contingent outcomes of how conflicts are portrayed and fought. That is a third reason for hope.

DEMOCRACY IS BASED on equality and freedom. These two principles are in tension with each other. Freedom—especially combined with unequal resources—can entrench or even steadily exacerbate political inequality, but without freedom there is also no way to fight back against such undermining of inequality.

Democracy means equal rights but also equal respect—a common life where people feel they can look each other in the eye and treat one another without the deference, or outright fear, characteristic of feudal or racial caste societies. Respect does not mean absence of disagreement. It's perfectly possible to have even deep disagreements without disrespect: not every difference of opinion is a difference of principle, and not every difference of principle denies the civic status of those one differs from.

In free societies, conflict is inevitable; the question is how conflicts are dealt with. There's also no such thing as democracy without losers; the question is whether the game is such that people take turns in making sacrifices for the sake of keeping the polity together. That is rendered easier if the thought is plausible that one's political opponents could just possibly be right. It's also made easier if one can imagine that one eventually finds oneself in the place where the opponent is now.

Democracy requires rules; these simultaneously enable and constrain. In a representative democracy, they institutionalize uncertainty. The latter sounds off-putting: Who values uncertainty as such, other than spectators who want a sports game to be as suspenseful as possible (even committed fans might not want that; they might be happy for their side to be so strong that a win is virtually guaranteed)? And yet uncertainty of outcomes within certain rules points to democracy's dynamic, and ideally even creative character. Democracy needs to remain open to new forms of representing ideas, interests, and identities; democracy dwells in possibility.

Who will most likely undertake such political work? Max Weber called parties "the children of democracy, of mass franchise, of the necessity to woo and organize the masses" (alas, these children have also been the orphans of political and legal theory). Now the kids have grown up, some have passed into old age, some have in fact died, but there are also newer generations. Parties are not automatically "divisive, distracting, and dangerous," as a pervasive antiparty suspicion that has always shadowed representative democracy would have it.[2] They are still the best way to realize the worth of individual democratic rights and deal with collective disagreements (including disagreements about who constitutes the people as such). Changing party systems are not necessarily a sign of crisis for democracy, and neither is a reshaping of the public sphere such that new and more actors can appear on the stage. The vision of a "hyper-democracy without parties but with citizens at the centre" (Beppe Grillo) will mean either less comprehensible politics altogether or the more or less hidden rule of particular individuals (such as Grillo).

Parties also provide the most plausible political machinery to counter the two secessions, or, to put it bluntly, Podemos-style, to mobilize those at the bottom and push back against those at the top. As Thomas Piketty has argued, "Everything depends on equipping groups of different origins and identities with the institutional, social, and political tools they need to recognize that what unites them outweighs what divides them."[3] There are no guarantees here, of course, but the fact that at least some party systems are offering citizens new tools and new choices is a sign for hope.

Parties and professional media ought to be regulated such that they fulfill their crucial functions for representative democracy: setting up political conflict by providing a vision of divisions; offering internal and external pluralism; structuring political time. It is important to have relatively low barriers for entry to these institutions; at the same time, it is perfectly legitimate for existing institutions to sustain core partisan commitments and a particular professional ethos even if it means excluding certain points of view or empowering some members more than others.

Intermediary institutions must be accessible, accurate, autonomous, assessable, and thereby also accountable. This does not mean that they have to be nonpartisan (this is obvious for parties, less so for professional media). They aim not at finding the truth but at allowing citizens to take different positions on conflicts, a process both enabled and constrained by facts, even if facts are always fragile. While plenty of observers today fret about social media's undermining democracy, it's important to remember that these novel intermediaries have provided unprecedented access for citizens. Once more, the problems are not so much with the people as with bad regulation. It's not fashionable to say so, but increased access to public debate is a sign of hope as well. The question is whether the de facto monopolies can be broken up and whether business models that aren't based on "virality" and "engagement" (which reward radicalization) might succeed in a different legal framework. It's nice that a surveillance company like Facebook, which happens to have a social media thing going on the side, puts in an oversight board. But as long as Facebook remains at liberty to ignore what that board says, it's not regulation, it's a PR exercise.[4] Representative democracies have worked well when the function that intermediary powers like the press and parties needed to fulfill for citizens were clearly recognized—and they have worked especially well when those functions were legally specified by states that justify their regulations with reference to basic democratic principles.

What I've been calling the critical infrastructure of democracy is in serious disrepair in some countries. The best response is to regulate in line with basic democratic principles and encourage citizens themselves to assume responsibility for this repair by equipping them with the resources to finance both parties and media. Nobody can tell whether stressed and distracted citizens would take up the role of continuously shaping their political infrastructure; after all, plenty already don't vote. Those with more resources (and interest in the political process) will no doubt come up with new ideas of how to preserve their influence, which has led some skeptics of reform to identify a quasi-Newtonian political law of motion or, sticking with physics analogies, has made them despair that there is such a thing as a hydraulics of political money: even if you block the stream of money one way, it will find another way to flow in.[5]

Claude Lefort underlined the open-ended process of

democracy when he described it as "a regime founded upon *the legitimacy of a debate as to what is legitimate and what is illegitimate—a debate which is necessarily without any guarantor and without any end.*"[6] There is indeed no guarantee and no predetermined goal (such that we could ever say, "Now democracy is perfectly realized!"). But there are limits. Uncertainty—and the exercise of freedom in general—must be contained within two hard borders: people cannot have license to undermine the standing of their fellow citizens as free and equal members of the polity, and while everyone is entitled to their opinions, everyone cannot have their own facts.

Insisting on such borders does not mean that politics becomes reducible to rule following or to the perpetual policing of limits. Sometimes democratic action consists precisely in breaking and reshaping the rules, or what the late civil rights leader and congressman John Lewis called "good trouble, necessary trouble." This is warranted especially when existing rules violate the core ideas of political freedom and equality. A distinctly democratic form of disobedience can also be justified when a political process is being blocked or has broken down in some other manner; it bears adding that those who disobey must be able to tell a plausible tale as to why protest is not just a matter of partisans' being bad losers. That such disobedience has been possible (which is not the same as successful) is a sign of hope.

THERE IS NO particular reason to be optimistic about democracy at this point; those bent on subverting it are at least as busy perfecting a populist-authoritarian art of governance as defenders of democracy are racing to issue crisis manuals. As we've learned, under such conditions courts will not necessarily save us, nor will other professionals; ultimately, only mobilized citizens can.

As Martin Luther King Jr. taught, optimism is not the same as hope. The former is about probabilities; the latter is about finding paths forward, irrespective of how likely it is that someone will take these paths. The paths are there; the rest is up to us. Democracy, after all, is not about trust (be it in individuals or institutions); it's about effort. The latter observation was offered by Edward Snowden, one of the figures of our time who became a rule breaker for the sake of restoring the spirit behind the rules.

Notes

PREFACE

1. Reinhart Koselleck writes that "in Greek antiquity crisis had clearly distinguishable meanings in legal, theological, and medical areas. The concept demanded hard alternatives: legal or illegal, salvation or damnation, life or death." See Reinhart Koselleck, "Krise," in *Geschichtliche Grundbegriffe: Historisches Lexikon zur politisch-sozialen Sprache in Deutschland*, ed. Otto Brunner et al. (Stuttgart: Klett-Cotta, 1982), 617.

2. Charles Taylor, one of the world's most influential philosophers (and not exactly a man of the demophobic right), does not hesitate to diagnose "a 'dumbing down' of electorates, in the sense that the grasp of the issues, and of what is related to what, declines among great swathes of the population." See Charles Taylor, "Is Democracy Slipping Away?," items.ssrc.org/is-democracy-slipping-away/.

3. It's easy to lose a sense of proportion here: 6 percent of U.S. citizens chose Donald Trump as the Republican nominee, and 28 percent of eligible voters made him president.

4. See, for instance, Jonathan Rauch and Benjamin Wittes, "More Professionalism, Less Populism," Center for Effective Public Management at Brookings, May 2017, www.brookings.edu/wp-content/uploads/2017/05/more-professionalism-less-populism.pdf.

5. Geert Corstens, *Understanding the Rule of Law*, trans. Annette Mils (Oxford: Hart, 2017), xx.

6. Political analysis—and the academic discipline of political science above all—always seems to be crowded out by something seemingly more robust and scientific. For a long time it was economics; now it's

psychology. For the recommendation of "mindfulness" as a response to polarization, see Ezra Klein, *Why We're Polarized* (New York: Avid Reader, 2020).

7. As Adam Przeworski observes drily, "Inferring the stability of democracy from responses to survey questions is a publicity stunt, not a valid scientific procedure." See his *Why Bother with Elections?* (Cambridge: Polity Press, 2018), 131.

8. True, all this is hardly new. Orwell observed in 1946, "It is almost universally felt that when we call a country democratic we are praising it: Consequently the defenders of every kind of regime claim that it is a democracy, and fear that they might have to stop using the word if it were tied down to any one meaning. Words of this kind are often used in a consciously dishonest way. That is, the person who uses them has his own private definition, but allows his hearer to think he means something quite different."

9. With the possible (complicated) exception of Italy.

10. For plenty of evidence, see the excellent book, by Nancy Bermeo, *Ordinary People in Extraordinary Times* (Princeton, N.J.: Princeton University Press, 2003).

11. Or, with a distinction familiar from administrative law: a focus on standards, as opposed to specific rules.

12. Steven Levitsky and Daniel Ziblatt, *How Democracies Die* (New York: Crown, 2018).

13. He adds, "The very idea that it would be possible to analyze political developments in terms of the decline of stabilizing, trans-partisan norms rather than substantive ideology is a political position." See Jedediah Purdy, "Normcore," *Dissent* (Summer 2018), www.dissentmagazine .org/article/normcore-trump-resistance-books-crisis-of-democracy. Corey Robin has gone so far as to say democracy *is* norm erosion. I wouldn't, but there's truth in this aphorism.

14. Ibid.

15. Melissa Schwartzberg, *Counting the Many: The Origins and Limits of Supermajority Rule* (New York: Cambridge University Press, 2013).

16. As Dewey put it, "The old saying that the cure for the ills of democracy is more democracy is not apt if it means that the evils may be remedied by introducing more machinery of the same kind as that which already exists, or by refining and perfecting that machinery. But the phrase may also indicate the need of returning to the idea itself . . . and of employing our sense of its meaning to criticize and re-make its political manifestations." John Dewey, *The Public and Its Problems* (1927; Athens: Ohio University Press, 1954), 144.

17. Christian Meier, *Die Entstehung des Politischen bei den Griechen* (Frankfurt am Main: Suhrkamp, 1980); Melissa Schwarzberg, *De-*

mocracy and Legal Change (New York: Cambridge University Press, 2007). As the philosopher Raymond Geuss observes, "Really significant political action . . . is action that, for better or for worse, neither simply conforms to existing rules nor intervenes . . . to find craftsman-like solutions to specific problems, but that changes a situation in a way that cannot be seen to be a mere instantiation of a preexisting set of rules." He adds, "It creates new facts, violates, ignores, or even changes the rules . . . [T]he fact that such disruptive change of the existing systems of action is always at least a possibility is one of the things that gives politics its special character." See Raymond Geuss, *Politics and the Imagination* (Princeton, N.J.: Princeton University Press, 2010), 41. David Graeber draws a somewhat similar contrast between truly freewheeling—and potentially terrifying—*play*, on the one hand, and *games* where rules are unambiguous; he writes, "Who hasn't dreamed of a world where everyone knows the rules, everyone plays by the rules, and—even more—where people who play by the rules can actually still win? The problem is that this is just as much a utopian fantasy as a world of absolute free play would be." David Graeber, *The Utopia of Rules: On Technology, Stupidity, and the Secret Joys of Bureaucracy* (Brooklyn, N.Y.: Melville House, 2015), 205. This contrast between play and game is not available in many other languages.

1. FAKE DEMOCRACY: EVERYBODY HAS THEIR REASONS

1. With the possible exception of India: there the RSS is a highly mobilized mass force systematically engaged in violence.

2. This symbolic message (which is never merely symbolic, but has very real consequences) can usefully be compared with Sandra Day O'Connor's endorsement test developed in *Lynch v. Donnelly*: "Endorsement sends a message to nonadherents that they are outsiders, not full members of the political community, and an accompanying message to adherents that they are insiders, favored members of the political community." As so often, treating people as inferior and excluding them can then produce the very evidence which appears to prove that unequal treatment is justified.

3. For some examples of what Trump's populism has meant on the ground, see Dylan Matthews, "Donald Trump, the Family Separation Crisis, and the Triumph of Cruelty," *Vox*, June 19, 2018, www.vox.com /2017/1/28/14425354/donald-trump-cruelty; Seth Harp, "I'm a Journalist but I Didn't Fully Realize the Terrible Power of U.S. Border Officials until They Violated My Rights and Privacy," *Intercept*, June 22, 2019, theintercept.com/2019/06/22/cbp-border-searches-journalists/; A. C. Thompson, "Inside the Secret Border Patrol Facebook Group

Where Agents Joke About Migrant Deaths and Post Sexist Memes," ProPublica, July 1, 2019, www.propublica.org/article/secret-border -patrol-facebook-group-agents-joke-about-migrant-deaths-post-sexist -memes.

4. Larry Diamond, *Ill Winds: Saving Democracy from Russian Rage, Chinese Ambition, and American Complacency* (New York: Penguin, 2019), 106.

5. Kate Manne, "The Logic of Misogyny," *Boston Review*, July 11, 2016, bostonreview.net/forum/kate-manne-logic-misogyny.

6. David Miller, *On Nationality* (Oxford: Oxford University Press, 1995).

7. Bálint Magyar, *Post-Communist Mafia State: The Case of Hungary* (Budapest: Central European University Press, 2016).

8. Quoted in David Frum, *Trumpocracy* (New York: HarperCollins, 2018), 53.

9. Ernst Fraenkel, *The Dual State: A Contribution to the Theory of Dictatorship* trans. Edward Shils (New York: Oxford University Press, 2017).

10. Kim Lane Scheppele, "Hungary and the End of Politics," *Nation*, May 6, 2014.

11. Dan Kelemen, personal communication.

12. To be sure, more or less prestigious names are being dropped by leaders here or there and can serve as signals about political orientations; in that sense, the name-dropping is important, even if the point is not the imminent translation of some comprehensive worldviews into practice. But then the crucial question is this: A signal directed at which audiences? And why do these audiences matter? Especially in Russia—a prime contender today for a great power with philosophical pretensions—the name-dropping appears more about satisfying committed nationalists (and, to some extent, *siloviki*, the representatives of the national security state) than an indication of the actual sources of policy. I am indebted to Guillaume Sauvé and Ivan Krastev for discussions on this point.

13. Benjamin R. Teitelbaum, *War for Eternity: Inside Bannon's Far-Right Circle of Global Power Brokers* (New York: Dey Street Books, 2020).

14. Larry Bartels, "2016 Was an Ordinary Election, Not a Realignment," *Washington Post*, Nov. 10, 2016, www.washingtonpost.com/news /monkey-cage/wp/2016/11/10/2016-was-an-ordinary-election-not-a -realignment/.

15. Voters arrived at that fateful point after traversing a long path (that had been paved since Hillary's husband's time in power). Newt Gingrich recommended that Republicans use the following words when talking about Democrats: "betray, bizarre, decay, destroy, devour, greed, lie, pathetic, radical, selfish, shame, sick, steal, and traitors."

Lilliana Mason, *Uncivil Agreement: How Politics Became Our Identity* (Chicago: University of Chicago Press, 2018), 132.

16. I am indebted to Cristóbal Rovira Kaltwasser for discussions on this point.

17. I am indebted to Kim Lane Scheppele for this point.

18. Kim Lane Scheppele, "The Party's Over," in *Constitutional Democracy in Crisis?*, ed. Mark A. Graber, Sanford Levinson, and Mark Tushnet (New York: Oxford University Press, 2018), 495–513.

19. No wonder almost a third of Americans say they have lost friends because of politics. Roderick P. Hart, *Trump and Us* (New York: Cambridge University Press, 2020), 239.

20. Ivan Krastev, "The Fear of Shrinking Numbers," *Journal of Democracy* 31 (2020): 66–74.

21. Jérôme Fourquet, *L'archipel français: Naissance d'une nation multiple et divisée* (Paris: Seuil, 2019).

22. Ivan Krastev, *Ist heute schon morgen? Wie die Pandemie Europa verändern wird*, trans. Karin Schuler (Berlin: Ullstein, 2020).

23. For this argument about functional elites and their self-reproduction in national contexts, see, for instance, Michael Hartmann's work, such as *Die Abgehobenen: Wie die Eliten die Demokratie gefährden* (Frankfurt am Main: Campus, 2018).

24. I am grateful to Ivan Krastev for stimulating thoughts in this context. Technology also plays a role, of course: British aristocrats after the world wars felt indebted to those who had died in the trenches; by contrast, it would not occur to anyone to thank a drone.

25. Of course, the opposite turned out to be true: Trump had meant it literally when he talked about the wall, but he had not been serious when he had made promises about doing something for the downtrodden.

26. See Peter Thiel, "The Education of a Libertarian," *Cato Unbound*, April 13, 2009, www.cato-unbound.org/2009/04/13/peter-thiel/education-libertarian.

27. See also Evan Osnos, "Doomsday Prep for the Super-rich," *New Yorker*, Jan. 30, 2017.

28. Emmanuel Saez and Gabriel Zucman, *The Triumph of Injustice: How the Rich Dodge Taxes and How to Make Them Pay* (New York: Norton, 2019), 77–78.

29. "Transcript: Trump's 'Winning, Winning, Winning' Speech," *Tampa Bay Times*, Feb. 24, 2016, www.tampabay.com/opinion/columns/transcript-trumps-winning-winning-winning-speech/2266681/.

30. Jeffrey Winters, *Oligarchy* (New York: Cambridge University Press, 2011).

31. We can leave aside here the question of whether the ultra-wealthy have inherited their resources or whether they are what Daniel Markovits describes as the meritocratic working rich dominating the United States today. Markovits notes, "Eight of the ten richest Americans today owe their wealth not to inheritance or to return on inherited capital but rather to compensation earned through entrepreneurial or managerial labor." See his *Meritocracy Trap: How America's Foundational Myth Feeds Inequality, Dismantles the Middle Class, and Devours the Elite* (New York: Penguin Press, 2019), 89.

32. For Aristotle, the difficulty was how to distinguish oligarchs and aristocrats. Wealth might be a sign of greed and corruption, but it could also be an indication of virtue. See the excellent discussion in Gordon Arlen, "Aristotle and the Problem of Oligarchic Harm: Insights for Democracy," *European Journal of Political Theory* 18 (2019): 393–414.

33. Jacob S. Hacker and Paul Pierson, *Let Them Eat Tweets: How the Right Rules in an Age of Extreme Inequality* (New York: Simon & Schuster, 2020).

34. In Athens, the wealthy generally served in the cavalry, the hoplites (sometimes identified by historians as the "middle class") in the infantry, and the poor tended to be rowers in the navy (*thetes*). Radical democracy meant a majority of *thetes* in the assembly. Mogens Herman Hansen, *The Athenian Democracy in the Age of Demosthenes: Structure, Principles, and Ideology*, trans. J. A. Crook (Norman: University of Oklahoma Press, 1999), 126.

35. Wolfgang Merkel has coined the term "two-thirds society" for this phenomenon: the bottom third has effectively disappeared from political life completely. See also Brice Teinturier, *"Plus rien à faire, plus rien à foutre": La vraie crise de la démocratie* (Paris: Robert Laffont, 2017). For empirical evidence, see Armin Schäfer and Hannah Schwender, "'Don't Play if You Can't Win': Does Economic Inequality Undermine Political Equality?," *European Political Science Review* 11 (2019): 395–413. They conclude starkly, "Moving from the most egalitarian to the most unequal countries depresses turnout—all else being equal—by 7 to 15 percentage points (depending on the exact model), which is comparable in magnitude to the effect of compulsory voting. Within Germany, where institutional variables do not differ, relatively deprived regions have significantly lower levels of turnout. Finally, we find that turnout declines for all income groups in unequal countries but particularly strongly for low-income groups. Our findings, therefore, unambiguously support the relative power approach—the rational abstention approach—that expects inequality to have a negative impact on political engagement. Our analyses show that in more

unequal countries, fewer people turn out and vote. The idea that inequality mobilizes the poor to greater political activism because 'more is at stake' clearly does not have any empirical grounding."

36. Claus Offe, "Participatory Inequality in the Austerity State: A Supply-Side Approach," in *Politics in the Age of Austerity*, ed. Armin Schäfer and Wolfgang Streeck (Cambridge: Polity Press, 2013), 203. Thomas Piketty adds that we should not assume that those who secede/abstain are by default racists; as Piketty puts it, "If the less advantaged truly supported anti-immigrant movements, their turnout should be at a peak today. The fact that it is very low clearly shows that many less advantaged voters are not satisfied with the choices presented to them." *Capital and Ideology*, trans. Arthur Goldhammer (Cambridge, Mass.: Harvard University Press, 2020), 754.

37. Milan W. Svolik, "Polarization Versus Democracy," *Journal of Democracy* 30 (2019): 20–32. As Svolik puts it, "The political acumen of Chávez, Orbán, or Erdoğan lay in their ability to draw political battle lines along societal cleavages that were only simmering when these leaders were first elected. Once they succeeded, elections confronted their supporters with the choice between their partisan interests on the one hand and democratic principles on the other." For detailed evidence on whether voters are willing to act as a check on undemocratic behavior by politicians from the party with which they identify, see Matthew H. Graham and Milan W. Svolik, "Democracy in America? Partisanship, Polarization, and the Robustness of Support for Democracy in the United States," *American Political Science Review* 114 (2020): 392–409. The authors observe that "voters are about 50% more lenient toward violations of democratic principles by candidates from their own party."

38. Larry M. Bartels, "Ethnic Antagonism Erodes Republicans' Commitment to Democracy," *Proceedings of the National Academy of Sciences*, Sept. 15, 2020, www.pnas.org/content/pnas/early/2020/08/26/2007747117.full.pdf.

39. Josiah Ober, *Athenian Legacies: Essays on the Politics of Going on Together* (Princeton, N.J.: Princeton University Press, 2005); Andreas Kalyvas, "Democracy and the Poor," in *Thinking Democracy Now: Between Innovation and Regression*, ed. Nadia Urbinati (Milan: Feltrinelli, 2019), 57–76. Kalyvas emphasizes that plebeian democracy meant not dispossession of the rich but countering their ability to translate economic power into political power.

40. Lenz Jacobsen, "Im Bund mit den Ängstlichen," *Zeit Online*, Nov. 28, 2015, www.zeit.de/politik/deutschland/2015–11/alternative-fuer-deutschland-parteitag-frauke-petry-hannover.

41. Jedediah Purdy, *This Land Is Our Land: The Struggle for a New Commonwealth* (Princeton, N.J.: Princeton University Press, 2019), 15.

42. Krastev, "Fear of Shrinking Numbers"; Catherine Fieschi, *Populocracy: The Tyranny of Authenticity and the Rise of Populism* (Newcastle: Agenda, 2019), 162.

43. To be sure, confirmation of a vision at the ballot box does not signify carte blanche; the implementation of a vision is constrained by the possibility of the present minority gaining office and reshaping the conception of the people yet again.

44. The contrast between forming and finding was first suggested by Ernst Fraenkel. Note, for instance, Narendra Modi claiming, "I am merely the medium" and "it is the people whose voice is resonating." Sunil Khilnani, "The Idea of India Says Persuade, Not Dictate," *Times of India*, Aug. 15, 2017, timesofindia.indiatimes.com/india/the-idea-of-india-says-persuade-not-dictate/articleshow/60063019.cms.

45. The dilemma is nicely laid out in Jonathan White and Lea Ypi, "The Politics of Peoplehood," *Political Theory* 45 (2015): 439–65.

46. Note that, contrary to a common image of populists as unruly and norm breaking, they in a certain way actually belong on the first side of the dilemma: the norm is that the people are those who the populists, as unique representatives of the people, say the people are.

47. It seems rather insufficient to say, where such exclusionary measures dominate, "they usefully alert us to the pressing need to promote counter-perspectives and act as a provocation to do so." See White and Ypi, "Politics of Peoplehood," 456.

48. Anna Stilz, *Territorial Sovereignty: A Philosophical Exploration* (New York: Oxford University Press, 2019).

49. As Josiah Ober has pointed out, a group seeking the benefits of social cooperation without a master is rare but hardly unknown; it's not absurd to assume a group seeking non-tyranny, although, as Ober concedes, it may well be that "things have happened in the past (good, bad, just, unjust)." See his *Demopolis* (New York: Cambridge University Press, 2016), 37–38.

50. Stilz, *Territorial Sovereignty*, 98.

51. Ibid.

52. Fabio Wolkenstein, "Populism, Liberal Democracy, and the Ethics of Peoplehood," *European Journal of Political Theory* 18 (2019): 330–48.

53. Christoph Möllers, *Das Grundgesetz: Geschichte und Inhalt* (Munich: C. H. Beck, 2019), 103.

54. Some hold that democracy requires the justification of all decisions that end up coercing others. Borders affect not just those inside them but also those who are kept out by them; hence the latter must be part of the decision-making process. The conclusion is that ultimately,

from the point of view of a consistent democrat, the demos must be nothing less than global. The same conclusion appears to follow if one adopts a somewhat weaker criterion and argues that virtually all decisions in a democratic state—whether coercing others directly or not—have effects on noncitizens, and because all affected by a decision should have a say in it, we once more end up with a call for something like world democracy.

A conventional response to this position is that one simply can't conceive a political machinery that would allow a global demos to determine a collective will (let alone consistently implement universally binding decisions) without turning into some kind of tyranny. Another objection would emphasize that there are very different and yet legitimate ways of implementing the principles of freedom and equality; peoples disagree about the particulars even of basic political rights; everyone might have their own reasons for disagreeing, but these might all be perfectly good ones—grounded, for instance, in diverging historical experiences, diverging value commitments that touch on basic rights (but don't uniquely determine them), diverging views of the empirical effects basic rights might have on different people, and so on. Note how the "it's gotta be global" view achieves the opposite of what the defenders of an ethnic perspective want: it expands the people to the absolute maximum (and, to be consistent, aliens would also have to be included in debates over whether they could be excluded from Earth). But on one level the two apparent extremes have something in common: they stop a democratic conflict over peoplehood in its tracks; the size of the people is given; forms of togetherness are not fought over and reshaped over time. I am not suggesting a moral equivalence between the two views; there remains much to be said for a conception of peoplehood that, in light of a commitment to reciprocity, is sensitive to externalities. Wolkenstein mentions the campaign for Scottish independence as an example of actors who tried to justify their aims to both insiders and the most relevant outsiders (the rest of the U.K. and the EU). See Arash Abizadeh, "Democratic Theory and Border Coercion: No Right Unilaterally to Control Your Own Borders," *Political Theory* 36 (2008): 37–65; and Wolkenstein, "Populism," 343–44.

55. Quoted in Adam Przeworski, *Democracy and the Limits of Self-Government* (New York: Cambridge University Press, 2010), 27. This is another way of saying that a political people isn't actually an "entity" at all but an ongoing pluralistic process; see Jürgen Habermas, "Constitutional Democracy: An Uncertain Union of Paradoxical Principles?," *Political Theory* 29 (2001): 766–81.

2. REAL DEMOCRACY: LIBERTY, EQUALITY, UNCERTAINTY

1. If one agrees with this understanding of political equality as foundational, one may well ask how the world's largest democracy can at the same time be a caste society. A plausible answer is that India's constitution contains not just a set of rights and procedures; it is an ongoing pedagogical and policy program to transform society and systematically reduce status hierarchies. See also Madhav Khosla, *India's Founding Moment: The Constitution of a Most Surprising Democracy* (Cambridge, Mass.: Harvard University Press, 2020).

2. Philip Pettit, *On the People's Terms* (New York: Cambridge University Press, 2012), 84–88.

3. Social and political equality are different phenomena: the entrepreneur in sneakers and T-shirt can be easygoing and even resist the temptation of de facto patronizing me with his manner, but we are unlikely to be equals politically, unless the critical infrastructure of democracy is such that it assures some measure of equal opportunity to engage in politics.

4. Elizabeth Anderson, *Private Government: How Employers Rule Our Lives (and Why We Don't Talk About It)* (Princeton, N.J.: Princeton University Press, 2017).

5. I am grateful to Jean Cohen for this observation.

6. Dexter Filkins, "James Mattis, a Warrior in Washington," *New Yorker*, May 29, 2017.

7. Johnny Cash, of course (true, the song was written by U2, but the theoretical insight emerges in the Cash version only).

8. John Rawls argued that such "burdens of judgment" made persistent pluralism in a modern democratic society inevitable but not inherently problematic. John Rawls, *Political Liberalism* (New York: Columbia University Press, 1993).

9. I am indebted here to the excellent discussion of the tensions between equality and freedom in Arash Abizadeh, "Representation, Bicameralism, Political Equality, and Sortition: Reconstituting the Second Chamber as a Randomly Selected Assembly," *Perspectives on Politics* (forthcoming).

10. Clearly, what exactly the criteria are for treating others as equals is a complicated question; for some of the complications, see G. A. Cohen, "Notes on Regarding People as Equals," in *Finding Oneself in the Other*, ed. Michael Otsuka (Princeton, N.J.: Princeton University Press, 2013), 193–200.

11. In this book I leave aside the complicated question of compulsory voting, of which I'm broadly in favor: we make it a duty to pay taxes to

sustain our common life; we can make it a duty to vote (including "none of the above") to maintain our shared political life.

12. Note that a simple majority decision (as distinct from an election with a campaign, and so on) also satisfies the condition of ex ante equal chances, as well as equal respect. On such unique characteristics of majority decision, see Kenneth O. May, "A Set of Independent Necessary and Sufficient Conditions for Simple Majority Decision," *Econometrica* 20 (1952): 680–84; Charles Beitz, *Political Equality* (Princeton, N.J.: Princeton University Press, 1989), 58–67.

13. The difference makes a difference: Trump has always played himself in every cameo in a film and on TV, whereas an actual actor needs to have a capacity for empathy and trying to understand other people's lived experience from the inside. As Leo Braudy observes, "Reagan's experience as an actor, far from trivializing his performance as president, allowed him to project a much more complicated character than he may have actually possessed." Quoted in James Poniewozik, *Audience of One: Donald Trump, Television, and the Fracturing of America* (New York: Liveright, 2019), 210.

14. Abizadeh, "Representation, Bicameralism, Political Equality, and Sortition," 6.

15. Hansen, *Athenian Democracy*, 250, 313–14.

16. This is a stylized contrast between ancients and moderns to test our intuitions; the claim is not that the Greeks themselves necessarily held this view. After all, the assembly, as a decision-making body, actually issued decrees (while *nomothetai* formulated general laws), so citizens chosen by lot did not "govern" in our modern sense. The assumption was that citizens were capable of occupying an office (if old enough: one had to reach thirty or even forty for certain offices), not that decision-making power should be given to a randomly chosen individual. Even Hansen, generally skeptical of the idea that lottery was primarily equality-affirming, draws this contrast, though: "Oligarchs went in for election and the holdings of posts by individuals; democrats chose the lot and collegiality" (ibid., 237).

17. Bernard Manin, *The Principles of Representative Government* (Cambridge: Cambridge University Press, 1997).

18. Note that this is a theoretical argument; historians are skeptical that the Athenians used sortition to affirm equality; rather, it was employed "because it safeguarded the powers of the people, prevented conflict and counteracted corruption." Hansen, *Athenian Democracy*, 84.

19. E. E. Schattschneider, *The Semisovereign People: A Realist's View of Democracy in America* (Boston: Cengage, 1975), 68.

20. Hansen, *Athenian Democracy*, 138, 204.

21. Of course, it's not quite as simple as that: there can be vote-counting errors (leading to endless disputes); in some countries you can get more votes and still lose—the world's supposedly leading democracy being an example of this. Then there are the numerous doubts that social choice theorists such as Kenneth Arrow have cast on the promise of "unambiguous outcomes." To be sure, cycling seems less of a problem in the so-called real world than in social theory, and as Andreas Schedler has pointed out, elections' margins of error are not like statistics: "The potential errors of elections are not inferential, but organizational." Andreas Schedler, *The Politics of Uncertainty: Sustaining and Subverting Electoral Authoritarianism* (New York: Oxford University Press, 2013), 111.

22. Of course, this was also true in the ancient assembly, except that the Greeks did not count individual votes but relied on estimates (which could be challenged by the losers).

23. Przeworski, *Democracy and the Limits of Self-Government.*

24. Walt Whitman, "Election Day, November 1844"; https://whitman archive.org/published/LG/1891/poems/329.

25. I owe the pair "propose-impose" to Adam Przeworski.

26. And, as Cas Mudde puts it memorably, liberals are people who love to be scared (personal communication).

27. In the United States, I can look up in one second online whether my neighbors have registered for a party; hence, I know how they vote (unless they strategically try to influence the party that they in fact oppose). The United States is an outlier in this regard; other democracies protect the data—and anonymity—of their citizens much more.

28. Bernard Manin provides the strongest counterargument, also fully applicable in our day: "With open voting, you as a voter certainly do not select those who control your vote, but they self-select: You vote under the eyes of those who are interested in you. In practice, this means that open voting does not place each voter under the control of the general public, but under the control of his social environment . . . They are just a small and limited group. There is no reason to expect this limited group to be vastly less particularistic, selfish, or narrow-minded than the person whose vote they control." See Bernard Manin, "Why Open Voting in General Elections Is Undesirable," in *Secrecy and Publicity in Votes and Debates,* ed. Jon Elster (New York: Cambridge University Press, 2015), 211.

29. Przeworski, *Democracy and the Limits of Self-Government.*

30. As conceded even by Jason Brennan, *Against Democracy* (Princeton, N.J.: Princeton University Press, 2016).

31. John Stuart Mill, "Thoughts on Parliamentary Reform," in *Essays on Politics and Society,* ed. J. M. Robson (Toronto: University of Toronto Press, 1977), 332.

32. Ibid., 333.

33. When agreeing to a widening of the franchise, Gladstone wanted voters to demonstrate nothing less than "self-command, self-control, respect for order, patience under suffering, confidence in the law."

34. Of course, one cannot discriminate openly by advocating against a candidate on the basis of race or gender, for instance; an open election wouldn't address this problem, because one could still hide one's true motivations.

35. Abizadeh, "Representation, Bicameralism, Political Equality, and Sortition," 7.

36. Jean-Jacques Rousseau, *The Social Contract*, trans. Victor Gourevitch (Cambridge: Cambridge University Press, 2018), 114.

37. Ibid., 51–52.

38. The difference between the ancient polis and modern representative democracy is not reducible to one between direct and indirect democracy. Athens had elections for something plausibly understood as representative offices, and plenty of present-day countries offer referenda, popular initiatives, and so on. One major contrast, though, is the role of popular jury courts (which did not feature anything like a public prosecution service and which were not staffed by the rich; ordinary people were paid to sit on them), which played a crucial role in keeping wealthy elites in check. As Paul Cartledge puts it, "The *demos* exercised its *kratos* in the courts." Paul Cartledge, *Democracy: A Life* (New York: Oxford University Press, 2016), 117.

39. I thank Cas Mudde for this observation.

40. Ellen Meiksins Wood, *Peasant-Citizen and Slave: The Foundations of Athenian Democracy* (New York: Verso, 1989).

41. Hansen, *Athenian Democracy*, 318.

42. Ober, *Demopolis*; Josiah Ober, "Epistemic Democracy in Classical Athens," in *Collective Wisdom: Principles and Mechanisms*, ed. Hélène Landemore and Jon Elster (New York: Cambridge University Press, 2012), 118–47.

43. An obvious complication is judicial review, which losers can use to overturn majority decisions in a representative body.

44. It's sometimes suggested that the distinctive feature of populists is that they assert the role of an unconstrained people against ossified procedures. Maybe. But note that there is no procedure-less democracy. What do grassroots movements whose sincere desire for democracy is above suspicion do first? Like Occupy Wall Street, they endlessly debate what fair procedures (General Assembly, and so on) consist of. Michael Kaplan, "Prohibiting the People: Populism, Procedure, and the Rhetoric of Democratic Value," *Constellations* 26 (2019): 94–115.

45. Sam Wang, "Why Trump Stays Afloat," *New York Times*, Oct. 29, 2016.

46. A tilted playing field is characterized by systematically unequal access to state institutions, resources, and the media; see Lucan Ahmad Way and Steven Levitsky, "Why Democracies Need a Level Playing Field," *Journal of Democracy* 21 (2010): 57–68. It is probably not an accident that if one looks at elections worldwide between 1788 and 2000, incumbents won 80 percent of the time. Przeworski, *Democracy and the Limits of Self-Government*, 167.

47. Quoted in Allan Lichtman, *The Embattled Vote in America* (Cambridge, Mass.: Harvard University Press, 2018), 248.

48. Danielle S. Allen, *Talking to Strangers: Anxieties of Citizenship Since Brown v. Board of Education* (Chicago: University of Chicago Press, 2004).

49. Jennifer Hochschild, "Four Ways to Lose Politically," *Political Theory* (forthcoming).

50. Jeffrey K. Tulis and Nicole Mellow, *Legacies of Losing in American Politics* (Chicago: University of Chicago Press, 2018). In an era when left-wing parties often ditch leaders after one election loss, it is worth remembering just how often transformative figures such as Brandt and Mitterrand got defeated—before they finally won.

51. The problem is of course that in many of today's democracies one can reasonably hold the view that not everybody does get their say. That does not result in a blank check for any kind of disobedience, but it does legitimate a certain type of democratic disobedience, about which I'll say more in chapter 4. Daniel Viehoff, "Democratic Equality and Political Authority," *Philosophy and Public Affairs* 42 (2014): 337–75.

52. Daniel Markovits, "Democratic Disobedience," *Yale Law Journal* 114 (2005): 1897–952.

53. See House of Commons, April 10, 1826, *Hansard*, vol. 15, hansard .parliament.uk/Commons/1826-04-10/debates/9539b799-a397-487e -9839-65bee9e441e8/CommonsChamber.

54. An interesting test case for this idea is a democratic party seeking secession. In Canada, the Bloc Québécois was attacked as a disloyal opposition, even when, on the basis of its election result, it was designated as the loyal opposition. As one MP charged in 1995, "Mr. Speaker, I address some comments to Her Majesty's Loyal Opposition, currently the Bloc Québécois supported by the Liberals, with specific reference to the words loyal and opposition. According to the Oxford dictionary loyal means faithful, trustworthy, true, steadfast in allegiance and devoted to the sovereign or government of one's country. In the House the Bloc is certainly not loyal to Her Majesty or to Canada and is openly plotting against the government to set up a separate Quebec." See www.ourcommons.ca/DocumentViewer/en

/35-1/house/sitting-265/hansard#HERMAJESTY'SLOYALOPPO
SITION.

55. Tocqueville argued that "one supports itself by power . . . the other by
public opinion. Its lever is public favor; its arms in the struggle it sustains are ardent convictions and disinterested passions, which it gives
birth to and sustains in the nation." The opposition's "great power,"
he claimed, "always resides in sentiments and in general ideas."
Quoted in William Selinger, *Parliamentarism* (New York: Cambridge
University Press, 2019), 153.

56. It also derives some benefit from it: a coherent opposition makes a
government more coherent. Martin Van Buren, for instance, realized that the presidency of James Monroe was in fact marred by the
weakening of the Federalists, because it made for more factionalism
inside the national party (Monroe had actually run unopposed in
1820). See Richard Hofstadter, *The Idea of a Party System: The Rise
of Legitimate Opposition in the United States, 1780–1840* (Berkeley:
University of California Press, 1969), 228–29. As Van Buren put it,
"In the place of two great parties arrayed against each other in a fair
and open contest for the establishment of principles in the administration of Government which they respectively believed most con-
ducive to the public interest, the country was overrun with personal
factions." Martin Van Buren, *Inquiry into the Origin and Course of Political Parties in the United States*, ed. his sons (New York: Hurd and
Houghton, 1867), 3–4.

57. Quoted in Nadia Urbinati, *Representative Government: Principles and
Genealogy* (Chicago: University of Chicago Press, 2006), 236.

58. John M. Murrin, "Escaping Perfidious Albion: Federalism, Fear of Aristocracy, and the Democratization of Corruption in Postrevolution-
ary America," in *Virtue, Corruption, and Self-Interest*, ed. Richard K.
Matthews (Bethlehem, Pa.: Lehigh University Press, 1994), 118–19.

59. The Leader of the Opposition also receives the same salary as a cabinet minister.

60. Beitz, *Political Equality*, 229.

61. I am riffing here on the nice formula "the minority should have its
say, and the majority should have its way" in the Venice Commission's *Opinion on the Relationship Between the Parliamentary Majority and the Opposition in a Democracy: A Checklist* (2019), www
.venice.coe.int/webforms/documents/default.aspx?pdffile=CDL
-AD(2019)015-e.

62. Note how this strategy relies on the assumption that voters will not
appropriately assign blame for a government's seeming inaction. That
assumption does not uniformly hold across democracies; much will depend on the state of intermediary institutions, professional media in

particular. The Bannon quotation is from Hacker and Pierson, *Let Them Eat Tweets*, 206.

63. This idea of a running discussion between government and opposition goes back to Hans Kelsen, who also thought it would result in corresponding compromises between the two sides.

64. Andreas Schedler, "Democratic Reciprocity," *Journal of Political Philosophy* (forthcoming).

65. Ibid.

66. I am grateful to Armin Nassehi on this point.

67. See as an example afd.nrw/aktuelles/2017/06/keine-demokratieklausel-mit-den-systemparteien/.

68. Even in the absence of anti-system parties, the fragmentation of party systems can have the effect of making the idea of a loyal opposition as a government in waiting much less plausible, because very diverse opposition parties might simply not be able to form a coherent alternative. See Florian Meinel, *Die Vertrauensfrage: Zur Krise des heutigen Parlamentarismus* (Munich: C. H. Beck, 2019), 36–38.

69. A particular question is whether opposition parties should ever boycott elections. Conventional wisdom has it that they shouldn't, but there are no context-independent answers here. If it's a presidential election, the argument for boycotting is stronger, because, unlike in a parliament, an opposition will simply not occupy one office (but not lose all representation and leverage). Another variable is whether a regime is already clearly perceived as undemocratic by important outside observers; if it isn't, a spectacular boycott might change minds (or sometimes suitably embarrass outside actors who do not want to acknowledge the ongoing destruction of democracy; think how a complete boycott of legislative elections in Poland or Hungary might have put pressure on the EU Commission).

70. With thanks to Tomasz Koncewicz.

71. Obviously, there is a gray area here: not all cases have one correct decision; and in any case, not all judgments by courts in non-democracies are issued on order from the rulers (the fact that packed courts in Moscow and Budapest sometimes act like independent institutions only serves to confuse outside observers and makes it harder to discern that on the cases that really matter to Putin and Orbán, they tend to fall in line).

72. Adam Przeworski, *Democracy and the Market* (New York: Cambridge University Press, 1991). As Andreas Schedler has pointed out, "The politics of uncertainty transcends the boundaries between democratic and authoritarian regimes." In democracies certainty about procedures is combined with uncertainty about substantive outcomes; in autocracies certainty about substantive results goes with uncertainty about

the procedures. The result? According to Schedler, "While weak democracies can be just as fragile as weak autocracies, consolidated autocracies can never be as safe as consolidated democracies." Schedler, *Politics of Uncertainty*, 26.

73. From his play *Jumpers*.

74. Przeworski, *Democracy and the Market*, 10. The presence of parties is clearly not a proof of democracy. As Erica Frantz points out, "91 percent of authoritarian regimes featured at least one political party in the post–World War II period at some point while in power." See her *Authoritarianism* (New York: Oxford University Press, 2018), 76. Some autocrats have made a point of showcasing "independence" as proof of democracy; under the Belarussian dictator Lukashenko, "nominal independents conquered 48 percent of legislative seats in the 1995 elections, 73.6 percent in 2000, 89.1 percent in 2004, and 93.6 percent in 2008." See Schedler, *Politics of Uncertainty*, 90.

75. I owe this formulation to Sam Moyn.

76. If that picture were correct, an Elizabeth Warren would already be president. I owe this observation to Cas Mudde.

77. Christopher H. Achen and Larry M. Bartels, *Democracy for Realists: Why Elections Do Not Produce Responsive Government* (Princeton, N.J.: Princeton University Press, 2016). Even these realists concede that "so long as a free press can report dubious goings-on and a literate public can learn about them, politicians have strong incentives to avoid doing what is widely despised. Violations occur, of course, but they are expensive; removal from office is likely. By contrast, in dictatorships, moral or financial corruption is more common, because public outrage has no obvious, organized outlet. This is a modest victory for political accountability" (ibid., 319). In the age of populist authoritarianism, we are learning that it might not be so modest, after all.

78. Roslyn Fuller, *In Defence of Democracy* (Cambridge: Polity Press, 2019), 55–61, offers a whole range of reasons to be skeptical of the conclusions drawn from what she calls the "Sharknado" of political science.

79. Ibid.

80. The counterargument is that at the time the federal government had no instruments to provide assistance.

81. I am indebted to Tali Mendelberg for this point.

82. It's also not a sign of impartiality, though: shortcuts are conditioned by stereotypes, as Walter Lippmann already observed almost a century ago. Walter Lippmann, *Public Opinion* (New York: Harcourt, Brace, 1922), 96.

83. Arlie Russell Hochschild, *Strangers in Their Own Land: Anger and Mourning on the American Right* (New York: New Press, 2016), 228.

84. E. E. Schattschneider, *Party Government* (New York: Holt, Rinehart, and Winston, 1942), 37.

85. Lawrence Lessig, *They Don't Represent Us* (New York: Dey Street Books, 2019), 7.

86. Martin Gilens, *Affluence and Influence: Economic Inequality and Political Power in America* (Princeton, N.J.: Princeton University Press, 2012).

87. For an accessible rendition of the tough-luck test, see Philip Pettit, *Just Freedom: A Moral Compass for a Complex World* (New York: W. W. Norton, 2014).

88. As Cartledge, building on the work of Moses Finley and demolishing Thucydides's tendentious account of Cleon, points out, demagogues "were supposedly low-class—or at least lower-class—politicos who brought democracy into (deserved) disrepute, since they merely pandered to the base desires of the unwashed masses; whereas Pericles had led the People and even forthrightly told them what they ought to decide and to do. That, however, is all pure ideology, modern as well as ancient. The word *demagogos* by itself means 'leader of the demos' (in the sense of all the People); it is only when such leaders or would-be leaders are viewed from an oligarchic-conservative standpoint that it comes more often to mean 'rabble-rouser' or misleader of the masses." He also notes that one could be a major leader in Athens without holding any office. Cartledge, *Democracy*, 115–16.

89. Adam Przeworski and John Sprague, *Paper Stones: A History of Electoral Socialism* (Chicago: University of Chicago Press, 1986).

90. Quoted in Hacker and Pierson, *Let Them Eat Tweets*, 27–28. I am indebted to them for the Private Willis versus Disraeli contrast. German has an explicit distinction between *Darstellung* and *Vertretung*—showing a conflict between groups and acting for one group in a conflict.

91. Michael Saward, *The Representative Claim* (Oxford: Oxford University Press, 2010).

92. "The People Lose Patience," *Economist*, Aug. 29, 2020.

93. "A New World: Real Opposition Politics Beckons for the First Time," *Economist*, July 4, 2020.

94. Schattschneider, *Semisovereign People*, 10, 105.

95. Ibid., 16.

96. Alexander A. Guerrero, "Against Elections: The Lottocratic Alternative," *Philosophy and Public Affairs* 42 (2014): 135–78.

97. Though one could promise them lucrative positions after serving in the lottocratic body (for instance, in the amorphous world of think tanks and the political entertainment complex so highly developed on the American right). I thank Steve Macedo for this insight.

98. Abizadeh, "Representation, Bicameralism, Political Equality, and Sortition," 8.
99. Urbinati, *Representative Democracy*.
100. Jane Mansbridge, "Rethinking Representation," *American Political Science Review* 97 (2003): 515–28.
101. Maria Paula Saffon and Nadia Urbinati, "Procedural Democracy, the Bulwark of Equal Liberty," *Political Theory* 41 (2013): 441–81.
102. Unless one instituted an imperative mandate.
103. David Plotke, "Representation Is Democracy," *Constellations* 4 (1997): 19–34.

3. CRITICAL INFRASTRUCTURE

1. One might ask why the discussion is limited to parties and media and does not include other institutions that are usually seen as intermediaries, such as NGOs, trade unions, and employer associations. I don't mean to deny the importance of the latter, but to put it bluntly: one can imagine a representative democracy without them, whereas one cannot conceive of one without parties and media. I thank Dan Kelemen for pressing me on this point.
2. Of course, access is not the same as success. Especially in the case of professional media—as opposed to blogging and such—a given market might sustain only so many quality products (and there is evidence that competition, under some circumstances, can positively degrade an information environment and lead to decreasing political participation). See Julia Cagé, "Media Competition, Information Provision, and Political Participation: Evidence from French Local Newspapers and Elections, 1944–2014," *Journal of Public Economics* 185 (2020), doi .org/10.1016/j.jpubeco.2019.104077.
3. And when it comes to elections, it's about moving bodies to the right place at the right time—a question of logistics, which in turn is conditioned by the available infrastructure. See Eitan Hersh, *Politics Is for Power* (New York: Simon & Schuster, 2020). The full name of the paper was *Relation aller Fürnemmen und gedenckwürdigen Historien*.
4. David Roberts, "Donald Trump Is the Sole Reliable Source of Truth, Says Chair of House Science Committee," *Vox*, Jan. 27, 2017, www .vox.com/science-and-health/2017/1/27/14395978/donald-trump -lamar-smith.
5. Bob Woodward, *Fear: Trump in the White House* (New York: Simon & Schuster, 2018), 205. Trump also observed, "Many of our nation's reporters and folks will not tell you the truth and will not treat the wonderful people of our country with the respect that we deserve," and "Unfortunately, much of the media in Washington, DC, along with

New York, Los Angeles in particular, speaks not for the people but for the special interests and for those profiting off a very, very obviously broken system." As Jedediah Purdy has pointed out, the tweets could also be seen as a "mode of governance, a minor form of entertainment and a soft, plausibly deniable mode of state terror." Purdy, *This Land Is Our Land*, 61. Jeff Tulis has pointed out that Trump's inaugural had a highly unusual structure—such that it could best be understood as a series of tweets.

6. Marshall McLuhan and Quentin Fiore, *The Medium Is the Message* (New York: Random House, 1967), 22.

7. Urbinati, *Representative Government*.

8. Following Carl Schmitt's critique of parliamentarism, there remains the mistaken belief that parliaments are mainly about *parlare* (think how during Weimar the Reichstag was regularly dismissed as a *Schwatzbude*—a talking shop). But parliaments above all make decisions, and plenty of procedures exist precisely to force decisions and cut off talk (think of the limits of even the filibuster in the U.S. Senate).

9. John Stuart Mill, "Considerations on Representative Government," in *On Liberty and other Essays*, ed. John Gray (Oxford: Oxford University Press, 1991), 282.

10. Charles Taylor observes that there is both a topical and what he calls a "metatopical" understanding of the public sphere, with the latter knitting together "a plurality" of topical spaces "into one larger space of nonassembly." But, *pace* Taylor and to some degree Habermas, it is not by definition apolitical; this view makes Taylor assert that a politically constituted ancient *koinônia* could not feature a public sphere. Charles Taylor, *Modern Social Imaginaries* (Durham, N.C.: Duke University Press, 2004), 86, 92.

11. Jürgen Habermas, *Strukturwandel der Öffentlichkeit: Untersuchungen zu einer Kategorie der bürgerlichen Gesellschaft* (1962; Frankfurt am Main: Suhrkamp, 1990). Witness also Mill writing, "The newspapers and the railroads are solving the problem of bringing the democracy of England to vote, like that of Athens, simultaneously in one agora; and the same agencies are rapidly effacing those local distinctions which rendered one part of our population strangers to another; and are making us more than ever (what is the first condition of a powerful public opinion) a homogeneous people."

12. Ibid.

13. Jefferson to Francis Hopkinson, March 13, 1789, founders.archives.gov /documents/Jefferson/01-14-02-0402. The more partisan he became, the more Washington denounced parties. Hofstadter, *Idea of a Party System*, 99.

14. *Federalist*, No. 10, avalon.law.yale.edu/18th_century/fed10.asp.

15. Quoted in Hofstadter, *Idea of a Party System*, 28.

16. Alexis de Tocqueville, *Democracy in America*, trans. Arthur Goldhammer (New York: Library of America, 2004), 600–601.

17. Edmund Burke, *Thoughts on the Cause of the Present Discontents*, archive.org/details/cihm_44099/page/n3/mode/2up.

18. Pierre Bourdieu, *In Other Words: Essays Towards a Reflexive Sociology*, trans. Matthew Adamson (Stanford, Calif.: Stanford University Press, 1990), 138. The political theorist Nancy Rosenblum observes that conflicts "do not spontaneously assume a form amenable to democratic debate and decision . . . someone must create the lines of division over social aims, security, and justice. Party rivalry is constitutive. It 'stages the battle.'" Or consider Gramsci: "One should stress the importance and significance which, in the modern world, political parties have in the elaboration and diffusion of a conception of the world, because essentially what they do is to work out the ethics and the politics corresponding to these conceptions and act, as it were, as their historical 'laboratory.'"

19. Hannah Arendt, "Truth and Politics," in *Between Past and Future* (New York: Penguin, 1977), 227–64. Of course, "facts" are not out there waiting to be discovered and then assembled into partisan agendas. As Walter Lippmann put it in characteristically pithy fashion, "The facts we see depend on where we are placed, and the habits of our eyes." Lippmann, *Public Opinion*, 80. In other words, facts follow political function.

20. Rawls, *Political Liberalism*.

21. Arendt, "Truth and Politics."

22. Hans Kelsen, "Foundations of Democracy," *Ethics* 66 (1955): 1–101.

23. Christopher Lasch, "Journalism, Publicity, and the Lost Art of Argument," *Gannett Center Journal* (Spring 1990): 1–11.

24. In some countries, parties are not constitutionalized, and yet practices and laws (such as prohibition of defection) have evolved so that party democracy is clearly seen as legitimate, and patterns of partisanship are recognized as indispensable for a functioning democracy. India is an example.

25. It does not follow that every single institution that conceivably contributes to democratic political will formation does itself have to be democratic. As Giovanni Sartori remarked drily, "Democracy on a large scale is not the sum of many little democracies."

26. Justice Scalia, writing for the majority of the Supreme Court, observed that a blanket primary "forces political parties to associate with—to have their nominees, and hence their positions, determined by—those who, at best, have refused to affiliate with the party, and, at worst, have expressly affiliated with a rival."

27. As an extreme case: In *LaRouche v. Fowler* (1998), the D.C. Circuit Court held that the Democratic Party could exclude delegates for Lyndon LaRouche (whom they had failed to keep off the ballot), because the latter was not a Democrat (and, more particularly, he was a racist).

28. Russ Muirhead discusses the pros and cons of such "epistemic partiality" in "The Case for Party Loyalty," in *Loyalty*, ed. Sanford Levinson, Joel Parker, and Paul Woodruff (New York: New York University Press, 2013), 229–56.

29. Jonathan White and Lea Ypi, *The Meaning of Partisanship* (New York: Oxford University Press, 2016).

30. This is clearly a much more plausible account for decision by assembly, or even deliberation, and much less so for mass membership plebiscites. For the difference, and an overview of empirical trends, see Thomas Poguntke et al., "Party Rules, Party Resources, and the Politics of Parliamentary Democracies: How Parties Organize in the 21st Century," *Party Politics* 22 (2016): 661–78.

31. Aradhya Sethia, "Where's the Party? Towards a Constitutional Biography of Political Parties," *Indian Law Review* 3 (2019): 1–32.

32. "That is why reciprocal equality preserves cities . . . since this is also what must exist among people who are free and equal . . . For they rule and are ruled in turn, just as if they had become other people. It is the same way among those who are ruling, some hold one office, some another." Aristotle, *Politics*, trans. C.D.C. Reeve (Indianapolis: Hackett, 2017), 1261b1, 23.

33. Hersh, *Politics Is for Power*.

34. On the wider significance of intraparty democracy, see also Scheppele, "The Party's Over."

35. Article 21 of the German Basic Law states, "The political parties participate in the formation of the political will of the people. They may be freely established. Their internal organization must conform to democratic principles. They must publicly account for their assets and for the sources and use of their funds as well as assets." The Party Law in turn regulates the specifics of internal democracy to a degree of detail that one might well consider an infringement of the right of free association. In general, constitutionalizing parties has become the norm in Europe; see the excellent overview by Ingrid van Biezen, "Constitutionalizing Party Democracy," *British Journal of Political Science* 42 (2012): 187–212. As van Biezen points out, only in three European countries (plus the U.K., for obvious reasons) do parties receive no mention in the constitution: Denmark, Ireland, and the Netherlands. The earliest constitutionalization occurred in Iceland in 1944, followed by Austria in 1945, then Italy, and then Germany.

36. Technically, they are unincorporated private associations. At the same

time, courts, and not internal arbitration panels, decide many cases about who can join, who gets to vote in primaries, whether parties can have all-women short lists, and so on.

37. Of course, private clubs, in many contexts, are also not at liberty to discriminate, even if some associations (religious ones, above all) can be exempted from some provisions of antidiscrimination law.

38. Nixon v. Herndon, 273 U.S. 536, 540 (1927).

39. Quoted in Adam Przeworski, *Crises of Democracy* (Cambridge: Cambridge University Press, 2019), 63.

40. Dennis F. Thompson stresses periodicity, simultaneity, and finality as properties of the democratic electoral moment; see his "Election Time: Normative Implications of Temporal Properties of the Electoral Process in the United States," *American Political Science Review* 98 (2004): 51–64.

41. Michael Schudson, "Was There Ever a Public Sphere? If So, When? Reflections on the American Case," in *Habermas and the Public Sphere*, ed. Craig Calhoun (Cambridge, Mass.: MIT Press, 1992), 142–63.

42. Jonathan White, "Rhythm and Its Absence in Modern Politics and Music," *German Life and Letters* 70 (2017): 383–93. White observes rightly that "institutionalised rhythms express the autonomy of democratic time."

43. Juan J. Linz, "Democracy's Time Constraints," *International Political Science Review* 19 (1998): 19–37.

44. The classic account is Daniel C. Hallin and Paolo Mancini, *Comparing Media Systems: Three Models of Media and Politics* (New York: Cambridge University Press, 2004).

45. Paul Starr, *The Creation of the Media: Political Origins of Modern Communication* (New York: Basic Books, 2004).

46. The Liberal Democrats' proposal was rejected by almost 67.9 percent of voters. Only 42 percent of citizens had turned up to vote in what remains the only U.K.-wide referendum unrelated to European integration.

47. Hallin and Mancini, *Comparing Media Systems*, 24. A similar story can be told about mass parties; countries that didn't have them at the end of the nineteenth century wouldn't develop them later. I am grateful to Cas Mudde for this point.

48. Victor Pickard, *Democracy Without Journalism?* (New York: Oxford University Press, 2020), 16.

49. Tocqueville, *Democracy in America*, 350.

50. Quoted in Natan Lebovic, *Free Speech and Unfree News: The Paradox of Press Freedom in America* (Cambridge, Mass.: Harvard University Press, 2016), 10. Benjamin Wittes and Susan Hennessey, *Unmaking the Presidency* (New York: Farrar, Straus and Giroux, 2020), 60.

51. David M. Ryfe, *Journalism and the Public* (Cambridge: Polity Press, 2017), 50.

52. Ibid., 602. A very charitable way of putting this is that both parties and papers serve as "epistemic trustees": they provide accurate information, but they also help make sense of that information in light of existing partisan commitments. See White and Ypi, *Meaning of Partisanship*.

53. Pickard, *Democracy Without Journalism?*, 18. As Pickard also observes, news became a "by-product—a positive externality—from the primary exchange between media owners and advertisers." Ibid., 66.

54. Robert Post, "Data Privacy and Dignitary Privacy: Google Spain, the Right to Be Forgotten, and the Construction of the Public Sphere," *Duke Law Journal* 67 (2018): 981–1073.

55. Ibid., 1036–37.

56. Hallin and Mancini, *Comparing Media Systems*, 34.

57. To be sure, opinions were expressed by widely read syndicated columnists including Lippmann himself.

58. Matthew Pressman, *On Press: The Liberal Values That Shaped the News* (Cambridge, Mass.: Harvard University Press, 2018).

59. Quoted in Lebovic, *Free Speech and Unfree News*, 161.

60. Pressman, *On Press*.

61. Nicole Hammer, "From 'Faith in Facts' to 'Fair and Balanced': Conservative Media, Liberal Bias, and the Origins of Balance," in *Media Nation: The Political History of News in Modern America*, ed. Bruce J. Schulman and Julian E. Zelizer (Philadelphia: University of Pennsylvania Press, 2017), 126–43.

62. Richard Butsch, "Six Decades of Social Class in American Television Sitcoms," in *Race, Class, and Gender in Media*, ed. Gail Dines and Jean M. Humez, 4th ed. (Thousand Oaks, Calif.: Sage, 2015), 750–65.

63. Poniewozik, *Audience of One*, 25.

64. Upton Sinclair, *The Brass Check: A Study of American Journalism* (Pasadena: published by the author, 1919), 222.

65. This de-radicalization went so far that, for instance, the Italian Communist Party supported a political system mostly designed to exclude them from power. I am grateful to Carlo Invernizzi on this point.

66. Timothy Snyder, "Fascism Is Back. Blame the Internet," *Washington Post*, May 21, 2018, www.washingtonpost.com/news/posteverything /wp/2018/05/21/fascism-is-back-blame-the-internet/?utm_term= .a73641422a11.

67. Katherine Viner, "How Technology Disrupted the Truth," *Guardian*, July 12, 2016, www.theguardian.com/media/2016/jul/12/how -technology-disrupted-the-truth.

68. Yochai Benkler, Robert Faris, and Hal Roberts, *Network Propaganda:*

Manipulation, Disinformation, and Radicalization in American Politics (New York: Oxford University Press, 2018).

69. Ibid. The expression "conservative entertainment complex" is from Levitsky and Ziblatt, *How Democracies Die.*

70. In 1980, more than 90 percent tuned to one of the major networks; by 2005 that number was down to 32 percent. Lessig, *They Don't Represent Us,* 79.

71. Stefano DellaVigna and Ethan Kaplan, "The Fox News Effect: Media Bias and Voting" (NBER working paper no. 12169, April 2006), www .nber.org/papers/w12169.

72. The story is told in Brian Rosenwald, *Talk Radio's America: How an Industry Took Over a Political Party That Took Over the United States* (Cambridge, Mass.: Harvard University Press, 2019).

73. In the absence of professionally produced news, citizens are not necessarily left to their own devices: quite apart from professional producers of disinformation, there are plenty of actors on the scene paid to influence (without lying) but without any commitment to professional norms of the kind journalists have. In 2014 there were still 47,000 professional journalists in the United States; by contrast, the number of PR consultants stood at 264,000. Similar proportions hold elsewhere. Timothy Garton Ash, *Free Speech: Ten Principles for a Connected World* (London: Atlantic, 2016), 192.

74. Patrícia Campos Mello, "Empresários bancam campanha contra o PT pelo WhatsApp," *Folha de S.Paulo,* Oct. 18, 2018, www1.folha.uol .com.br/poder/2018/10/empresarios-bancam-campanha-contra-o-pt -pelo-whatsapp.shtml.

75. Luca Belli, "WhatsApp Skewed Brazilian Election, Proving Social Media's Danger to Democracy," *The Conversation,* December 5, 2018, theconversation.com/whatsapp-skewed-brazilian-election-proving -social-medias-danger-to-democracy-106476.

76. Silvana Krause et al., "Die brasilianische Präsidentschaftswahl 2018: Ein neues Paradigma der Finanzierung, Anti-Politik, und Soziale Netzwerke," *MIP* 25 (2019): 106.

77. Freedom House, *Freedom on the Net Report 2019: The Crisis of Social Media,* www.freedomonthenet.org/report/freedom-on-the-net/2019 /the-crisis-of-social-media.

78. I am indebted to Jay Rosen on this point.

79. To be sure, there are important differences here: journalists can easily become chummy with politicians, or at least adopt a kind of "savvy style" (as the media critic Jay Rosen has put it) to signal that they are part of an inside political game; by contrast, doctors do not collude with their patients in order to retain "access" (unless one counts as an analogy telling patients the diagnosis they want to hear).

80. As Trump put it at a rally in Iowa in June 2017, "I love all people, rich or poor, but in those particular positions, I just don't want a poor person. Does that make sense?"

81. And the answer? "You will come back, Michelle, we are going to make sure that the UK bounces back as strongly and as fast as we possibly can."

82. Clay Shirky, "Stop Press—and Then What?," *Guardian*, April 13, 2009, www.theguardian.com/commentisfree/cifamerica/2009/apr/13/internet-newspapers-clay-shirky.

83. Clara Hendrickson, *Local Journalism in Crisis*, Brookings, Nov. 12, 2019, www.brookings.edu/research/local-journalism-in-crisis-why-america-must-revive-its-local-newsrooms/.

84. Sam Schulhofer-Wohl and Miguel Garrido, "Do Newspapers Matter?" (NBER working paper no. 14817, March 2009, rev. Dec. 2011), www.nber.org/papers/w14817.

85. To be sure, this risks romanticizing front-porch democracy; after all, disputes among neighbors can be particularly bitter. In any case, many local problems require more than local solutions.

86. The situation of local newspapers does not necessarily parallel that of the national press. In the United States, what can generally be considered papers of record benefited from a "Trump bump" after 2016: citizens are concerned about the fate of U.S. democracy and are willing to invest in proper reporting.

87. David Runciman, *How Democracy Ends* (New York: Basic Books, 2018), 155.

88. Hence also the absurdity of Alexander Nix, disgraced head of Cambridge Analytica, claiming in front of the House of Commons Digital, Culture, Media, and Sports Committee, "We are trying to make sure that voters receive messages on the issues and policies that they care most about . . . That can only be good . . . for democracy."

89. Shoshana Zuboff, *The Age of Surveillance Capitalism* (New York: PublicAffairs, 2019).

90. Andrew Guess et al., "Avoiding the Echo Chamber About Echo Chambers: Why Selective Exposure to Political News Is Less Prevalent Than You Think," Knight Foundation, knightfoundation.org/reports/trust-media-democracy/.

91. Runciman, *How Democracy Ends*, 158. Lessig points out that "the science of digital addiction was driven most effectively by gaming companies." Lessig, *They Don't Represent Us*, 115. See also the report by the All-Parliamentary Group on Social Media and Young People's Mental Health and Wellbeing Inquiry at www.rsph.org.uk/static/uploaded/23180e2a-e6b8–4e8d-9e3da2a300525c98.pdf.

92. Manuel Horta Ribeiro et al., "Auditing Radicalization Pathways on YouTube," dl.acm.org/doi/abs/10.1145/3351095.3372879; Zeynep Tufekci, "YouTube, the Great Radicalizer," *New York Times*, March 10, 2018, www.nytimes.com/2018/03/10/opinion/sunday/youtube-politics -radical.html.

93. Richard S. Katz and Peter Mair, "Changing Models of Party Organization and Party Democracy: The Emergence of the Cartel Party," *Party Politics* 1 (1995): 5–31.

94. Paolo Gerbaudo, *The Digital Party: Political Organisation and Online Democracy* (London: Pluto Press, 2019), 5–6, 14.

95. Runciman, *How Democracy Ends*.

96. Karin Priester, "Bewegungsparteien auf der Suche nach mehr Demokratie," *Forschungsjournal Soziale Bewegungen* 31 (2018): 65.

97. Quoted in Gerbaudo, *Digital Party*, 81.

98. Enrico Biale and Valeria Ottonelli, "Intra-party Deliberation and Reflexive Control Within a Deliberative System," *Political Theory* 47 (2019): 500–526.

99. Chris Bickerton and Carlo Invernizzi Accetti, *Technopopulism: The New Logic of Democratic Politics* (Oxford: Oxford University Press, forthcoming).

100. I am indebted to writings by Jack Balkin on these points.

4. REOPENING

1. In the important case *Figueroa v. Canada* (2003), the Canadian Supreme Court provided reasons against requiring parties to field candidates in at least fifty constituencies and, more broadly speaking, for the role of smaller parties in the democratic process, because they "enhance the meaningfulness of individual participation."

2. "No Joke as Brazil Clown Tops Votes for Congress," BBC News, Oct. 4, 2010, www.bbc.com/news/world-latin-america-11465127.

3. Such a line of reasoning can also be deployed against an antitrust approach to political competition: a duopoly is acceptable, as long as it is beneficial to voters as "consumers of politics" (in parallel to Robert Bork's argument that monopolies are acceptable as long as they benefit consumers).

4. Samuel Issacharoff and Richard H. Pildes, "Politics as Markets: Partisan Lockups of the Democratic Process," *Stanford Law Review* 50 (1998): 643–717.

5. Brian Klaas, *The Despot's Apprentice: Donald Trump's Attack on Democracy* (New York: Hot Books, 2017), 106.

6. See Virginia Alvino Young, "Nearly Half of the Twitter Accounts Discussing 'Reopening America' May Be Bots," Carnegie Mellon

School of Computer Science, May 20, 2020, www.cs.cmu.edu/news /nearly-half-twitter-accounts-discussing-%E2%80%98reopening -america%E2%80%99-may-be-bots.

7. Julia Cagé, *The Price of Democracy: How Money Shapes Politics and What to Do About It*, trans. Patrick Camiller (Cambridge, Mass.: Harvard University Press, 2020), 239.

8. Garton Ash, *Free Speech*, 204.

9. To be sure, the self-presentation of Fox oscillates between objectivity ("we report, you decide") and supposedly transparent partiality, as when Bill O'Reilly claimed to offer news and analysis from a distinct working-class point of view. Reece Peck, *Fox Populism: Branding Conservatism as Working Class* (New York: Cambridge University Press, 2019).

10. Ibid., 69–70.

11. Ingrid van Biezen, "Political Parties as Public Utilities," *Party Politics* 10 (2004): 701–22; Leon D. Epstein, *Political Parties in the American Mold* (Madison: University of Wisconsin Press, 1986).

12. The supervision of party and media systems should ideally be delegated to politically balanced or outright depoliticized boards. The task of such nonpartisan bodies is not to reduce partisanship but to regulate political and professional rivalry. In practice, this will mean regulatory bodies staffed by figures associated with different political directions. Authoritarian populists like Poland's PiS immediately moved to make the staffing of regulatory bodies a matter of simple parliamentary majorities.

13. Hansen, *Athenian Democracy*, 316.

14. According to Lawrence Lessig, the relevant funders in the United States are less than 0.5 percent of the population.

15. In France and the U.K., 10 percent of "megadonors" account for more than two-thirds of the total of donations, according to Julia Cagé's study.

16. Public funding is, not surprisingly, under attack from populists. M5S brought about a situation in which public funding of parties effectively stopped.

17. Cagé, *Price of Democracy*, 74.

18. Ibid., 248.

19. Lawrence Lessig, *Republic, Lost: How Money Corrupts Congress—and a Plan to Stop It* (New York: Twelve, 2011), as well as Bruce Ackerman and Ian Ayres, *Voting with Dollars: A New Paradigm for Campaign Finance* (New Haven, Conn.: Yale University Press, 2004).

20. And parties could still charge membership fees. These have never really sustained most parties, which is not to say that they don't matter: laws

about public funding can be tailored in such a way that they reward the ability to attract a large membership (Germany being an example).

21. In New York City, six-to-one matching grants for small contributions encourage a similar attitude, except that contributions still tend to come from the top earners. In a better system citizens wouldn't feel their contribution has a real opportunity cost when money's tight.

22. Markovits, *Meritocracy Trap*, 53. Zephyr Teachout claims that representatives spend between 30 and 70 percent of their time every week raising money, in *Corruption in America* (Cambridge, Mass.: Harvard University Press, 2014), 252.

23. Sarah Kliff, "Seattle's Radical Plan to Fight Big Money in Politics," *Vox*, Nov. 5, 2018, www.vox.com/2018/11/5/17058970/seattle-democracy -vouchers.

24. To be sure, making perceptions of integrity a criterion is dangerous in contexts where integrity has been used as a weapon of exclusion of voters. Pamela Karlan, "Citizens Deflected: Electoral Integrity and Political Reform," in Robert C. Post, *Citizens Divided* (Cambridge, Mass.: Harvard University Press, 2016), 141–51.

25. This proposal of a survey as a quasi-constitutional tool can be found in Stein Ringen, *Nation of Devils: Democratic Leadership and the Problem of Obedience* (New Haven, Conn.: Yale University Press, 2013), 202–203.

26. As Bush put it at a fund-raiser, surrounded entirely by elderly white men in tuxedos, "Some people call you the elite. I call you my base." To be fair, the annual Al Smith dinner is supposed to feature self-deprecating jokes, yet Bush's supposed self-irony here (as with so many of his other remarks delivered with a smirk) plainly revealed the truth. See www.c-span.org/video/?c4506459/user-clip-haves-mores.

27. The initiative still prompted the public service to undertake a number of what were presented as important reforms: more investment in information gathering on the one hand, fewer texts freely available online on the other, so as not to engage in what private publishers had criticized as unfair competition.

28. Julia Cagé, *Saving the Media: Capitalism, Crowdfunding, and Democracy*, trans. Arthur Goldhammer (Cambridge, Mass.: Harvard University Press, 2016).

29. Stephanie L. Mudge, *Leftism Reinvented: Western Parties from Socialism to Neoliberalism* (Cambridge, Mass.: Harvard University Press, 2018), 74–75. Arguably Mirabeau was the first modern campaigning journalist. Gramsci would be another example. And maybe Boris Johnson. Of course, Marx also eventually had the benefit of being bankrolled by a capitalist, that is, Engels. Thanks to Cas Mudde here.

30. There's also the problem that supposedly nonpartisan nonprofit journalism in fact relies on partisan sources; see Magda Konieczna, *Journalism Without Profit: Making News When the Market Fails* (New York: Oxford University Press, 2018), 59–61.

31. Jay Rosen, "Questions and Answers About Public Journalism," *Journalism Studies* 1 (2000).

32. Norman Ornstein quoted in Jay Rosen's insightful essay "America's Press and the Asymmetric War for Truth," which has inspired a number of arguments in this paragraph. It can be found at www.nybooks.com/daily/2020/11/01/americas-press-and-the-asymmetric-war-for-truth/.

33. See Onora O'Neill, "The Rights of Journalism and the Needs of Audiences," *Kings Review*, March 18, 2013, kingsreview.co.uk/the-rights-of-journalism-and-the-needs-of-audiences.

34. Samuel Issacharoff, "Outsourcing Politics: The Hostile Takeover of Our Hollowed-Out Political Parties," *Houston Law Review* 54 (2017): 845–80; Daniel Schlozman and Sam Rosenfeld, "The Hollow Parties," in *Can America Govern Itself?*, ed. Frances E. Lee and Nolan McCarty (New York: Cambridge University Press, 2019), 120–50.

35. It also must be possible to come to some reasoned judgment about its internal pluralism (even if we saw that pluralism is a tricky criterion: it's possible to see whether there's a real possibility for debate, but we can't mandate that partisans or journalists, for that matter, disagree).

36. The basics of democratic political conflict of course also apply: opposition has its say; majority gets its way. Parties not observing such basics will rightly be seen as squabbling and pay a price at the polls.

37. The nonprofit Healthy Democracy has developed a model Citizens' Initiative Review process; see healthydemocracy.org/cir/.

38. John Gastil et al., "Assessing the Electoral Impact of the 2010 Oregon Citizens' Initiative Review," *American Politics Research* 46, no. 3 (2018): 534–63.

39. Lessig, *They Don't Represent Us.*

40. Much will depend on particular circumstances and the larger political structures in which referenda or initiatives are embedded: there is every reason to believe that direct democracy works well in Switzerland, where, through 2018, 641 national referenda have been held (we only ever hear about the seemingly irrational or illiberal ones, such as the ban on minarets). The turn against referenda in recent years has been prompted by opportunistic one-off votes such as Brexit—an advisory referendum in which no clear-cut concrete proposal was on the table and in which the state failed to ensure a level playing field. It also got the sequencing exactly wrong: it asked voters to approve a content-less treaty with the EU and afterward tasked a government

with negotiating the content. See John G. Matsusaka, *Let the People Rule: How Direct Democracy Can Meet the Populist Challenge* (Princeton, N.J.: Princeton University Press, 2020), 85–87, 150. It was actually Dominic Cummings who had proposed that there had to be two referenda: one on exit, one on a concrete proposal.

41. In an oligarchy, an even more direct pushback against the power of the wealthy would be the establishment of something like openly "plebeian" institutions, comparable to the tribunes in the Roman Republic. Something like a *panel of the randomly chosen poor* could be empowered to veto one piece of legislation per year or impeach particular lobbyists and lawmakers, or reject one Supreme Court decision per term. Obviously, such a formal entrenchment of class conflict runs counter to the notion of equal political opportunity discussed earlier; it also isn't obvious how such a structure would cope with changes in the way conflicts are understood. For some concrete proposals along these lines, see John P. McCormick, *Machiavellian Democracy* (New York: Cambridge University Press, 2011); see also Jeffrey Edward Green, *The Shadow of Unfairness: A Plebeian Theory of Liberal Democracy* (New York: Oxford University Press, 2016).

42. Przeworski, *Crises of Democracy*.

43. Wilders was eventually convicted of insulting a racial group, but cleared of charges of discrimination and inciting hatred.

44. Samuel Issacharoff, *Fragile Democracies: Contested Power in the Era of Constitutional Courts* (New York: Cambridge University Press, 2015), 37.

45. The original formulation of the idea of militant democracy can be found in Karl Loewenstein, "Militant Democracy and Fundamental Rights I," *American Political Science Review* 31 (1937): 417–32, and Karl Loewenstein, "Militant Democracy and Fundamental Rights II," *American Political Science Review* 31 (1937): 638–58.

46. Many invocations of the demise of the republic in 1933 tend to leave out what are hardly minor details. In particular, it is forgotten that no functioning democratic legislature authorized the effective end of democratic government. The Reichstag that voted for the "Enabling Law" of March 1933 could not be considered as such; deputies had already been imprisoned or were being severely harassed (even if it is a matter of debate whether the Nazis' "seizure of power" still took place within a democratic constitutional framework or outside it). Furthermore, Weimar had many repressive instruments for dealing with extremism, and many of them were used; the republic saw no fewer than twenty-eight party bans. In fact, from 1923 onward the Nazi Party was banned in the Reich, but it was allowed to be refounded in 1925; the political police in Prussia kept an eye on the NSDAP until 1932, but

never decisively weakened the party. See Gereon Flümann, *Streitbare Demokratie in Deutschland und den Vereinigten Staaten: Der staatliche Umgang mit nicht gewalttätigem politischem Extremismus im Vergleich* (Wiesbaden: Springer VS, 2015), 94. In general, accounts of militant democracy too casually suggest that the masses are consciously choosing "extremism" or even outright dictatorship at the ballot box.

47. Edoardo Caterina, "Die Ursprünge des Art. 21 GG: Die Idee der Parteiregulierung in Verfassungsdebatten der Nachkriegszeit," *MIP* 25 (2019): 60–73.

48. Alexander Kirshner, *A Theory of Militant Democracy* (New Haven, Conn.: Yale University Press, 2014).

49. Gerard N. Magliocca, "Huey P. Long and the Guarantee Clause," *Tulane Law Review* 83 (2008): 1–44.

50. This is not to deny the horrors of McCarthyism: the 1940 Smith Act in particular, which criminalized advocacy of overthrowing the U.S. government, did much damage.

51. There is a deeper paradox of militant democracy than the possibility of preventing death by suicide: countries that can have militant democracy probably do not need it, whereas those that need it cannot have it. Put differently, in any constitutional context where the most powerful actors can agree on what genuine threats to democracy are (irrespective of whether these threats emanate from the right or the left), and especially one where they can trust peer review as part of the process, there probably is such a strong democratic consensus that challenges to democracy will easily fail by themselves. Conversely, in highly polarized and unstable polities, characterized by deep disagreement and a tendency to deny the legitimacy of the political adversary, militant democracy might make sense, but the very facts of polarization and disagreement probably prevent the establishment of militant democracy. Even if militant democracy were possible, peer review would not likely be part of it, for one would either not regard other parties as peers or not really trust them. I am indebted to Christoph Möllers for this point.

52. Issacharoff, *Fragile Democracies*.

53. Svetlana Tyulkina, *Militant Democracy: Undemocratic Political Parties and Beyond* (London: Routledge, 2015), 72.

54. Quoted in ibid., 73.

55. The Venice Commission, evidently concerned about "over-banning" in a country like Turkey, has in fact explicitly endorsed the notion of a "political filter"—that is to say, a filter that lets only truly serious threats through. In somewhat different language, it has also underlined that banning ought to be a political and not a purely legal decision; the point is that parties, as opposed to prosecutors, for instance, are sup-

posed to be part of what the Venice Commission calls "political democratic" checks and balances. "Politics" is not a dirty word here; rather, it signals some faith in the political process (and the possibility that politicians might sometimes be in the best position to assess other politicians). See Venice Commission (European Commission for Democracy Through Law), *Opinion on the Legal and Constitutional Provisions Relevant to the Prohibition of Political Parties in Turkey* (2009), www.venice.coe.int/webforms/documents/default.aspx?pdffile=CDL -AD(2009)006-e.

56. Laurence Tribe and Joshua Matz bring out the logic of peer review when they write, "In some respects, Congress's political character can be a virtue, not a vice. Impeachment is a political remedy wielded by politicians to address a political problem. Their mastery of politics makes legislators savvy judges—both of the specific charges and of the broader circumstances. Nobody else in the federal government better comprehends the use and abuse of power, or can more capably assess whether the president has truly crossed the line." Laurence Tribe and Joshua Matz, *To End a Presidency: The Power of Impeachment* (New York: Basic Books, 2018), 141.

57. Jonathan Quong, "The Rights of Unreasonable Citizens," *Journal of Political Philosophy* 12 (2004): 314–35.

58. In their defense, it is often said that they are still trying to contribute meaningfully to public debate or that we cannot ask them to obey laws unless they have had their say, even if what they say turns out to be hateful. The trouble with such leniency is that even if what we might call for shorthand the haters don't come to power, there are still victims: law professors might say that burning crosses in African American neighborhoods is part of democratic discourse, but the psychological burden of that act of aggression is not borne by the law professors. More important, there is something paternalistic about forgiving, let's say, racist remarks because they supposedly point us, the sociologically competent diagnosticians of society's ailments, to the supposedly real problems ("economic anxiety," what else?). And, not least, there might often be ways of articulating certain views without denying the standing of fellow citizens; the indulgent libertarianism of some free speech advocates also liberates potential speakers from having to bother with finding such alternatives (in the course of which they might perhaps come to question their own political stance: now that I'm trying to prove that only minorities commit crimes or are taking all the jobs, I'm surprised to see that the empirical evidence just ain't there). See Ronald Dworkin, "The Right to Ridicule," *New York Review of Books*, March 23, 2006, www.nybooks.com/articles /2006/03/23/the-right-to-ridicule/. For the case for hate speech prohi-

bitions, see Jeremy Waldron, *The Harm in Hate Speech* (Cambridge, Mass.: Harvard University Press, 2014). For evidence that in the 2016 election, racial resentment drove perceptions of economic status and prospects, see John Sides, Michael Tesler, and Lynn Vavreck, *Identity Crisis: The 2016 Presidential Campaign and the Battle for the Meaning of America* (Princeton, N.J.: Princeton University Press, 2018).

59. That story is told in the documentary *Welcome to Leith*.

60. For an ingenious set of possibilities along these lines, see Corey Brettschneider, *When the State Speaks, What Should It Say?* (Princeton, N.J.: Princeton University Press, 2012).

61. Stephen Gardbaum, "Comparative Political Process Theory" (forthcoming).

62. For good measure, one Republican resigned shortly after Trump got his nominee through the Senate, making sure that the body had no quorum during a crucial election year.

63. Kim Lane Scheppele, "Autocratic Legalism," *University of Chicago Law Review* 85 (2018): 545–83.

64. The artist Maria Górnicka had people sing the constitution on-stage; the performance featured fifty-five people from different parts of the political spectrum. Susanne Baer, "The Rule of—and Not by Any—Law. On Constitutionalism," *Current Legal Problems* 71 (2018): 337–38.

65. Adom Getachew, "Living Constitutions," *Dissent* (Fall 2020), www .dissentmagazine.org/article/living-constitutions. See also Adam Clinton and Mila Versteeg, "Courts' Limited Ability to Protect Constitutional Rights," *University of Chicago Law Review* 85 (2018): 293–336.

66. For a less obvious example than right-wing militias, see the call for disobedience vis-à-vis the administrative state by Charles Murray in *By the People: Rebuilding Liberty Without Permission* (New York: Crown, 2015).

67. Prima facie, lawbreaking would seem inappropriate in situations where populists have not acquired power; by definition, they cannot have passed laws that one should flag as particularly unjust through open, conscientious, and well-publicized lawbreaking. Except that, as argued above, an opportunistic mainstream sometimes adopts precisely the laws that populists have been demanding. It might not always be evident that such laws then have a particularly anti-pluralist dimension; after all, as also suggested above, policies are not populist or non-populist as such. But one might still, in an indirect strategy of civil disobedience, break the laws in order to alert a majority to the ways that populists are gaining power through the opportunism of the supposed mainstream.

68. Amia Srinivasan, "The Aptness of Anger," *Journal of Political Philosophy* 26 (2018): 123–44.

69. Erica Chenoweth and Maria J. Stephan, *Why Civil Resistance Works: The Strategic Logic of Nonviolent Conflict* (New York: Columbia University Press, 2013). Of course, things are not so easy, and no strategy comes with guarantees. Resisters need to develop alternative visions for the future, mobilize participants in civil resistance across society, and find ways to bring about internal defections in the regime. The average nonviolent campaign lasts about three years.

70. As Margaret Roberts has shown with regard to China, smart authoritarians will try to avoid outright censorship whenever possible: censorship will draw attention to a story and serve as an incentive to jump the Great Firewall; much more effective is flooding (drowning the news) or friction (making access more costly by slowing connections, for instance). See Margaret Roberts, *Censored: Distraction and Diversion Inside China's Great Firewall* (Princeton, N.J.: Princeton University Press, 2018).

71. See the clip at www.facebook.com/TordaiBencePM/videos/4569 64691658893/?utm_source=InsightHungary&utm_campaign =4265fc2322-EMAIL_CAMPAIGN_2018_12_12_11_00&utm _medium=email&utm_term=0_af2f0a89f2–4265fc2322–106033 493.

72. Markovits, "Democratic Disobedience."

73. There is another paradox here: if democracy holds, there's no right to resist; if democracy is destroyed, a codified right will not serve as an excuse for resisters. The only plausible scenario is one of non-state actors succeeding with their resistance against all odds.

74. See the #wirsindmehr concert in Chemnitz, for instance: www.youtube .com/watch?v=p4GxBY_uXgg.

75. Markovits, "Democratic Disobedience."

76. Peter Beinart, "Left-Wing Protests Are Crossing the Line," *Atlantic*, Nov. 16, 2018, www.theatlantic.com/ideas/archive/2018/11/protests -tucker-carlsons-home-crossed-line/576001/.

77. Robin Celikates, "Disobedience and the Ideology of Civility," *Contemporary Political Theory* (forthcoming 2020).

CODA: FIVE REASONS FOR DEMOCRATIC HOPE (NOT OPTIMISM)

1. Erik Voeten, "No, People Really Aren't Turning Away from Democracy," *Washington Post*, Dec. 9, 2016, www.washingtonpost.com/news /monkey-cage/wp/2016/12/09/no-people-really-arent-turning-away -from-democracy/; and the online exchange at www.journalofdemocracy

.org/wp-content/uploads/2018/12/Journal-of-Democracy-Web-Exchange-Voeten_0.pdf.

2. Hofstadter, *Idea of a Party System*, ix; Nancy Rosenblum, *On the Side of the Angels: An Appreciation of Parties and Partisanship* (Princeton, N.J.: Princeton University Press, 2008).

3. Piketty, *Capital and Ideology*, 959.

4. I owe this formulation to Jack Balkin.

5. Samuel Issacharoff and Pamela S. Karlan, "The Hydraulics of Campaign Finance Reform," *Texas Law Review* 77 (1999): 1705–38.

6. Claude Lefort, *Democracy and Political Theory*, trans. David Macey (Cambridge: Polity Press, 1988), 39.

Acknowledgments

For carefully reading parts of the manuscript and offering very helpful comments and suggestions, I thank Hubertus Breuer, Robin Celikates, Peter Giraudo, Carlo Invernizzi Accetti, Dan Kelemen, Yannis Kevrekidis, Steve Macedo, John Morijn, Sam Moyn, Cas Mudde, Heidrun Müller, Grigo Pop-Eleches, Annie Stilz, and Nadia Urbinati. If I forgot anyone, apologies; if I made mistakes, also apologies—and I take full responsibility, of course.

I have benefited much from conversations about democratic theory with Chris Achen, Carles Boix, Charles de la Cruz, Madhav Khosla, Erika A. Kiss, Bálint Magyar, Wolfgang Merkel, Christoph Möllers, Kim Lane Scheppele, Paul Starr, Silvia von Steinsdorff, Balázs Trencsényi, and Nadia Urbinati. Thanks to Jamal Greene, Anna Kaiser, and Corey Brettschneider for helping with some intricate legal questions, and thanks to Jay Rosen for joining my seminar on media and democracy (via Zoom) for a very instructive discussion at a time when many U.S. media were evidently failing in their basic democratic duties. And thanks also to Nenad Stojanović for alerting me to the Oregon Model and inviting me to a conference in Geneva devoted to exploring the Model's normative and practical aspects.

Peter Giraudo provided excellent research assistance; his work—under the increasingly difficult circumstances of the pandemic—is reflected in many parts of the book.

I am very grateful to my agent, Sarah Chalfant, and her assistant

James Pullen for having faith in a project that aimed to become not just another product of the democracy defense industry. I also thank my editors Alex Star, Casiana Ionita, Ian Van Wye, and Heinrich Geiselberger; Alex and Heinrich in particular kept up a lively intellectual exchange over the years and pushed me without being pushy.

Thanks also to the Princeton Politics Department, especially its chair, Alan Patten, and the wonderful staff who, when everything stopped in 2020, kept everything going. Princeton's Center for Human Values is also gratefully acknowledged. I owe a large debt to the Wissenschaftskolleg zu Berlin, especially its rector and its general secretary, Barbara Stollberg-Rilinger and Thorsten Wilhelmy. Wiko provided time and a safe, healthy space as well as a truly critical infrastructure during the final stages of writing and revising. Support from the SCRIPTS (Contestations of the Liberal Script) research cluster in Berlin is also gratefully acknowledged.

Parts of this book draw on "Populism and the People," in the *London Review of Books*, May 23, 2019; on "Democracy and the Public Sphere," in *The Future of Democracy*, edited by Nadia Urbinati (Feltrinelli, 2019); on my contribution to *Constitutionalism Under Stress* (Oxford University Press, 2020), edited by Uladzislau Belavusau and Aleksandra Gliszczyńska-Grabias, and devoted to the tireless fighter for democracy, Wojciech Sadurski; on "Italy: The Bright Side of Populism?," in *NYR Daily*, June 8, 2018; and on "The Critical Infrastructure of Democracy" in *Philosophy & Social Criticism*; as well as a number of pieces published by *Project Syndicate*, where I thank my long-standing editor Ken Murphy.

This book was written in the shadow of the forty-fifth president of the United States, as well as the pandemic. But it is neither a contribution to Trumpology nor an exploration of the political consequences of COVID-19; nevertheless, it bears the marks of perilous times, which forced, among other things, a kind of *riduzione verso il principio*. During these times, my family stuck together and stuck it out with me. This book is dedicated to them, as well as to my students, at Princeton and elsewhere, who have taught me much, and who've kept faith that democracy rules.

Index

INDEX